Betty Tonsing takes us on her arduous journey, exposing the raw truth behind the seemingly modern facade of health care facilities. This is a must-read book for every healthcare professional and family caregiver.

Dale C. Carter, MBA, HFA,

Eldercare advocate and author

Betty's own poignant journal is supported with interviews heavily documented with medical research and factual statistics. I found her stories compelling, unsettling and thought provoking.

Lora Minichillo, JD

Patient advocate

Through her poignant journal, Dr. Tonsing demonstrates a deep insight and knowledge that transcends superficial or quick observations. She also has done painstaking research on this topic with hundreds of people from all walks of life. Through a research questionnaire that tapped into over 250 responses plus in depth interviews, other patient advocates have shared their own painful journeys, challenges, what worked and what they were able to change. This makes Betty Tonsing's book a wellspring of practical advice along with a number of gripping stories.

Joseph Pelton, Ph.D.

I am drawn to Dr. Tonsing's endeavor because for the last several years I have worked constantly to see my elderly mother and father through many difficult life stages. I believe all of us need the insights that Betty's book provides. I can only hope it is read widely as our entire system of health care is in need of improvement at a time when the challenges of demographics, technology and funding are more serious every month.

Donovan Russell, Ph.D.

Stand *in the* Way!

PATIENT ADVOCATES SPEAK OUT

Betty Tonsing, Ph.D.

Lulu Publishing Services rev. date: 01/08/2014

To George…….always, my special guy

Acknowledgments

George's illness was the saddest year of my life; yet in the sadness, there was also grace. I was acutely aware that I was given extra time to be with my special guy; I realized why he was so special and was able to savor every moment with him; and I felt a multitude of grace for all the people who were there for George and for me. This grace spilled over as I wrote this book.

Thank you to all the people on Facebook who posted my brief notice about the survey, and thank you to all the people who took the survey. Thank you to all those who agreed to be interviewed and for your willingness to be so forthright and personal about your own stories. Thank you to all those who were kind and helpful, introducing me to people you knew who might want to talk with me about their patient advocacy experiences. A special thank you goes to the Indiana Alzheimer's Association and to Dale Carter, who made an extra effort to connect me with people and with organizations to "spread the word." Thank you to Lora Minichillo, who took me under her wing to help me every way she could to get this book published.

Thank you to all of George's friends from literally all over the world who called George during his illness ... and to those few who were able to come to visit, again from all over the world. It was quite amazing. Thank you to Ann Pellegrino, Clerk of the Lafayette (IN) Friends Meeting (Quaker) for making the effort to come to the Indiana Veterans' Home and get to know George. Thank you to the wonderful Quakers who came to the hospital the last Sunday George lived for what they hoped was a meeting for worship with him; indeed, it was the most special meeting we could have asked for. Thank you again to the Quakers for helping officiate at George's funeral service and Mass. And thank you to the Rev. Ed Ruetz, our good friend, for simply being that ... a good friend.

Thank you for all the medical angels who eased George's pain and despair ... there were quite a few. Leading these angels were Carla and Angela at the Indiana Veterans' Home in Lafayette.

Thank you to Carol Bobay Vickrey, my friend of many decades, who from almost Day One was my own personal support group. I wonder how I would have managed that entire year without her friendship. Carol suggested from the very beginning, when we realized something was profoundly wrong, to keep a journal ... and become a voice for other patient advocates by writing this book.

George was a widower when I met him, and he was a lucky man to have had two loving families. Thank you, Lydia and Russell, for cheering your dad so very often with your "face time" calls ... that was new to him, and he loved it. David, I wish you could have been with him in some way. Thank you, Doug ... you were there always at the right time for your dad, and for me. Alyssa, who will soon be joining our family, you were there to support us, and you still do!

And ... to my beloved Eva and Joey, "Thank you" is not enough. You all brought joy to your dad's life to the very end.

Introduction

"Going in Circles"

On 10 May 2011, my husband had a routine knee operation. We anticipated that, following a few weeks' physical therapy and recovery in a therapeutic setting, he would return to his normal routine. That included daily drives to Starbucks in his truck for coffee and company. As a retired history professor, that also included consulting as a field editor for a scholarly press, and, as a Fulbrighter, being a grant reviewer of incoming proposals. As an avid outdoorsman, it included hunting and fishing. All that dramatically changed two weeks later, when a blood clot landed him back in the hospital, where he contracted pneumonia and a virulent bacterial cellulitis infection. For eleven months, he was in a stream of hospitals, acute care facilities, rehabilitation centers, and long term care nursing homes. He never came home.

A prolonged depression resulting from a combination of drugs, illness, and despair left him agitated, hostile, and assigned to the dementia unit, until appropriate drugs helped restore his gentle manner and astute mind. Throughout, I was his advocate. This was not the first time I had been in that role. Other hospitalizations always required my advocacy, but none to the extent of this.

When George had his initial operation, we had no idea all this would happen. Advocates are rarely prepared. It is like being thrown into the deep end of a pool in order to learn how to swim. Advocates must follow their instincts, utilize their personal knowledge of the person for whom they are advocating, explore relevant research, and develop the fortitude to push forward with questions, requests, and, sometimes, demands.

I started my personal journey as an advocate by keeping a journal, after George had spent a couple of weeks in the acute care facility, when it became apparent that he was falling into a deep despair and becoming very confused. All the attending medical personnel insisted he was suffering from dementia, though he had exhibited no previous signs. One day, feeling very helpless and out of control, he told me he was making no progress. He was afraid he was never coming home again. He felt he would never walk again: "I feel I am going in circles."

On the one hand, I had to take care of my husband's flagging spirits and assuage his growing despondency. On the other, I had quickly become alarmed by the growing number of issues and missteps that can emerge from a prolonged illness and residential recovery. I realized that I was not alone: others in this situation must surely experience the same issues and concerns. I began to meet more and more people who were going through similar circumstances, and the message I was repeatedly hearing was the same: What do people do who do not have someone as an advocate, when they are in a hospital for a serious issue? Or, for that matter, in a nursing home, a rehabilitation facility, or any facility that is long term resulting from a serious health care issue, immediate crisis or not? I also realized that, given my background and training, I could do something more than just keep a journal. I developed what I called the Advocacy Project.

A major part of this project was a survey that was reviewed by an advisory group of health and medical professionals, educators and researchers, and social service providers, all of whom are compassionate about how individuals are treated and cared for in our current health care system. The survey was distributed widely over social media and select national patient advocacy organizations. Over 250 people responded to the survey, and many of those asked to be interviewed. These were the objectives of the questions and their answers:

1. To help others when they need to become advocates;
2. To offer those who have already served as advocates an opportunity to "tell their story," good or bad, as it is therapeutic to share;
3. To enable the respondents to become part of the national discussion on health care reform;
4. To give the professional medical community vital feedback regarding the overall care of patients;
5. To help advocates fill, if possible, the current gaps in health care. Even though not everyone has an advocate, the stories that advocates share clearly reveal why their services make a difference; and
6. To correct what can be corrected in our health care system, and to applaud and commend what is wonderful and working.

Why was the project necessary?

- People within medical settings (hospitals, long term care and rehab facilities) are vulnerable as a result of surgery, illness, or injury; while under normal circumstances they might be fully cognizant and capable of handling their needs, here they are often unable to do so.
- Small community hospitals are being morphed into large, metropolitan, multi-story facilities with helipads, located on large, multiplex medical campuses housing several specialties. We are living longer and better lives as a result of fantastic research technology and medical advances, but in an increasingly impersonal medical world.
- Complications during hospitalizations (e.g., from infections, medication errors, less than competent doctors, etc.) are the third leading cause of death in the US, following heart disease and cancer. This has been repeatedly documented.

- MRSA, once exclusive to hospitals, is considered by some health officials as a contagious epidemic, which is now finding its way into the wider community including nursing homes, fitness centers, sports teams, and, reportedly, also the handles of shopping carts at your friendly grocery store. MRSA is deadly, with a mortality rate of at least 10-20% or possibly higher, according to some reports. People already sick and hospitalized are vulnerable, unable to shield themselves effectively against these virulent bacteria. Less deadly is cellulitis, but it will also leave patients gravely ill.
- Long term care in the United States cannot continue to sustain itself. Although it is a booming industry (encompassing nursing homes, assisted living, etc.), the increase in size of an aging population, bolstered by baby boomers living longer than ever, is outpacing and outstripping supply and taxing existing services. This will not change. Existing facilities are already stressed to meet a basic standard of care coupled with regulatory demands to effectively monitor individual patient needs.
- To manage costs, medical settings are increasingly using the services of CNAs (certified nursing assistants) for direct patient care. Less visible now are Registered Nurses (RNs) who have the skill and training CNAs do not have to carefully monitor patient care. RNs are increasingly "paper nurses" for floors, wings, and units, managing a team of less qualified medical personnel.
- Patients requiring occupational and physical therapy will, on average, receive these services for no more than 90 minutes a day, five days a week. For the remainder of the time, they do nothing. My husband wanted to know why he could not just go home and "sit." As it was, each time I visited him, the leg on which he had had a knee replacement was down, not up, whether he was in a wheelchair or a lounge chair. When I expressed concern about this, one of the nursing assistants took the small, plastic wastepaper basket nearby, turned it

upside down, and propped his leg up on it, before leaving the room. I was dumbfounded. This facility had a high rating for rehabilitation, and a flimsy waste basket was the best they could do? I complained to the administrator, but by the time a proper device was installed on his wheelchair and lounge chair, he was already being treated in the hospital for a blood clot.

- The world is flat and wired, and that includes medical settings. While technology is allowing for better integration of patient care – the VA hospitals were considered an early model by utilizing computers as part of the doctor/patient visit to capture information accessible by the entire system, including the pharmacists – it is also another barrier. A recent visit to the emergency room of a bustling metropolitan hospital revealed nurses with small notebook computers strapped to one of their hands. The hospital had begun using this technology that very day to capture vital information, which is a good idea, as the VA has demonstrated. However, who will get the most attention? The computer or the patient?

- "That decision is up to the doctor" is a regular response to cover numerous questions and concerns raised by patients (and their advocates) in all settings. For example, it appears to be irrelevant if a patient *knows* there is a serious error related to medications and expects an immediate correction. That decision will be made by the doctor, *when* the doctor can be reached, *if* the doctor can be reached, *whenever* the doctor will be making rounds again, which may not involve a routine schedule. This is now beginning to hold true for the "paper nurse" in charge as well. CNAs who increasingly have the most direct patient contact have the most limited decision-making ability.

Although we have the most advanced health care system in the world, it is understandable that mistakes will happen. People who are in hospitals, nursing homes, or rehab facilities need a personal advocate if for no other reason than to provide protection against harm and error, whether intentional or not. They cannot provide guaranteed protection. But the horror stories that are caught by advocates are too numerous to allow dismissal of the service and protection advocates provide.

The purpose of advocates is not to assume fault or blame on the part of the health care providers (doctors, nurses, social workers, hospital administrators, associated therapists). Advocates should take on the role of protagonist, not antagonist. They need to be alert and assertive. While considered both a blessing and a thorn, they are vital, while also, inevitably, sometimes in the way. If they are not well informed, their intentions may end up being more harmful than helpful. Minus the medical education of the professional health care providers, they must acknowledge the reality of their roles; at the same time, they cannot allow themselves to be shoved about or ignored. All advocates must know their rights and responsibilities, and so must the health care providers.

- Advocates want services in hospitals, rehab centers, and long term care facilities to be, first and foremost, patient-centered.
- As the inclusion of patient advocates becomes a goal of medical residential settings, resources such as training, workshops, and on-going support for advocates should be available. We believe hospitals do care; they are just overwhelmed. But they could host advocate workshops. The potential outcomes include good community relations, reducing the potential for litigation as a result of hospital errors, and cost savings for patients and the health system itself.
- Just as all patients entering residential medical settings today are asked if they have a living will and health directives, they should also be asked if they have an advocate or health representative.
- A consortium could be created involving all advocacy organizations (e.g., those addressing HIV/AIDs, Alzheimer's, cancer, health disease, mental health, etc.) committed to

identifying and training people who are willing to be an advocate for patients who do not have one, but need one. HIV/AIDS organizations, as well as Alzheimer's groups, have already been leaders in this area.

- The critical and often life-saving role of advocates must be included in the major discussions on health care reform in the US.

From this project, a book emerged. That was always my original intent ... to publish so that many others could read these poignant stories. This book contains my journal, passages of which remain painful to read even today. When I first began to keep the journal, a friend encouraged me to write while everything was "raw and immediate." Some people assume it was cathartic, but if that implies that writing meant that my own pain and grief were being released, the answer is No. In the end, I realized it was a love story to my husband.

What was cathartic is the knowledge that the survey, and subsequent interviews, could be shared with others. The results of these inquiries could help others who are also advocates, as well as those in the health field to better understand the powerful role of advocates and do a better job of integrating advocates into treatment. Of course, this also means that this book should be read by those in the health care field ... which suggests that it become part of the curriculum within medical training for CNAs all the way up to medical school.

What is the ultimate aim of this book? In a way, it is meant to alarm. Hospitals and nursing homes used to be forbidding places with long, dark hallways and unpleasant smells that combined cleansing detergent and ammonia with those of body fluids and death. Visitors were meant to feel they were in the way of crabby nurses, whose main intent seemed to be to remind people about visiting hour restrictions. Some would argue that too many nursing homes still smell this way. But today, the smell of latte floats through the air of most hospital foyers, replete with stores full of splendid gifts and flowers, while cheerful volunteers zip by in electric carts offering to take visitors to their destination. Visiting hours now are any time one can make it, and every effort is made to support families in times of health crises.

Why, then, do I think that above the door of every hospital and nursing home should be the sign: "Enter at your own risk"? Because every year 100,000 people die as the result of infections contracted while in the hospital; another 100,000 die from unintentional medical harm. If that number is not dramatic enough to paint a picture, here's another statistic: That is the equivalent of about eight jumbo jets crashing ... every week.[1] Moreover, the growth of for-profit nursing homes is out-pacing non-profit facilities. The for-profits lead in overcharging for services, while care suffers; they have incredibly high turn-over rates of personnel compared to home health programs; and they have a substantially higher incidence of abuse, infection, and pressure sores than non-profit and government facilities.

Every advocate I interviewed said that he or she should have asked more questions. This led me to think that we are being too polite. I want all patient advocates not to be afraid of their lack of professional training. I want them to stand up, speak out, and push back. I do not want them to be shoved around or ignored. I want them to know when to get out of the way, and when to get IN the way – and, most importantly, to know the difference.

Betty Tonsing, Ph.D.
www.patientadvocatesspeakout.com
Betty@patientadvocatesspeakout.com

---

[1]   A 747 jumbo jet holds, on average, 500 people, depending on the model.

My Journey With George

It started as a routine surgery.
10 May 2011

This has been a lousy spring! It is still cold and wet, as if winter will not let go. Hopefully, by the time George is home and ready to walk, the weather will be as it should be … warm and inviting. Because of his congestive heart failure and weakening heart, the major concern was surviving the surgery. And he did. He was clearly worried before the surgery. The possible outcome must have preyed on his mind. While in Eva's apartment before heading to the hospital and check-in, he was silent. Not talking with anyone. Taking the pre-surgical instructions in and out of his pocket, reading them over and over. But he survived. Yea!

George was acting rather strange following the surgery. The nurses had him up and on his feet the day after … which is normal. But he seemed delirious. He was telling happy stories, few of them true. I had never witnessed this before, with previous surgeries. Later a nurse told me it is called 'happy delirium' and not uncommon with "elderly" patients. Her words. She must think I am his daughter. Most people do. So irritating.

Next stop ... rehab
13 May 2011

Within the past three years, George has had two hip operations. The first one, while successful, ended up with six dislocations before a second surgery was imperative. He did not go into rehab after the first surgery. I was surprised the doctor did not suggest this. I told him that we lived in a two-story townhouse and that I worked all day, and I reminded him of his congestive heart failure. But the young doctor was confident all would be well. We were given an armful of useful aids, but not told how to use them.... I guess they assumed hands-on training was not necessary; we could just read the instructions. We figured out most items except the plastic 'thing' that George was supposed to use to put on his socks. We were completely baffled. And sure enough, he did not use it, and his first dislocation happened while he was trying to put on a pair of socks. It was downhill after that. The first dislocation sufficiently weakened the area to the point where George did not have a chance. Why the doctor waited so long before making the decision to have a second surgery – one more invasive and permanent than the original surgery – I do not know. After his sixth and final dislocation, the surgeon from the VA hospital who did his first hip replacement ten years earlier stepped in and performed the necessary, more invasive surgery, after which George went into rehab for about two weeks, and it made all the difference.

Recovery from a knee replacement is a lot trickier. I chose a place that was once a health sanitarium, and it is old ... no question. Today it is a long-term care facility and, like so many others, has integrated short-term rehabilitative care into its services. But it has a great reputation and is highly rated for physical therapy. It looks like a forbidding institution at first glance, but it appears warm and friendly inside. A very friendly and gentle St. Bernard is allowed to walk about from floor to floor, bringing cheer to everyone. I am told they separate the rehab patients from the nursing home residents and this makes sense ... this is what I want. Following his second hip operation, George was integrated with regular resident patients and he found it depressing.

Where are the other rehab patients?
16 May 2011

I was told that he would be on a rehab unit, but everyone seems like they are permanent and elderly patients in a nursing home. And everyone is in a wheelchair ... shouldn't some people be in various stages of recovery and using walkers and canes? This seems odd.

George does like the therapists, which is good! Occupational and physical therapy takes about three hours a day. True to form, he wonders why he has to be there otherwise. He is very, very bored. And I have no answers. They have already asked him why he is not participating in patient activities, but he does not wish to act as though he is a patient when everyone around him seems as though they are permanent residents.

He has developed a bladder infection. I am told that this seemingly innocuous infection can wreak havoc with people in long-term care facilities, impacting them mentally as well as physically. This has led to his wearing diapers, which I find disturbing. Are they necessary? Or just easier on the CNAs, who seem to be doing most of the direct patient care? There never seems to be enough nursing staff for all the patients, and when I question this I am told something about equating staff with patient populations and such. It does not matter. I will guess that no one who has someone they care about in a long-term care facility would argue with me that more staff are needed for direct patient care. But to the facilities it is all about 'cost containment.'

George wants out as soon as possible.

A wastepaper basket is the best they can offer?
18 May 2011

George is supposed to keep his leg up as much as possible. I remember when one of my staff members had a knee replacement; she could come back to work after several weeks only if she kept her leg up as much as possible. George almost never has his leg up. He is rarely out of his room, and is generally watching TV while in his wheelchair or in a regular chair, his legs dangling down in front of him, to the floor. Is there something the nurses know I do not know? Some new medical evidence that proves otherwise?

I asked about this, and got an immediate response. The nurse on duty (though I do not know if she was an RN, LPN, or CNA) took the plastic wastepaper basket from his room, turned it upside down, put a pillow on top of the bottom, and plopped his leg on this prop. Now, if George does not sneeze (he weighs about 225 pounds), his leg just might stay on top of this flimsy device.

I am in a facility that has billboards all over town broadcasting its reputation as five-star-rated for rehab. And a cheap wastepaper basket is all they can come up with to keep George's leg elevated? And I had to even ask about this?!?!

Stiches removed and all remains well.
23 May 2011

George had his stitches removed today. He had hoped that the surgeon would tell him that he could go with me to Louisville, Kentucky, while I mark US history papers for Advanced Placement. But not a chance! I do not think this really sunk in, but sometimes George chooses what he wants to listen to. Who does not? I told him that, as soon as I got back on 10 June, I would bring him home. They told me they would prefer he stay for at least six weeks, but he will be chomping at the bit. He told me the other day all he wished he could do is get in his truck and go to the store. Now that simple chore sounds like a party to him.

It will also be expensive. He does not have Medicare supplementary insurance, and he has only 20 days paid at 100% for rehab. After that, if he stays for as long as they have indicated, that would cost us several thousand dollars. We can do home care. We can make this work. We have done this before.

He is complaining of terrible pain. I understand that knee replacements are very painful, and his surgeon also reminded George of this. But he still complains, which is unusual for George. He was once quite the athlete. In high school he played every sport and learned to deal with pain. I wonder why he is complaining now.

So that explained the pain.
27 May 2011

I swam my usual mile this morning. By the time I got to my car, I had several voice messages on my cell phone, including one from our daughter who lives in Indianapolis. They had taken George to the Emergency Room after he complained of chest pain during physical therapy.

I am not in a panic. George's cardiologist once told him that chest pain is part of dealing with congestive heart failure, and this is something George has lived with now for over five years.

We know the Emergency Room doctor. He is fabulous! He dealt with a couple of George's dislocations a few years ago. He is more concerned about George's chest pain than his knee pain, and will run a series of tests. He is concerned about a blood clot. As he leaves the room, he says that a blood clot can cause this type of excruciating pain.

I return to work. I hate emergency rooms and am not a very patient person. There is little I can do, and the doctor says hours will pass before there is any news.

When it comes late in the afternoon, it is not pretty. The doctor calls personally. George does have a blood clot. Because of his congestive heart failure, he will have to stay overnight while they coagulate the blood for the procedure. It is a routine procedure, but there is a risk, given his compromised health condition. He also adds something that chills my blood. "Your husband is a very, very sick man. He will be in long term care for a very, very long time."

What does he mean? I am scared.

Success
28 May 2011

The procedure to remove the clot goes without a hitch. I missed seeing George before he went into the procedure, but he seemed very well coming back into his room. He was groggy, but doing well. Hopefully, this is just a step toward the home stretch.

But I wonder what this will mean to his rehab? Does he just pick it back up where he left off?

And what was it that the emergency room doctor was talking about? What did he mean?!?

What happened?
30 May 2011

George is almost completely incognizant. I cannot talk with him. He is barely audible. He needs to be fed, and it is all I can do to keep his hands out of his food.

He is shaking uncontrollably.

He has a fever, but it is not extremely high.

What is going on?

If the doctor does not know, who does?
1 June 2011

I do my own research, and I read that drugs can cause this type of shaking and reaction. What is he taking? I see George's doctor, and he too says he is combing over his medications to "find the culprit."

Now his shaking is getting worse. And he remains incognizant.

His chest is also full of phlegm. His roommate at the rehab facility was taken to the hospital because he developed pneumonia. George had expressed concern that he might also get pneumonia and was worried.

But no one seems to be acting with any great concern. And no one can explain the shaking. Am I supposed to think this is normal?

Where does he go after all this? He is sick ... no question. But how sick? And can the rehab facility handle this? I call the administrator and talk with her about it. I tell her my concerns about where he goes next, sharing with her the emergency room doctor's comment about being in a facility for a long time. I have no idea what that means, but I do know that I am worried as to how this will be paid for.

She tells me about two facilities in town that are called LTACs, or long-term acute care facilities. They are specialty hospitals for patients who must leave a regular hospital at some point, yet remain too sick to either go home or back into a regular long-term care facility. But one must be really sick for admittance. And that is determined by a strict set of insurance regulations. If one can get into such an LTAC, then Medicare pays 100% up to 45 days.

But the doctor had said that George would be in a long-term care facility for a "very long time." What happens if, after 45 days, George still needs care? I have no idea what is going on or what will happen next.

I decide to go to the US history readings. If I stay, I will be obsessed at the nurses' station, demanding answers. Eva is coming up from Indianapolis to "check out what is happening." My 'take charge' daughter. I feel relieved all around.

Is this good news?
3 June 2011

George is sick enough to go into an LTAC. I guess this is good news. At least I know it is covered by Medicare. I had not heard of these places before now, but Eva's report seems comforting. She tells me that the facility is small and the medical staff plentiful and intense. He will get a lot of focused care and attention. She also reports there are various patients floating about in various stages ... some in wheelchairs, some with walkers, and some patients walking on their own. She describes one woman as a regular speed demon in her wheelchair. Already this sounds positive and upbeat. Her text messages are pouring in. She is on top of things.

Then she texts that he is being seen by a doctor, who will be his attending physician. This is a private facility, owned by a small group of doctors, and his regular doctors do not have privileges. Is this another version of 'out of network'? But I accept that ... I have no choice. Eva continues texting the doctor's evaluation of her father. I go for a swim in the hotel pool, assured that Eva has this under control.

When I return, Eva has a new text. While evaluating George, the doctor turns and says: "How long has your father had Parkinson's?"

Is this the other shoe dropping? Parkinson's? Eva continued: "It took this doctor about five minutes to diagnose Dad with Parkinson's." It can be diagnosed that quickly? On just an examination? And how did this escape his other doctors whom he has been seeing for years?!

I am learning all kinds of new things.
4 June 2011

Until this week, I had never heard of LTACs, and few I ask have either. Most people I have asked who have lived in South Bend all their lives have not heard of this particular place ... but remember what the building was originally used for! And now PICC lines.

They have inserted a PICC line in George. His hemoglobin is down, whatever that means … I will research it. And the antibiotics. His son Doug is visiting. Doug reports that the purpose of the PICC line is to get the drugs closer to the heart, and the PICC lines are more effective than just regular IVs. This all sounds very high-tech and specialized. But again, this is called a specialty hospital. He certainly sounds better on the phone, and that is reassuring. He came into this facility still shaking and incognizant, and today already he is showing remarkable improvement. He may very well lick this. Where does George get all this reserve?

Remarkable recovery
6 June 2011

George seems to be doing so well! His voice sounds strong. He is, of course, bored, and does not seem to be very engaged in too much physical therapy. I told him that he had to get out of his room as much as possible. He was there to recover, and he had to demand to be kept engaged. I am not there and cannot tell much of what is going on. But he sounds so good … far more coherent than when I left last week. This must be one amazing place.

What am I going home to?
8 June 2011

The readings are over. I leave today, first for Indianapolis, and will overnight with Eva. I am somewhat nervous as to what I am going back to. George had to have been terribly sick to be admitted into the LTAC. The mortality rate for these places is high, but people are very sick upon admittance. I assume he is recovering, but very uncertain as to what happens next. The blood clot clearly derailed the routine recovery and schedule we had planned.

I took Eva to dinner tonight. No one has a sense of how sick George is, but everything has certainly been dramatic. I told her that, if something happened to her father and he did not recover, I was most likely going to seek contract work overseas. George and I met while working overseas; we spent thirteen years there, and I miss the work. It was the most rewarding and beneficial work in which I have ever been engaged. We both loved it, and I miss it. Before I get too old and am unable to do this, I would love five more years overseas.

Carol called at midnight. I have not heard from her in years. She heard through the Facebook grapevine that George was sick. Carol ... it is midnight! Call you tomorrow.

Does Donald Trump get treated here?
9 June 2011

The LTAC has beautiful surroundings! I have driven up and down this road several times and had no idea anything was behind this thick grove of trees. The place is serene and well landscaped, perched on a bluff above the St. Joe River, a winding pathway inviting walkers. The foyer of the hospital is quiet and softly lit. The receptionist is very friendly, the décor is pleasant, and the hallways are flanked by offices of various specialists and administrators. This feels like the type of place where Donald Trump would go for treatment. I turn a corner, and George is in the main room of his unit, looking out the huge windows that overlook the river, waiting for me. While he looks OK, the two IV bottles to which he is attached cancel out any thought that he is leaving anytime soon. He is sitting in a large common area that serves eight rooms, each with two beds, but most are occupied by only one patient. All the nursing staff are wearing simple gowns of specific colors: one color for CNAs and a second for RNs and LPNs. The doctors can wear what they want. There are also physical therapists, occupational therapists, respiratory therapists, and wound specialists ... all walking swiftly about. The place is impressive, and I feel confident. Of course, he is ready to leave. The nurse in charge of him today tells me he is doing OK, but that is it. He is taking two antibiotics: Vancomycin and Piperacillan/Tazobactam. I am told that Vancomycin is one of the most powerful antibiotics one can take. I have no idea how long he will be on these drugs.

Meeting the doctor
10 June 2011

Today I met George's doctor. He is very confident about himself. He says he is also an attorney. That he has been here for a year, and owned a hospital in a major city where he was previously. I wonder why he would walk away from "owning" a hospital ... and did he own the entire hospital? Again, I am learning new things. He says he has no confidence in the VA system where he did his residency following med school at an elite school on the east coast. He says that owning a hospital – which a group of doctors do with this LTAC, and I assume he is also one of the owners – gives assurance that they have an increased stake in patient recovery, other than the VA system where doctors simply work their hours. Although I am impressed with his confidence, it is also off-putting. This doctor has a lot to say, clearly more than most doctors would express to a patient's family, and on the first meeting. Perhaps since this place is so specialized and patient care more intimate, this is part of the process. It seems to be a far closer relationship with the doctors than the usual quick and impersonal hello. This guy is anything but impersonal.

I begin to ask him about his diagnosis of Parkinson's ... how it could have been missed by all his previous doctors, some of whom George has seen for years? He slaps the table: "He has Parkinson's! That is all there is to it. He has Parkinson's." And by this exclamation, I am to question no further?

Let's do what we always used to do.
12 June 2011

The doctor wants George to spend as much time out of his room as possible. And bring nothing from home ... no pictures, nothing personal. He wants to begin the transition period of George leaving, even at this point. That is how he sees it. George is here to get over the infection of cellulitis; get rid of the PICC lines; and head full-steam into physical and occupational therapy, so he can go home, as soon as possible. This place is only a way station ... not his home. And he wants George to go home as a husband, not me serving as a nursemaid. All this sounds good to me!

I brought coffee and the *New York Times*. This is what part of our Sundays was about: good coffee and the *New York Times*. And outdoors, where the sun could shine on his face ... another good therapy the doctor suggested. Sunshine and warmth. We talk about the US history readings; George looks forward to going next year, or at least he hopes: "I have a feeling I am not yet out of the woods."

Next Sunday is Father's Day. I wonder if George can come home for the day. Joey is away on training for the National Guard, but Eva can come up. He will sit in his own chair, watch his own TV. We will grill. It will be wonderful. He will have to go back, but what a nice break. A return to his home and life is coming. Hang in there!!

Too much 'upper body strengthening' ... come on!
13 June 2011

George has been here since 3 June, and still he has not engaged in physical therapy. I complain and speak directly to the head therapist. That gets action. He quickly explains they have been working on building up George's upper body strength, but I counter that a whole week of that seems overkill. In the hospital, the day after surgery, they had him up walking, and in two days, on a PT plan. And he was very active with PT at the previous rehab center. We go immediately to the PT room, where the therapist works with George. He does well enough, and with assistance and the wheelchair right behind him, uses the walker to make his way back to his room. The physical therapist seems pleased, and they will start a daily routine of this. I remind him that the goal is to go home, that we live in a two-story townhouse, and that I work all throughout the day.

Don't they read medical charts?
14 June 2011

George's legs were really swollen today. I went to the nurses' station to ask if perhaps his Lasix should be increased, only to be told he was not on Lasix. Oh, yes, he is! I replied. For over five years now, he has been on Lasix. The nurse informed me that, according to the list of drugs he came with from the hospital, Lasix was not on the list … and therefore he was not taking Lasix. I told her his legs were swollen. Surely they knew he had congestive heart failure, and Lasix was commonly prescribed for patients with CHF. While in the hospital, his blood pressure dropped to 80 over 40, and he was taken off almost everything, including his blood pressure medication and Lasix. Further, the first thing I brought with me when I arrived from my business trip was his list of drugs, which I asked to be placed in his chart. Did anybody read this and take it seriously? I was willing to accept that his own doctors did not have privileges at this specialty hospital, but I did not expect any doctor at this place to change his treatment without consultation. This doctor, so quick to diagnose Parkinson's, which I still question, surely he is aware that diuretics are a common prescription for CHF. And did no one notice his swollen legs? Were they waiting for a full-blown CHF episode to prove the point? "The doctor will be in later," was her calm reply. In a scene out of the movie *Terms of Endearment*, I said I was not waiting for the doctor to 'come later.' Sometimes he came, sometimes he did not. And his hours were not regular. I was not willing to wait. I wanted the doctor contacted, immediately.

When I went back to George's room, I told him he was not on Lasix and that was why his legs were swelling. "Is this my fault?" he asked. I wanted to cry. Like any of this was his fault.

When George was still in the first rehab facility following the initial surgery and before the blood clot, he was getting really grungy. The bed baths were losing ground and I inquired as to when he would be able to have a shower. It had been almost three weeks since his surgery. The head nurse looked at the chart and confirmed that he should have begun showers two weeks after surgery. What happened? I asked. "The chart was not carefully read," was all she could say. Understaffed? Yes. All these places are.

The cellulitis hangs in.
16 June 2011

George is back in bed, and has been now for two days. A bit of fever, and he seems to be drifting mentally. The cellulitis is hanging in there. It has been two weeks of antibiotics. When are they going to work? And I guess this means no day trip home for Father's Day. As well, the nurses told me rather abruptly that no one is allowed to leave on day trips, as this is a violation of Medicare regulations; if any attempt is made, they are to report this to the administrators immediately. This makes the whole place feel like a prison!

Father's Day
19 June 2011

We still had a nice Father's Day. I took my portable grill and we had a cookout on the patio. I also took several yummy side dishes, and it was nice. I took a video to watch as well. George liked it all, but seemed strangely quiet. I do not think he feels very well, but he is not saying much. He really is so full of antibiotics at this point … he could be feeling a reaction to it all. But he is not tracking very well, not able to hold a conversation. This is a real departure from the first week. I am worried.

George nosedives.
20 June 2011

George is again gravely ill. The fever has returned. His knee is swollen, red, and hot. He does not want to get out of bed. He is again shaking violently, and, when he is able to talk, makes little sense. In fact, there has been little sensible conversation at all of late. I am telling myself this is all drug-related. Fever-related. Illness-related. This will not last.

Do they know something?
23 June 2011

George is getting out of bed again, but with great difficulty. He is like dead weight, and the CNAs are afraid to lift him on their own, so they use a lift. And once out of bed, he just sits in his wheelchair, staring out the window. He still cannot track a normal conversation. Friends are calling him, but then they call me later, asking what is going on. I have tried talking with the nurses, but they always seem to be busy. Either that, or they are avoiding me. I have loads of questions. One nurse did sit down with me for a bit of time. She said sometimes this happens with surgery and grave illness, and the drugs may make it worse as well. Many things could happen as a result. Nothing is explained very clearly. I tell her I am assuming he will recover, be as before. She offers no comment, and her silence is deafening.

It is time the doctor and I talk again. Clearly, something is going on, and I need to know what is happening with George. He is now going in a direction that to me is unexpected, but is it? This doctor has been chatty before; now I need serious information. I leave my cell phone number at the desk with a request that he call at his convenience, and soon.

All they see is a frail old man.
24 June 2011

All they see is a frail old man. An elderly gentleman, sitting hunched over in his wheelchair. Wetting his diapers, which they call *briefs*. I try to tell them what his life was like before surgery, a routine surgery that was meant to give him a quality of life, relief from pain, and the ability to walk again briskly that he needs to maintain health. The blood clot changed all that. Then came the pneumonia and the infection. All the progress made in two weeks of rehab gone. And now they tell me he is confused. Some are bold enough to call it by name – dementia. I say that the day before surgery, he was in his truck – this 'elderly old man' – driving to Starbucks for coffee. I also try to tell these people that he is a field editor for a scholarly press, and, as a Fulbrighter, helps review proposals for grants. I am told intelligence has nothing to do with who gets dementia or Alzheimer's. Remember Ronald Reagan? President of the United States! And that offered no protection from getting Alzheimer's. Several of the nurses are sympathetic. I like most of them. They are doing a good job, and some are indeed medical angels. But the tone is clear. Accept it. We know what we are talking about. Not you, married to this man for 28 years. What could you possibly know? We are the experts. We see this all the time. And we see people like you family members all the time, not willing to accept what we know. We are the experts.

No call from the doctor
25 June 2011

I think the doctor is ignoring me. He has not called. I did see him in the parking lot the other day, and he clearly saw me … but made no attempt to talk with me. This may not be a big deal to him, but it is a very big deal with me.

I leave another request at the nurses' station that he call, again leaving my phone number, which is clearly also in the chart.

Quality of Life
26 June 2011

It started out as a routine knee replacement. Today, a common surgery. It was going to restore a quality of life. Yeah, sure.

Who *is* this doctor? Where did he come from?
27 June 2011

I am so fed up with this doctor. He continues to ignore me. He does not keep regular hours at the hospital, so there is little hope of catching him there for a conversation. I decided to send him a fax with my list of questions, making it easier when we meet. I used a search engine to get his office fax number, and oh, my!

I know that lawsuits are part and parcel of being a doctor – a beloved family member dies, and a lawsuit may be in the works. As a result, malpractice insurance is so expensive and a reason so many doctors choose safer areas of practice. This doctor has a lawsuit – maybe there are others. But the one that I found all over the search engine (literally) is about selling controlled substances to undercover agents. I could not tell from the legal language the status of the lawsuit, but there it was. And it seemed, given that he is a lawyer, that he is trying to represent himself, although another search of his name revealed that, at least as of May this year, he was not licensed to practice law in the state of Indiana … because of failure to apply for a license.

And there is an issue of yet another failure to practice. In 2004, the Iowa Board of Medical Examiners denied him a permanent medical license. The Board determined that he "engaged in professional incompetency, practice harmful or detrimental to the public and unethical or unprofessional conduct in violation of the laws and rules governing the practice of medicine in Iowa. The Board reviewed information indicating that [he] failed to provide appropriate mental health treatment to three children and that he inappropriately routinely billed for services at a higher level than the care that was provided according to his medical records." (6 February 2004)

I call Eva. Do I report this immediately to the hospital? Is it possible that they did not do a background check on this doctor? Would that do any good? If he is part of the private network within this hospital, is it likely they all have something unseemly to hide? Do I just yank George out of there right now? But, so gravely ill?! Should I call his own doctors and alert them of this? Where would George go? My own research on LTACs tells me that this is the type of care he needs … he certainly cannot go home or to a regular long-term care facility. Eva is concerned that, if I reveal too much about this doctor at this point, his care toward her dad could be harmful. But I am worried also that care under this doctor is already harmful.

This guy is on my intense radar screen.

Cavalier doctor
29 July 2011

I am visiting George, and in waltzes the doctor. He informs George that he is on an antibiotic so powerful and at such doses that it is the equivalent of taking out a rabbit with a cannon. The guy does not lack humor. It is confounding that this infection is so virulent. It is not possible, he states, for George to remain on antibiotics forever.

It is, however, possible that the infection has attacked the new knee joint and, if that is the case, it will have to be removed. The only way to determine if the knee is infected is either to aspirate fluid from the knee, or simply to take George off the antibiotics. Without antibiotics, if an infection remains, it will return with a vengeance.

With great nonchalance, the doctor says that that an orthopedic surgeon (and I assume one within this very network I consider dubious) will be asked to perform the surgery. George would remain at this LTAC for six weeks during the appropriate recovery time before a second operation is performed to install a new knee joint. Then, saying not another word to me, he walks out of the room as though he had just announced George's teeth would be cleaned the next day.

George did not understand one word: "Does this mean I am leaving tomorrow?" he asks.

Doctor, you are fired!
30 June

George called early today. He said he had been offered a job at the hospital. He figures if he is going to be there for a long time – possibly forever – then he could at least be of some use.

What is going on?

I left immediately for the hospital to meet with the Director of Nursing. She confirms she had this conversation with George that morning. No, a job had not been offered; instead, he offered to work … for free. George has hit a wall, an emotional wall. He must get out of this place as soon as possible. I want him moved to the rehab hospital that has been set up as the next step toward his recovery. And I want this doctor off his case. I tell the Director of Nursing about the doctor's visit with George the night before. Given George's heart condition, he might not survive another surgery so soon after the surgery in May. The fever seems to be subsiding … is it not possible that he could remain on antibiotics for a longer period of time? At least long enough – perhaps a few months – to get him through this stage? And under no circumstances would he have surgery through this particular network. He would return straightaway to his own doctors he has been seeing for years, who have given him excellent care. And that would include his bevy of doctors and surgeons at the VA hospital in Indianapolis. Could that not be my choice? Yes, she replied. I could choose that. I could overrule the doctor. What would be the doctor's reaction? Would he respect this? "He likes to have his way," was her reply. But this was my decision … she did not feel that George was in a state of mind to participate in the discussion, and I had the medical power of attorney for this decision.

They have ordered an aspiration to remove fluid from George's knee to determine if an infection remains. Because of the upcoming holiday weekend, this cannot be scheduled until next week. It really is best, she says, that he stay in the facility until this procedure can be performed. I object. But I do trust her. The nursing staff seem competent. It is the doctors I do not trust at this point.

He can stay the weekend, but I want him out of this facility and out from under this doctor's care as soon as the weekend is finished.

This doctor must think he is a god.
1 July 2011

I wrote the doctor yet another long note, which I personally delivered to his office and faxed to the facility, so the administrator could see my comments. Yesterday we were supposed to meet at 7 p.m., a time he requested. This call came from a nurse, who said he wanted to discuss George's situation. But he did not show up. I called much later that night, and it seems he finally came about 11 p.m. Who on earth is going to wait for a doctor until 11 p.m.?! I am fed up with his cavalier attitude and have expressed concern about the care he is giving George. While I was at the hospital earlier today, the administrator wanted to meet with me. She had her own copy of the fax and was concerned. She spoke with the doctor, and he said he would like to set up another meeting, but could not do so until the afternoon. He could not give a specific time. There are six hours to the afternoon, I told the administrator, and I was not about to sit there for those six hours waiting to see if he showed up. His ear seems attached to a cell phone … perhaps he could use his phone to call me when he was on his way to the facility, and I would come straight away. I too am a working professional, and I expected this as a professional courtesy. She agreed.

I left and was on my way to an appointment, when I got a call from the hospital. It was about 11:30 a.m. Was I aware that the doctor was there and meeting with George? Did anyone call me? No … and can this guy not tell time? He requested an afternoon meeting … what time zone was he working in?

Within twenty minutes, the doctor called me. Nice as can be. Full of information. He had a long meeting with George. He told him that he was no longer taking antibiotics … in fact, he's now been off for two days. This was news to me as well. Other than the aspiration, this was the only way they could tell if the infection remained. Within days, they would know. A backup plan was underway. The doctor told me that he explained the gravity of the situation to George and that, while surgery was a very regrettable step, it was also a necessary one. Long-term continuation of antibiotics was not a plausible choice, and he had seen horrid results from these infections left unabated. In the end, the patient was miserable, close to death, and it was not worth it. The surgery, though risky, was necessary for George's hoped-for recovery. He was aware that I have power of attorney, but he considered that George was cognizant and understood completely what he was saying. He told me that George had agreed to the surgery, if it came to that. In his opinion, George's cognizant agreement overruled any weight I might have with my power of attorney.

Goodbye.

Within minutes, George called. "Did you know that I was no longer taking antibiotics?" he asked. "I might get sick!" That was all he understood from the conversation. "Did the doctor talk to you about a second surgery?" No, he did not recall that at all. And George is "cognizant" enough to make a decision, indeed! Last week the medical staff were all over the place about his loopiness, insisting that I had simply to accept that he had dementia. And today, he is cognizant enough to agree to this risky surgery by unknown doctors!

Really? Seriously?!
2 July 2011

I was able to visit George during the day today; I think I should do this more often. He was with a small group of other adults in his unit for an occupational therapy session. The fourth of July is this weekend, and for whatever strange reason, the young therapist thought it would be a useful exercise for these grown adults – none from the dementia unit – to make American flags out of construction paper. I understand the *purpose* of the exercise – to practice small motor skills, as each pasted white stars and stripes on blue and red paper in as perfect placement as possible. But really, was this the best exercise she could come up with for this purpose? I looked at the adults sitting at the table. They were all compliant. Why? At this point, is the place so boring that this is something to do? I was furious.

I guess I must add that George's stars and stripes were in order. Gold star?

Meanwhile, it is day three off antibiotics. No sign of fever. The knee is no longer swollen, red, or hot. Not even warm. We have to wait six days.

"Can you pick me up?"
3 July 2011

George called mid-day. He was still at the university. But he did not have his car. Could I please pick him up?

George, are you there? This is scaring me. You are my best friend. The one with the best advice of anyone I have ever trusted in my life. You are my rock! Please, snap out of this!!

For the first time ever, he cries.
4 July 2011

I want to see George's medical records, but the nurses are reluctant. It seems they need permission from administration to let someone other than the patients see their medical charts. I remind them I have power of attorney as well as medical power of attorney. I should have this right. I want to see what this wacky doctor has been writing. And what strange rules ... I question if such a rule would apply in a normal hospital setting. I am very suspicious of this 'private doctor-owned' facility. I guess they can make up their own rules. And hire whomever they want!

There, word for word, is pretty much exactly what the doctor told me in his phone conversation with me. He acknowledges that the family "does not want re-surg: <u>but</u> they are not fully informed ... pt is COMPETENT & it's HIS DECISION." The doctor does state he hopes it is not necessary ... and it was kind of him to acknowledge such. Inhumane, otherwise. But he continues to stress that George understood what he was explaining and approved, "<u>if needed</u>." He went on to say that the "wife ... understands the 'best bad' choice principle & now concurs <u>IF</u> we need surg." The doctor went on to write, "I told her she & I spoke <u>because</u> George so authorized it & that I respect patient autonomy in a competent pt – over family wishes though I want family on board." Bald-faced lie. I never concurred with this doctor's actions or coercion of my husband's so-called agreement.

The attending nurse was reading this medical note with me and said there was not a nurse who has taken care of my husband who would agree that George was cognizant enough to make such an informed decision. Also, every person in that unit by this stage knew my full-blown objections to further surgery and my increasing angst and concern about this doctor.

But it is the Fourth of July! Let us celebrate the best we can. We have another BBQ and watch yet another video. Then George wants to help me carry things out to the car ... he wants to help. I am sure he is feeling very helpless at this point. How will he react when he sees the car? I find out soon enough. He does not recognize the car. Not at all.

We take a walk about the parking lot. Surrounded by trees, it is pleasant enough. We have grown tired of the confinement of the small patio that is also the 'smoking' room. Ugh. In short order, a CNA comes to retrieve George, asking, "What are you doing out here?" as though he were a child. It is obvious we are taking a walk, and it should be obvious we are not running away. I am quickly learning that everything is about liabilities. We seem to be in an off-limits area, which I find puzzling, since we are still on the grounds. George needs to come back inside the facility, where I am sure the liability coverage works best. "George, would you like to get ready and change for bed?" I could not resist. "Do you go to bed at 6 p.m.?" Her body language tells me that some of the staff here are very tired of me. Too bad.

On the way back to his room, George gets angry and starts to cry. He is still in 'diapers' and they need to be changed. "You will never do this to me again," he snaps. "This is embarrassing!!" We have never talked about this. All our conversations have always been when he will get well, and when he will get out. Now he seems convinced he is never getting out. I cannot get him to stop crying. In the small commons area, others are staring. It is a holiday, and other families are about.

Where is this going? I have been married to George Carter for 28 years, and never have I seen him cry.

He is infection-free! I hope....
5 July 2011

I have never prayed so hard in my life, and he did it. This infection seems licked! Now maybe I can sleep again! I would call in the middle of the night … did he have a fever? How was the knee? Were there any signs of this coming back? And I would have long conversations with whoever was on duty. I may never meet these medical angels of the night … but bless them. They saw me through my own torment and fear. And he did it! George has incredible reserves!!

Now on to the next step. I told him that the road home was through this next final step … another specialist hospital, this one focused on rehab. It should take about two-three weeks. He needs to get out of that wheelchair. On to a walker, then his cane, and by that time … home.

His mind is still a concern. He gets to the rehab hospital before I do. Likes it, he says. It is like an apartment, he says. I know the place is small, a converted small community hospital, with just a few rooms. How specialized is it?

When I arrive, it looks like it was before … a small, community hospital. There is nothing like an apartment setting.

When I find his room, he asks straight up: "Do you think this is enough room for us?"

He thinks I am going to be staying here with him.

"He co-fabulates."
7 July 2011

George has seen a psychologist at this new facility. I have no idea why one was not asked to evaluate him at the previous hospital. Since he has been here, he has made little sense, and the psychologist is concerned about his mental condition. He only hedges toward a conversation about dementia. Talks about how George 'co-fabulates.' I had to Google this once home. It's something about making things up when someone does not know an answer. I wonder about some of the things the doctor thinks George is making up. We have both lived pretty exotic lives! What could sound like 'tall tales' – sleeping in the bush with lions nearby, crouching in a bathtub under a mattress while an army is staging a deadly night raid in your apartment building, and in yet another unstable country keeping our bags packed in case the US Embassy calls alerting immediate evacuation – all really did happen! He will continue to do evaluations, but will recommend that George begin taking Aricept, which is a medication for dementia.

Meanwhile, he has again seen the young man who works with speech therapy. This rehab hospital works in partnership with the previous LTAC. I am with George during this evaluation. He did very well! I am rooting so hard for George to turn this around. He answers the questions quite well, except he cannot remember what season it is. George has been in a hospital since early May. All he knows is that, outside the windows, the sky is blue and there are leaves on the trees. I do not see the alarm in not knowing the season after all he has gone through, but the young therapist finds this concerning.

Big change for the better
8 July 2011

George seems to be doing SO much better. The nursing staff call it 'night and day.' Mentally, he is responding so well now. A bit of 'loopiness' remains, but he is far more cogent than when he entered this facility. The psychiatrist visits with him as well and, in my opinion, makes a bit of a strange evaluation. I had shared with the psychiatrist – who acts a bit odd – that I feel George has been experiencing depression. The psychiatrist is aware of my husband's rather prestigious academic background, and perhaps his line of questioning takes that into consideration. He asks George if he has ever been treated for depression, which he has not except for one brief period years ago, and George never dwelled on it much. He rarely discussed it, and I cannot recall why he was depressed other than perhaps feeling that life was not moving in ways he wanted it to. His career seemed to have halted with age. This happens to a lot of people. He used the resources of the VA, which are very limited, for psychological counseling, so nothing came of it. I think he may have even taken Prozac for a brief period, but even my memory is dim about this. George does not talk about that, and I do not bring it up. The psychiatrist asks him straight out: "Do you think you are experiencing depression?" To which George says, No. The psychiatrist seems to accept this. He says only that George is probably suffering from a vitamin B deficiency and he will have him tested for this. He says also that his overall system is quite depleted, and that is very true! He adds that his health needs to be optimized and, once that happens, George is likely to have remarkable improvement. I say that I feel starting him on Aricept is likely to interfere with optimizing his health; perhaps we should see how George recovers before he starts any other mind-altering drugs. He has been on so much already. The psychiatrist agrees. But the psychiatrist does spend some time talking about dementia, noting that, as the American population is living longer than ever before, dementia or Alzheimer's is likely to afflict an increasing percentage of older Americans. The psychiatrist is going to order a CAT scan of George's brain to rule out – or in – any damage that may have occurred to his brain during his illness, such as mini-strokes or TIAs.

As I leave the floor, the psychiatrist further stresses with me that, in his view, George does not have dementia. His physical health needs to be improved, and they also need to get him moving in physical therapy. This will all make a huge positive difference for him. And those B vitamins!

As I drive home, I am thrilled! I am happy for the first time in weeks. This is all going to be OK. I call several friends with the wonderful news.

He is crying again.
12 July 2011

George is crying again. Now it seems uncontrollable. He is not sleeping at night, and I know he is exhausted mentally and physically. He is still wearing 'briefs' – and I ask the nurses to take them off. But he has limited control of his bladder, and they do not want him to 'pee' on the floor while at physical therapy. Why would he do this? He has no bladder infection. What is going on? He wants to leave, but he is not making very good progress with physical therapy. I wanted to take him home when he was much further along. This is not working out.

And he is still 'loopy.'
14 July 2011

When I came to the hospital today, one of the nurses pulled me aside and asked how long we were married. Twenty-eight years. Well, apparently he told the nurse we were getting married in a couple of days. I told the nurse that I really could not take any more of these reports. Every time I arrive at the hospital, there is a new report of some wacky story George told that day. I am fully aware he is slipping, and like crazy. And I cannot continue hearing about it each and every time. I am now getting very scared.

"He has run out of generals."
15 July 2011

I had another conversation with the psychologist today. I have not seen him since that one and only visit he had with George. And I had to remind the staff about the Vitamin B deficiency, as he has not yet started that regime. A CAT scan was done, but there is no report yet, which seems strange. But the psychologist has continued his battery of tests, and he is concerned. He is aware that George has had quite an extensive academic background; his use of words reveals not only this history but also his acute intelligence. He says that people with higher levels of intelligence have resources they can pull from as their minds descend into dementia or Alzheimer's, and he feels George has been doing this for quite some time. And now he is, in his words, "running out of generals." He is on the "battlefield alone"; based on the outcome of the tests, the psychiatrist feels that George has mid to advanced dementia.

I am shocked. I would not doubt that, before this, it is likely George had early stages of dementia. Eva and I thought he was just hard of hearing when, during a conversation, George would say something off the wall and in no way connected to the conversation. I was going to have his hearing tested after his surgery. He also had not been tracking very well, and now I realize it was quite possibly early-onset dementia. But does one go this quickly from early-onset to advanced? Possibly, he said, if events have been traumatic, and his illness has indeed been traumatic for his mind and body.

I am not at all prepared for this. I walk around the corridors of this small hospital. Everyone else is recovering and will be going home soon, shedding their walkers and canes. George is not recovering. Will he ever?

I am scared to death.
18 July 2011

I am bringing George home. I feel the eyes following me from those who think I am making a mistake. There is no mistaking that he is mentally deteriorating and he is not physically ready. Not by any measure. While he was still in the LTAC, I met a woman whose mother was in the facility. She had arrived a few days after George was admitted, when I was still in Louisville. She watched him as he moved about the commons area, reading parts of the paper, looking for the "more interesting sections," as she put it. Without knowing his background, she knew he was intelligent ... "not likely to talk to *me*," she said. Of course, how could she have known his very personable nature? He loves to talk with everyone! She told me that she figured he would not be at the LTAC very long. Then the cellulitis gripped his body and mind, and everything changed. She could see the change. She had the look of tolerance on her face that one has for those with dementia. Be kind. Be patient. Listen, and then gently move away. There is no conversation, not when George says, each time I come, 'This is my wife,' and everyone already knows that. What he was doing just days before his surgery now becomes a part of every conversation I have with people. This is not George. He was driving his truck every day, doing errands. He was an editor for a scholarly press. He was reviewing Fulbright proposals, because he *is* a Fulbright Scholar. With a sidelong glance, she asked: "Do you expect him to be what he was before?" Yes, I said, with my own sidelong glance. Certainly that is not a crazy expectation!

At the rehab hospital, he rallied the first few days ... and now he has mentally nosedived.

I told them he needs to come home. 'Experts' all agreed that he will require 24/7 care. Could I provide that? What on earth does that mean? That if I am alone with him in our humble home, I do not sleep? I asked how long would this 24/7 be needed. It depends, said the 'major domo' nurse – the discharge planner, and I think that gives her some kind of power – on his cognitive abilities. All was quiet. Just she and I are talking. Of course, they all know he is 'loopy.' Silly wife ... she is not accepting the facts of her husband's serious mental condition. Forget what he was doing just days before surgery. No one can look at me. With profound authority, the discharge planner tells me that perhaps his cognitive abilities will not ever return. This is, of course, substantiated by his bizarre comments at this fine hospital – this nine-room, 18-bed facility owned by doctors, some with questionable qualifications.

What if they are right? It is true that major trauma associated with surgery and illness can create an onset of such mental confusion that, if George had an early stage of dementia going into this – and that is likely – it is now compounded.

So what does this mean? It almost feels like a life sentence. Everything about my life is about to change. Forget the national job search. Forget going overseas again, even with a short-term grant. Forget going with gusto into an exciting new job opportunity. Forget even going to meetings I enjoy. One of the doctors said I could explore some of the possible adult day care programs. That will be the new normal.

I am scared to death.

Keep your hands off my husband!
19 July 2011

Everyone knows I am taking George home. I am feeling upbeat, I think. I went to the farmers' market today. We have a special market here in town, and I love it! Once the harvest season starts in the spring with asparagus, with few exceptions I buy all my vegetables and fruit at the farmers' market, and today I wonder if I can keep up this routine I find so relaxing. It does take more time than running down to the local corporate grocery store near our house.

As I arrive, I am told by the doctor who is generally at the nurses' station that the Chief Medical Officer visited with George that day. He said almost in the next breath that what makes him the Chief Medical Officer is his level of ownership in this private hospital, leaving the clear impression that he is a significant investor. I am sure that once they were out of his mouth the doctor regretted these revealing words. I was not impressed with the credentials. I was impressed with what the desk doctor said next: that he confirmed the diagnoses of Parkinson's, depression, and dementia in my husband and ordered drug treatment to begin immediately.

Not so fast! This sounds more like saving one's own backside! I asked how often this 'doctor' had met with George, and the desk doctor's halting response followed with the words "not very often" were enough. I would guess not at all, I replied ... and then added that not one prescription ordered by this doctor was to be administered to my husband. George was not under this doctor's care, nor the care of any doctor in this facility, nor in the LTAC. Within 24 hours he would once again be under the care of his actual doctors. I was furious. What incredible action on the part of this so-called doctor! What kind of a place is this?

Coming Home
20 July 2011

It was an incredible struggle getting George into the car. The nurses shouted "Good luck!" as we drove away. I am sure that is what they say to everyone leaving, but their forced cheer left me with a chill. We stopped by Burger King on the way to get a favorite treat – Iced Mocha Joes! We are having quite a heat wave right now. People will be waiting for us when we arrive to help me get George out of the car and into the house, and now I wish we could just take a long drive and go to Mongo State Park *and* Lake Michigan, which are in opposite directions. But we take our time as best as we can, as I point out familiar landmarks that George says he recognizes.

He makes a comment that he thinks he was over-medicated in the hospitals, but he has heard me say that very same thing, and I wonder if he is just mimicking my observations.

As we drive into our complex, he does not recognize anything. It is strange that he should have recognized the grocery store and the colleges, or so he said. I am hoping that, once he is inside the house, his eyes will light up and the healing of his mind will begin.

But he does not recognize our home. He likes it! He finds it comfortable! But he does not recognize our home.

Still no recognition
22 July 2011

George appears more alert. He rarely leaves the chair, however. He does everything from the chair, including using a bedpan. Hopefully, the home healthcare nurses and therapists will move him along. But he does appear more alert. I made an appointment with his regular physician for next week and will be anxious to hear what he has to say. I also had to make arrangements with an ambulance to help transport him, as I simply cannot get him out of here in his wheelchair on my own. And he cannot use the walker … even after all this time.

I'm concerned that he still does not recognize our home. "Does this place look like where we used to live?" he asked today. George, we have lived here five years. Oh.

This is so lonely….
23 July 2011

I have been married to George Carter for 28 years. I was long a single woman, quite independent at age 35 when we got married. This solid rock of a man was calm where I was scattered, peaceful where I was volatile, reassuring where I was always reaching … giving me great security. I had lived independent so long, and rather enjoyed it. But when we got married, I immediately became forgetful. Where did I put the house keys? What appointments? The usual everyday routines escaped me. I figured I had been long waiting for someone to take care of me, and here was my prince so ready to do just that. Our 14-year age difference put him in a different generation. And his first marriage must have also prepared him to play the role of taking care of me. Whatever the explanation, I simply forgot all my usual independent abilities; for that period of time, it was wonderful. I was being taken care of.

In time, my independence returned. It would have been strange if it had not!!

Then we got Joey, adopted at six months. Eva, adopted at four months, was so healthy. Not a minute of problems or concerns. But Joey came packed with plenty. Both were from Taiwan, but Joey was born two months premature, which often means a death sentence in a developing country. As an emerging nation, Taiwan is far more advanced than that, but he was in a public hospital with no one to visit and love him, which sick babies desperately need. He also required a few blood transfusions for reasons we never understood. We had no idea what his illness was about, other than the hospital reports that were not easy to read or understand. We did not think orphanages foisted off sick babies. After all, they gave us healthy Eva. How wrong. Joey was so sick. Infantile epilepsy. He was hospitalized three times the first two months with us for acute asthmatic bronchitis. One night he was so sick we called the US Ambassador and the border patrol to open the gates between Lesotho and South Africa so we could get Joey to a hospital. George did that. He was my rock. That night, I remember his holding Joey, 10 months old, choking hard on his cough, spittle coming out of his mouth. Joey's eyes were focused on George, spelling fright. George somehow knew that, if we did not act, he would not make it through the night. Yet he did not panic. He was calm. He was reassuring. He did what we needed to do. The gates opened around midnight. And Joey was OK.

Now I am alone with George. He remains ill. Desperately ill? I do not know. He has little strength to improve physically. And I remain scared to death of his mental status. Three times today he pulled off the gauze wrapped over his bloody arm wound. Yet he does not know why. This morning, looking at the *New York Times*, he shook his head as he commented that he could not understand what had taken place in the senseless carnage in Norway by one demented man. That is the old George. Will I see more of that? This afternoon, bone-tired, he was making senseless comments about racetracks.

I brought Joey's twin bed downstairs to get him out of the confinement of the brown La-Z-Boy, no longer a source of comfort. He is now in a comfy bed, having taken Tylenol PM. He is sleeping.

His body and mind are still so in need of sleep … deep sleep. Will he wake in a few short hours and do crazy things? I must sleep as well.

I am lonely. My strong prince is not there. My best friend. I am there for him, I guess. I get angry. Frustrated. Yell when I should not. I have never had his patience. And I am also doing things I thought I would never want to do or be willing to do, but really am so happy to do now. I have this time with him. Hoping possibly the time will come again when we are trekking up the shores of Lake Michigan and over to tranquil Mongo, casting lines at which fish do not bite.

This is my prince. I so wish I had my strong, reassuring prince back. I fear he is gone. I cannot talk with him anymore. We have conversations, but there is no substance … just conversation. I am alone. Forget about going back overseas! That was really selfish. What was I thinking? I just want George back!

Woman, you are harming this man!
24 July 2011

George either fell or got out of the bed in the middle of the night. I could not get him back into the bed. I put the mattress on the floor, and, with tremendous effort, was able to get him on top of the mattress, but he remained restless. I finally lay down with him, hoping that would comfort him, wishing so badly we could once again be in our own bed, just cuddling. I had to wait until 7 a.m. to go to the Fire Department to ask them to help me get him off the floor. I did not want to call 911, so I drove down to the fire station and asked if a couple of firemen could come to the house and help. I guess this cannot happen casually. With lights flashing, up came the fire truck, with several well-equipped firemen in their boots. It was still blazing hot, so they just wore t-shirts. At least the siren was not wailing! And they could not just get him up off the floor. Procedures had to be followed. Blood pressure. Lots of questions. George looked a mess, having been up most of the night, I am sure. I had to give his brief medical history. They felt he should go to the hospital. I resisted.

"Sir, how are you feeling?" they asked. "Not very well." He should go to the hospital, they insisted, this time glaring at me as they walked out the door.

George, will you please stop this nonsense?!

I did not make it.
27 July 2011

Forget the bed. On Sunday night he slept in the brown chair, but I think the ordeal that night was again his tearing off his band-aids, and I was out of gauze. Those wounds risk infection and need to be covered. So I had to go shopping at CVS at 4 a.m. to buy more gauze. At the store, I stared at the shelves. Will life be like this now forever? Or for as long as ...?

On Monday, the home nurse, occupational therapist, and physical therapist arrived. Arrangements were made for a bath on Tuesday and Friday. Also a speech therapist. His vital signs were excellent. His primary care physician called, responding to my fax Friday about his medications. He asked that George start taking his allergy medication again, and said that it was OK to take Ambien 5 mg to sleep. We looked forward to seeing Dr. Scheel that Wednesday, to talk about all his medications, what had happened over the past 2.5 months, and if he should indeed be on Aricept for dementia. This was mostly to see a doctor we trust.

Long day, bone tired. Nice supper. We talked about Obama and Boehner's speech on the debt ceiling. I asked him if he wanted to listen to it and he said quite coherently, "Listening will not make a difference." No, indeed. About 9:30 he was ready to sleep. The plush rocker is inviting and ready. Chris Botti provides a soothing background. He is asleep immediately. Maybe this is the ticket. He so desperately needs sleep. He is physically and mentally exhausted.

Again I wonder if I should drink wine. I need to relax as well. But 24/7? What does that really mean? If I have too much wine and fall happily asleep, and a crisis occurs with George, I am not 'off duty.' Does this mean no breaks? For how long? I take my chances. Of course I will not drink too much, but I also need to relax. I fall sleep around 11 p.m.

At 1 p.m. I am awakened by a soft rustling noise downstairs. What is that? I gingerly make my way down the steps, and see that somehow George has pushed the chair all the way back against the window. The rustling sounds are the vertical blinds, several of them yanked off and lying on the floor. George has his legs draped across the arm of the chair, and he is naked. He is still wearing a 'diaper' at night, but it has been torn to unrecognizable shreds, scattered in wet clumps all over the floor. He seems so oblivious to what happened.

Earlier in the day, the physical therapist showed us how to get George out of this very soft rocker, and it worked. I was able to get him on his feet and over to the other chair. Now that he is wearing new clothes, I persuade George to try to sleep again. As I vacuum the floor, he sits amused in his chair, as though it were 2 in the afternoon instead of morning. He sees nothing wrong with any of this.

I probably should stay downstairs, but I am exhausted and beginning to feel a bit catatonic. Maybe this will not work. Maybe I cannot 'patch' this up.

I decide to go back to bed. Anxiety creeps over my body and, most especially, my chest. I do not want a panic attack, and I am fearful of a heart attack. I am a very fit and healthy 63-year-old, but this is taxing. I am not winning this battle, and it appears George is not either.

I doze off at about 5 a.m., and wake up at 7. All seems quiet downstairs. Perhaps our evening's crisis is over and done with. Perhaps George stayed in the chair and is still sleeping. Maybe I can slip off to the farmers' market for some fresh produce. But no, he is again on the floor. I have no idea how he got there. At least his clothes are on, with the exception of his shirt. He thinks he has had a heart attack, but is showing no signs of this. He does complain of heart palpitations, which I am sure he has. He has had quite an active night! He talks very coherently about congestive heart failure … so clear, so logical, and so disconnected to what is going on. He wants to go to the hospital. I cannot decide between calling 911 and getting assistance from the maintenance staff to help George off the floor and into a chair. It is only a week, just barely. Do we need more time? I am also certain this will happen again. But am I giving up? If I call 911 and George goes to the hospital, that is a serious step in all this. He wants to go to the hospital. But I do not tell him that, if he does, he is not coming home anytime soon.

The same firemen as the crew Saturday evening come out again. By their looks at me and at George, I know what is going through their minds. They are young. They have seen a lot, but I do not need their judgment at this moment. Seeing a lot and knowing a lot are two different things.

At the hospital, there appear no signs of cardio concern. He will spend the night on the cardio unit. I call the Indiana Veterans' Home to see if George can get in. He needs to go somewhere for more attention and more therapy. I will wait to see what the VA says, praying he gets in. He has been seen by the VA for almost 20 years, and I have the most confidence in their system at this point. He cannot come home, and I doubt I can afford any other care. And at this stage, I am tired of working with people I do not know and may not trust.

So, I did not make it. I could not fix this. As the ambulance drove away from our home, I could feel pressure leaving my body like air leaving an overinflated tire. I am sorry, George. At this stage of your recovery – or not – I cannot do this. I so wanted to make all this work. Being home – which you never recognized – my cooking, vitamins, personal care, stimulation, company, none of it worked. The time was too short. A week was probably not enough. I will never know.

Wrist restraints
28 July 2011

Someday it may happen to you. In all my years of marriage to George Carter, he never once used a swear word. He never once raised his voice. He never once got angry, lost his temper, yelled, screamed, or hollered. Thank heavens our kids were as good as they were … discipline was a complete non-event!

While we were waiting for him to be admitted to a room, he kept wanting to hold my hand … kissing my hand. So sweet, so tender. For whatever was going on in his mind, he thought it would be good idea if we got jobs working on a community project, helping people. Perhaps he was thinking of all our years overseas when that was our principal life experience.

But when I arrived at the hospital early today, they told me that he got very aggressive. He was highly agitated. He tried to hit people and yelled nasty things at them. He kept trying to get out of bed, wanting to leave the floor. He probably would have, had he been able to walk.

Now he is being transferred to another floor. They seemed glad to be rid of him. One of the nurses wondered if I intended to take him home: "He is quite a handful," she stated. When I found his room, he was heavily sedated. Good thing. He desperately needs to sleep. He desperately needs to calm his raging storms. And he was restrained. Around the waist so he would not fall out of bed. And his wrists tied to the bed. Oh, my God. This is what they do to crazy people, right? My calm George, whose beautiful blue eyes I fell so deeply in love with, a man I relied on all our days together for his reassuring peaceful manner, restrained. So he will not hit people. So he will not fight. Fight what? And whom? George, what is going in that fine mind of yours?

I could not stay. I could not watch this. I could not wait until he woke up to discover his wrists tied to the bed.

He cries a lot.
31 July 2011

This is just like 'the frail old man' story. At the other places, you were quickly labeled with dementia, sitting like a frail old man in a wheelchair … making loopy comments that people smiled at. But, still, what a nice man. Too bad the wife does not accept what is going on.

Now he is a frail old man who cries a lot. Still, a nice man! Now he is no longer trying to hit people. But he "cries a lot." And he does cry a lot. Now so often that I have come to expect it when I visit.

The first time I ever saw George cry in our entire marriage was toward the end of his stay at the LTAC. Out of the blue. Clearly frustrated. A nurse in the unit had asked a couple weeks earlier if he had ever experienced depression. He had not, but given everything, he was headed straight toward that brick wall. Can somebody please pay more attention to this and less to dementia and Parkinson's?!

Well, there was another time, maybe. We were living in Oregon, and spent the weekend in the mountains. The kids and I were either skiing or snowboarding. George used to be quite the skilled skier, but now weight and age slowed all that down, and he sat in the lodge, reading a book, even though he wanted so dearly to ski. He was quite upset that night, missing the days past of his more agile youth. He did not really cry, but he sure came close! I told him to lose 75 pounds and he would be skiing down any mountain he wanted! But before all that happened, we headed back toward the plains and prairies of a broader Midwest landscape.

During the shift change, his nurse was introducing him to the new nurse on the evening shift. She told her some things she needed to know regarding his specific care … and for whatever reason she needed to add … He cries a lot.' I could not disagree. He does. Perhaps she said this so the new evening nurse would not be alarmed … this is just what he does. The new normal.

Next step
1 August 2011

George was to be transferred to the Indiana Veterans' Home today. He did finally get accepted. But his numbers for taking Coumadin are 'off,' way off. They need to be normal before he can be transferred. I hope this delay does not mess things up. George has been acting so crazy. When he is not crying, he is simply mad. He asked me the other day if I had brought a gun with me. He told me we were going to need it to "get out of this place." Has George lost his mind? I really do not want any of this shared with the Veterans' Home. They might not take him. I told them he needed rehab for a knee replacement. I guess I need to be careful, because I am sure all of this will be in his chart, and they *will* get his chart. I just need to get him into this facility. I have checked other long-term care facilities and the cost would be exorbitant. I am just finished with every other place … at this point, I simply want the VA to take care of him. My trust level right now is very low.

"What was he like before all this?" 2 August 2011

I let the ambulance get a head start toward Lafayette before I head south. I want George admitted before I show up. Maybe he will behave and not act crazy and just settle down. He wants to go back to 'that place" he was "before"… the home he did recognize. He has had it with hospitals. I told him he was going to see his doctors in Indianapolis and, before that happened, which would be soon, we had to stay in another VA facility for a short while. I am lying and feel very sneaky. I have never acted like this before in our marriage.

When I find his room, he looks pathetic in his bed. It is as though he was just deposited there: did they think he was going to 'rest up' from his trip? He is already agitated and wants out: "This place is dreadful!" George must wonder why I am not responding to his demands to go home, such as he remembers "that place."

I am told Dr. Goodman wants to meet with me. He is the Chief Medical Officer for this entire large four-building facility serving hundreds of veterans and their spouses. Now, THIS is a Chief Medical Officer unlike the ones at the rinky-dink facilities where

George was all summer, before I brought him home. The very first question this man posed to me was, "What was your husband like before all this?" – meaning I assume, the operation. So, the game is up. No more pulling punches. I guess it did not take this bevy of experienced folks long to figure out George has more than just a host of physical maladies. The place is full of veterans in all stages of need, so I am sure they have seen it all.

As I am talking with the doctor, George is brought in in his wheelchair. He was asking for me. He will join our conversation, which may be difficult because there is a great deal to discuss about his mental condition. I told the doctor about his being diagnosed with Parkinson's and he did a brief examination, enough to determine that he does *not* have this disease. Some of the nurses who had visited us from home health care had been a bit stunned to hear this diagnosis as well.

In the conversation, he asks George where he taught; he offers only the simple reply: "Everywhere." I elaborate on 'everywhere.' George had been an editor of the Daniel Webster papers at Dartmouth; an NEH fellow at Yale University; a fellow at Lambeth Palace in London; a scholar in residence at UCLA; a professor at the University of Wisconsin in LaCrosse; a Fulbright Scholar in Africa and Central Asia and a Senior Fulbright Specialist in the Middle East. The doctor looks at George in a very tender way. He sees a lot of soldiers who once led vigorous lives come at last to the Veterans' Home coping with physical and mental challenges that all but strip away their once youthful armor. Dr. Goodman very quietly says: "We are going to take care of you."

"This is the Gestapo!"
3 August 2011

After spending the night in Indianapolis with our daughter, I arrive around noon today. I am so exhausted! I stop at the main switchboard to ask about someone I have to see who has papers that need to be signed, when I get a call via the Switchboard. George is looking for me: "Where is my wife?" I am told to come to his floor as quickly as I can. Is he OK?

George is at the nurses' station, in his wheelchair. "These are all racists!" he shouts. "Fascists!" And the head nurse, Angela, "heads up the Gestapo." Angela, who is busy with a chart, just looks up to check out my reaction. No one appears to be rattled by all this. I am assuming this is not terribly uncommon.

I had a brief conversation with Angela the day before, enough to sense that George was in good hands on this head nurse's floor.

I can do nothing for his agitation, and I do not know what they are going to do. Restrain him as they did in the hospital? Dope him up?

I have a long drive home, so I do not stay very long. There can be no conversation with George ... what would we talk about? He has already decided he does not want to be in this place. Does not *need* to be in this place. There is nothing wrong with him. He wants to leave.

Before I go, we take a long walk around the grounds. The place is on 250 acres and is beautiful. I have never seen a long-term care facility with such an expansive landscape. Veterans are everywhere, at all levels of personal mobility. There is an adjoining veterans' cemetery that looks like a smaller version of Arlington. The original Commandant's home, still standing in a grove of trees, is now closed up, next to other original structures; perhaps in a better economic climate funds for restoration could be found. The place was built toward the end of the 19th century for Indiana Civil War Veterans who had become aged and infirm. Inside the main building is a very nice library, which I find unusual as well, graced with several comfortable wingback chairs next to windows and bird cages. A bird aviary is in the main hallway along with a large- screen TV with more comfortable chairs and couches. There is a long line of rockers farther down another hallway adjoining a second building, all of which look out over the grounds, and several tables with games and puzzles. I am told there is a woodworking shop if George is interested, and there is a smoking room, which is open much of the day for the veterans so they do not have to go outside. That is very accommodating, considering that any staff who want to smoke have to leave the buildings and cross a road to light up. There is a fairly large auditorium that hosts a whole range of ongoing activities including workshops on veterans' issues, Bingo every Saturday and Sunday, and weekend Protestant and Catholic church services. Mostly I am impressed with the staff, who almost to a person appear to care genuinely about the veterans. I am sure there is more than one sour apple, but for the most part, the veterans are treated with tremendous respect and dignity. As they should be.

But George does not care about any of this. Before I leave, he is in a terrible crying rant about his involvement in the Korean War. All the people killed. How horrible it was. I have never heard him express any of this before.

This is the second time within days!
5 August 2011

What is going through your mind? This is the second time within less than a week you got up too fast, fell, and off you go to the emergency room, again! The first time you fell on your hip. Because you grimaced, x-rays were needed to rule out a fracture. You joked with the nurse, wanting bells and whistles on the ambulance, 'getting your money's worth.' And the bills mount. Now again, this evening: Doug and Eva had just left two hours ago, and off you go again: standing up too fast for anyone to stop you, even though a CNA was right there. You fell on your knees and your head. You complain that your head hurts, and off you go again for x-rays. Do you want more bells and whistles? George, this is not a game! And the bills mount.

What demons are running through your head? I know you want out of there. That is all you complain about. And you could leave if you could walk! If you could just get into a car or the truck. But you will not cooperate in physical therapy. You balk. You act ugly with people. Even though they are professionals, their feelings must be hurt. We cannot get through to you that the ticket out is your ability to be mobile. And that alone might not be your ticket out. If you are not cognizant – and you are not! – you cannot leave. I cannot try that experiment again. When we were home, you were becoming unhappy. That Sunday, late in the afternoon, you asked why we were not doing something. I so wanted to bring you home, to go off to Lake Michigan, to Mongo, even to Quaker meetings with you! But I could not get you out of the house by myself, not with you in a wheelchair. And what if you needed to pee? This you did not seem to understand. I began to see the looks: your chin in your hand, stuck, dumped, moody, and getting depressed. So just being home was not enough.

So here you are. If mobile, you could take trips out. This place is not the prison the other facilities were. But you have become your own worst enemy. I am glad there are too many miles between me and the VA. If there weren't, I would be expected to drop everything and rush off to the Emergency Room, like a good wife. Crazy. No one can seem to reason with you. Have you created this? Are you at all aware? What will it take?

And the bills mount.

The Dementia Floor
6 August 2011

George has been moved to the dementia floor, though not necessarily because he has dementia. An evaluation is still needed to make that final determination despite the obvious signs, and everyone here in this facility is in some shade of mental gray! But since he has arrived he has left the building and wheeled his chair down near the bus stop. Few buses come onto the grounds, but he does not know that. He simply read the sign that says 'Bus Stop' and figures one will come. They are concerned that he is trying to run away; and for his safety, he has been moved to the dementia unit. He can still leave the floor if someone is with him, and everything else is like other units – except

I do notice that the eating utensils are all plastic with no knives, just forks and spoons. The elevators require a special key for them to come to that floor and that is to avoid the people getting on an elevator when no one is looking.

I accept this. I think I am still in a state of mild shock over it all. But I understand the move. And it does not seem to faze George one bit. He thinks all the people on the dementia floor are just fine, and tells me about different ones he is meeting. A few months ago this would have been transparent to George and he would have felt sorry for those on this floor, but not now.

He did not even know he was home.
7 August 2011

I thought when I brought George home, light bulbs would go off in his mind and eyes. He wanted to come home since Day One in regular rehab, 'back then' when everything was still normal and OK. Over time, he began to refer to our home as "your apartment." I would tell George, it is *our* home. And he would nod, *OK*. Just to make me happy. But he did not believe it was his home. It was just *my* home.

But all that would change as we drove into the complex. Things would look familiar. The cloud in his mind caused by all the drugs and fever and illness and stress would lift. It did not. He seemed to remember Martin's grocery store, Saint Mary's College, the dome of Notre Dame … or so he said. But not where we lived. And yet … we were about to enter the front door. That would do it!

It did not. Not his comfy chairs. Not his slippers. Not the living room full of bookcases and artifacts from our lives in Africa, the Middle East, Central Asia. Not the bird feeders. He used to call me often to talk about the ducks visiting in the back yard fighting over the corn with the squirrels and the rabbits. Nothing struck a spark. He thought it all looked nice! Probably thought he would be comfortable in this place. But not yet *his* place.

It occurs to me that, when he is alternating among being aggressive, angry, and sad, now that he is once again in a 'facility,' he does not mention being home. I see this as perhaps a blessing. For all his misery, since he did not realize he actually was home – something he wanted so badly – then perhaps he will not have the pain of missing it all over again.

When visiting him at the VA home this weekend, I found him ranting again about how he hated the place; how he did not like the people; how no one knew what they were doing; how he was not going to do physical therapy because they did not know what they were doing there either. The only place he thought was any good was the university. He liked that place. He thought the people he saw there were good, kind, knew what they doing. He thought he would make progress there and wanted to go back to the university. He was not sure where it was exactly: northern Iowa? Even when George is loopy, he references things which were part of his life. He is a retired professor, so talking about universities makes sense. And we did once live in Iowa and had a grand time there. I pressed him about this place he liked so much. Surely he was not talking about the facilities he was in before coming home? He wanted to go back to *those* places? He complained nonstop! Then it hit me. We live on University Park Court, in the University Park Apartments. All he could recall from that was 'university.' In his mind, he was not home; he was just in another facility. Quite a nice one. He was the only resident, except for me looking after him night and day. Cooking good food. Watching whatever he liked on TV. Being waited on. In comfy chairs. Cool and quiet as a heat wave raged outdoors. And those people from Memorial Home Care were terrific ... he had their complete attention. Just another facility. Could he go back?

Now I am all alone.
8 August 2011

I signed papers today that give complete access to George's checking account to the VA. His income – all of it Social Security – will now be used to cover his co-pay. I will no longer have access to this account. His income is now *their* income. That part of our partnership is now finished. Money that was once used to buy groceries, gifts for birthdays and Christmas, cards for special occasions, a fishing license, coffee at Starbucks … now belongs to them. And rightfully so. It is his fair portion to pay. They will put about $30 a month into a trust fund that he can draw from when he likes. But it is so strange. Not ours. Not his contribution to our financial household. Not his. And not mine. Certainly not mine. And so another part of our partnership, our marriage, is finished. I am so alone.

It was only a T-shirt.
15 August 2011

We always enjoyed the AP US History readings. Crazy, considering that we read for eight hours a day, seven days straight, starting at 8 a.m. with strictly defined breaks. Not quite the schedule we normally keep in our independent lives. But we enjoyed it! Our plan was that George would have as quick a recovery as with his hip operations and off we would go. There was concern about it being so soon after the surgery, but we would hope for the best.

And then his world crashed. We did not yet know it was crashing. He just got real sick, but reports were that he was getting better. So we did not know – or I did not know – that his world was ending.

He has a series of t-shirts from these readings. Collecting them is a big deal. A phrase chosen from one of the readings is inscribed on the back … a phrase that everyone will understand, accompanied by peals of knowing laughter. This year's color is a really nice forest green, a color that will look good on George.

Laundry services in long-term care facilities are notorious for chewing up and ruining people's clothes, and they also often get lost. I said I would do his laundry, thank you. But I learned quickly not to have anything 'favorite' among his clothes. The sign "family will do laundry" could have been written in several languages and posted all over his room, and his clothes would still make it to the facility's laundry room – sometimes with his cell phone still in his pocket. Clearly his favorite t-shirts were going to stay home, and most especially the AP t-shirts, which are classics.

So it was when he was safely home that he got to wear his newest nifty AP forest-green shirt. In fact, he wore it the last night he was home. And in the chaos in the Emergency Room I did not notice it had been removed. I found his other clothes later, but not the shirt. It was only a t-shirt, but it was symbolic of a time, now perhaps the last time, when our lives still encompassed the longed-for and cherished routine we had known for so long. Now gone.

Cellulitis ... again!
22 August 2011

The call came Friday afternoon. George was again taken to the Emergency Room. He legs had been swelling all week, and that was one concern. But he also had cellulitis, and this needed immediate treatment.

The only cellulitis George and I know – and I doubt that George even remembers – is a wallop. Last time George had it for about a month, and a very bad month it was. High fever, lots of shaking, total lack of cognition – these took over his entire body. He was very, very sick. One nurse told me she was concerned that George's leg would have to be amputated. Surely the new prosthesis would get infected ... how could it escape this raging infection?! If he has cellulitis again, he will not make it. He simply cannot go through that all over again. This time it will no doubt attack the prosthesis.

But I guess there is cellulitis, and there is cellulitis. And this time George got a break. No PICC lines. No Vacomycin, mother of all antibiotics. No shaking. Not even a fever. An IV antibiotic for sure ... and the main reason why he had to go to the hospital. Still treated quite seriously. But this antibiotic comes in a small tube and is finished in about 30 minutes. Before, he was on two incredibly powerful antibiotics that came in bags, each dripping into his system for several hours a day. The nurses must wonder why I am so casual about this, and I am not sure that the good people at the VA facility really are clear about just how sick George has been. It is amazing this guy remains walking on the earth.

So this was a pass. Back to the VA by Sunday. And on the way back, a very nice drive for about three hours ... visiting parks and picking up a picnic lunch. This time George got lucky.

Just when I thought the crying was over
27 August 2011

Today is our wedding anniversary. When I parked the car outside the drugstore to buy some cards, I started to cry, again. I was reminded of what George said before all this began, when he was still in regular rehab after surgery, chomping at the bit to get home. Back when it was all still 'normal.' All he wanted to do was to get in his truck and go to a store. Stuck in a wheelchair and working on slow progress to walk again, he still remembered his truck. Credit card slips in his wallet reveal that, every day, the week before his surgery, he was at Starbucks. Was that his usual habit? Or did he just have a feeling? If it had all worked out, he would probably have come to this same drugstore to buy cards for me. He spent a lot of time looking for just the right card. But better than the card were his own words. George always wrote something special ... always.

I was told that he was really sharp this week. Carried on normal conversations. Very astute. I wondered what to expect. No miracles, of course. But I do not feel hopeless.

He was OK. He did seem more alert, which was good news. So I started talking with him like the old George, like old times. And he responded. But he always responded in the past, like a good husband. Was he *really* getting it?

The weather is still hot this late summer, and going outside will remain a treat for a long time to come. I had a couple of Starbucks coffees and my weekend newspapers. Let's go outside to read! And that is when I noticed. He barely reads anymore. And he rereads stories in the newspaper. The book I brought him – a history book, one of his Christmas presents – remains unopened, although he says he is reading it. He was an avid reader. He may have had early stages of dementia before all this happened, but he was still an avid reader.

We had dinner in one of Lafayette's nicest restaurants. A chic place, the kind we always liked. It was a good choice. He was still alert and we could talk, although not with a lot of depth. He does not seem to have any idea of how sick he has been, what has happened, how long all this has gone on, all the places he has been … and if I broach it, it seems painful to him. What does he remember?

Then it began. Are we in Monticello? No, George, Lafayette. Where did he get the name Monticello? Not sure, heard it on the news about the hurricane, some town in Virginia. What is Joey doing this weekend? He is in drill. Why? He is in the National Guard. The Guard? Did you forget that? Yes. And then … 'they' were asking what he was going to do after Christmas, when the semester is over. Would he be staying at the university? (Who is 'they'?) He wondered if he would be staying, since, after all, he is not teaching. Again he asked about the university, where he was 'up north.' Would he be returning there? He liked that place. And then, just to put an exclamation point on the entire troubling conversation, he licked his knife.

After dinner, we took a drive before returning to 'campus' and his 'dorm.' A recliner had been put in his room so he could get out of his wheelchair and spend time reading and watching TV. But he immediately asked if he could go to the 'lounge.' This is a series of chairs across from the nurses' station. Everyone on the dementia floor seems to congregate next to the nurses' station, and George is no exception. This is what he wants to do, and the nurses are used to it. They now have a comfortable stool that George uses to keep his feet up. His attending CNA was gently prodding him to go to his room and go to bed ... it was getting late: "George, what can I do to convince you to go to bed?" Does he do this every night? Yes. He does not like to go to bed. So he sits in the brightly lit lounge, hub of all activity, and enjoys 'watching the world go by,' as he puts it. Not reading his books. Not connecting to the outside world he can view on TV. Not even sports. Here is his new world. A world I cannot share ... one I am certainly not ready to share. So I left his 'dorm' and went to *my* new normal, and cried.

I miss the phone calls.
29 August 2011

It was mostly silly stuff. The kind of sweet chatter that binds couples together, way outside the heady conversations that belong to high-intellect dinner parties. And long, long after one is trying to impress the other in a courtship. Oh, we most assuredly did the 'heady conversations.' That was our fun! Having people over for dinner for sumptuous meals (I am a yummy cook!), delicious wine, and deeply stimulating conversation. No one-upmanship in our scholarly household, though scholars we are. Just thoughtful conversations – and sometimes fast exchanges – on the issues of the day.

But between us, just simple conversation. George was often home alone. I have been the 'breadwinner' for years. He never quite took to taking on activities in this college community. He was content with the world he created that included friendly chats with the folks at the grocery store and Starbucks on his frequent forays, the fellows at the Mongo nature and hunting reserve who must surely miss him by now, the woman who cleaned our house, and our fabulous neighbor who often baked goodies to his delight. And our phone calls.

When Tiger Woods was playing, I always got a call. I do not know if he was a big fan. I am, and he catered to me. We moaned that he was not yet out of the abyss. The antics on our patio were a frequent topic. I would hear how the squirrels, rabbits, and ducks were squaring off over the cornhusks, and he would bet on the ducks ... surely a leftover from his Oregon days! If there was breaking news, he would call to see if I was watching TV, which always baffled me. Why on earth would I be watching TV? That was *his* world! He would call toward the end of the day, wondering when I was coming home. He was always patient with my crazy schedule. "I'll be here!" he would say, with a smile in his voice.

George had his cell phone with him for the longest time during this crazy ordeal. At the first rehab center, the walls were too thick and the place too old to hold a signal. So we had to rely on the landline ... yet we managed. It wasn't the same as his cell phone, but this was only temporary, after all. Soon he would be home. It was a mild inconvenience. We had no idea what would happen next.

I was thrilled that the LTAC was high tech enough to allow cell phone usage. And call he did! Often throughout the day ... when he was not seriously ill. And *that* was often enough. I will never forget when I got a call one afternoon, the week that George was so sick with the virulent infection that I thought surely he was going to die ... and then his number flashed on my phone. George was calling! My heart leaped out of my chest. Oh, the joy of still being in love! I was so excited. His conversation was clear, so amazingly clear. He had trouble hitting the numbers, and someone helped him. But there was his voice, the voice I fell in love with so many years earlier.

"Betty. How are you?" "How am *I*? George. You have been so sick!" "I know," he says. "I have been worried about you," I yell. "I am worried about *you*," he replies, in that gentle manner of his, always so assuring. I left immediately, got some special treats we could munch on as we again spent time together, just doing nothing. I was confident that surely this awful period would pass.

Again and again he called. Several times a day. Increasingly, as he moved on to yet another new facility. Terribly impatient, mostly depressed. When was I coming? When was he leaving? And I always promised him the same, because I believed in the same … soon. Soon I would bring him home.

And I kept that promise of home.

There were no phone calls when he was again in the hospital. Oh, a few, but not many. He had no cell phone. And the room phone was often out of his reach. He would have a nurse help him call me, and he was always crying. It was so hard. We had no conversations. Just sadness.

He has called a few times from the VA facility, but the calls have dropped off. Initially, he was still reaching out to me, so depressed, so sad. I guess the medications are helping with that now. But he is again creating a new world, and I guess there is not much regarding that to talk about with me. I do not belong in that world. It is not about our patio and our little nature reserve. Nothing in the mail has arrived to invite us anywhere. I need nothing 'from the store' or the post office. And he is not coming home for dinner.

He wants to stay on the dementia floor.
1 September 2011

It was all arranged. George was to be moved. He may have 'mild' dementia (OK, maybe 'mild to moderate,' depending on whose report one reads). At the second rehab hospital he was reported by the psychologist to have 'moderate to severe' dementia, so I guess he is improving, but he really does not belong on the dementia floor. He was put there when he first arrived because he kept trying to escape. It wasn't exactly like scaling the side of a prison wall, but after our walk about the grounds the afternoon he arrived, he remembered quite well that all he needed to do was get on the elevator and the doors would open automatically on the first floor, taking him outdoors. For his 'own safety,' he was moved to the 'second floor,' which I knew full well was the dementia unit. Everyone at the veterans' home is in a state of gray, including George. If one had full physical and mental ability, there would be no need to live there. But on the dementia floor, people tend to be in advanced stages of either dementia or Alzheimer's. And George, while continuing to say loopy things (since he still thinks he is living in a dorm on a university campus – which he considers second-rate – and is waiting to see what they will ask him to teach), is otherwise very clear and conversant.

So, off he was to go to another floor – take your pick, George. You can get back on that elevator and come and go as you please. Take your meals in the cafeteria on the first floor of the Mitchell Building. Go to the library. Go outdoors! And I will hope you forget about escaping again. But when the moment arrives, you do not want to go. You want to stay on the second floor of MacArthur. You are comfortable, happy, secure. And I am more than disappointed. Getting off that floor would have been a step toward the normal life I still think, in the back of my mind, that you are returning to – at some point, I hope. The head nurse on that unit whom I respect and like a great deal acknowledges your ability to make this decision. And you are adamant. We talk. You will leave if 'you want me to, Betty,' your voice making it clear you do not want to leave this world that has brought you safety and security. I tell you I am disappointed, which is a really unfair thing for me to say. I know full well that you are not as cognizant as I am so hoping you could be. And you cry. I am making you cry. You do not want to disappoint me, and I am now only adding to your confusion and pain. Carla comforts you and lets you go back to the dining room so you can have your supper … you are eating supper now at 5 p.m. daily, hours earlier than our usual 8 p.m. habit. I can visualize you making your way down the hallway, in your new home, your new world.

I spend much of the rest of the day, and the next, crying.

Resentment
2 September 2011

So, you are happy. If you fall, someone is there to pick you up. When you scrape your arm or leg – which is often (and I always get a call) – someone is there to bandage you up. When you need to use the toilet, someone is there to help. When you need anything, someone is there with a fix. And you are happy, secure, comfortable. Well, I cannot say for sure about happy.

And when I come, the questions simply get transferred to me. Betty, I need a band-aid. I need to go to the toilet. I am cold. I want to move now. I cannot keep sitting in this wheelchair.... I bring along things I would like to read, journals and magazines I would like to catch up on ... perhaps we could read the papers together, over the Starbucks coffees I always bring and which you expect. But that does not happen for very long. You get restless easily and want to continue having your wheelchair moved about. Or you have to use the toilet again. Or you are simply bored. I am not a wife, I am not a friend ... I am simply an extension of the veterans' home.

I thought I was doing pretty well for the longest time, keeping up a tremendous pace and not really feeling strained. But lately I have felt incredible stress, so now I worry about a heart attack or stroke of my own. I feel I am wound very tight. George may be somewhat out of it, but I am not and cannot afford to be. I own a business, which is really floundering this year. A national job search has been derailed since all this began. I am not teaching this semester, which is a huge disappointment. I love being in the classroom, teaching. The bills are mounting like crazy, and there is little money to pay for them, even a fraction of them. I deal with that. I have dealt with all this, all the moves from one place to another. Fighting and advocating on your behalf. Fending off what I felt were crazy diagnoses. Working so hard to get you patched up and back home and normal again – whatever that means. Coping with the failure of all that, and the likely reality of where this is all headed.

And you do not have a clue. Gone is my husband, my partner, my friend. Gone is the person I could talk to, someone I used to count on to help patch things up for me. You are almost like a 'Stepford' spouse in your responses as we talk: yes, no, yes some more. And when you do offer your own comment, it is not grounded in reality: Are we in Monticello? What is the name of this university? Is this northern California? At the speed this is all moving, I am waiting for the day you do not recognize *me*.

Do not think for a moment that resentment is not a part of all this.

Try 'being alone' on for size.
3 September 2011

I never noticed it before. I have lived and traveled all over the country and the world, it seems all my life, and often alone. If I had waited for someone else to do anything adventurous, it would never have happened. I had been single for so long, waiting until I was 35 to get married. I am sure my parents had given up on me! And when I did, my friends were shocked. I was very independent by the time I got married.

Being married is not my only identity. But after 28 years of a pretty good marriage, you really are used to having someone with you – most especially if that person is your best friend, as George has been my best friend. I still miss having the children living at home and likely always will. I really like having my family around me!

George's health issues prevented him from joining me in many of my sports, but we often were still together. George would grab his book and perhaps a carafe of coffee and, while I skied, he would read in the lodge. While I biked, he would find a park bench. While I stormed down to the icy waters and sandy beaches of Lake Michigan, he would find a shaded picnic table up on the grassy knolls above the dunes. When I golfed, he would ride around in a cart. We were still together, and we also had our fun rituals after the 'workout.'

We loved having people over for dinner – I love to cook, and we so enjoyed the intellectual banter of a stimulating evening. We had our favorite shows on TV and always looked forward to the British comedies and the PBS News Hour. We stuck by Tiger Woods as he struggled to regain his footing, and George kept an eye on the crockpot while I attended Notre Dame home games with a flock of out-of-town guests.

Now the house is quiet. I look over at his chair and wish he were in it, watching his beloved ESPN or just snoozing away. I wish he were making his coffee, working on the computer, setting the table, folding clothes, reading manuscripts, listening to his favorite CDs. I have not had time to get ready for this.

He cries, I cry.
6 September 2011

George cries now so easily. In 28 years of marriage, I never saw him cry, not once. And now, so easily. He cries when I get ready to leave. He cries when he asks about Joey, our son, and when am I coming for a visit. He cries when we talk on the phone. He cried when we had dinner for our anniversary, and he cried when he gave me his card – which Joey bought for him – and realized he had forgotten to get a gift. He cried. He cries often.

I cry too. But never in front of him. I wonder if our pain is different? He is depressed. Is he also afraid we are leaving him? That I am leaving him? I cry because *he* has already left.

Am I still an advocate?
10 September 2011

This book I am writing is about advocacy. And that is how I have felt for all this time with George. I needed to be so alert and assertive. On top of things. Now the VA is taking care of him. I see him once a week. For a day, often two. Only part of the days. It is a long drive round- trip. I still intervene, but have basically let them take charge. I make suggestions or ask things, and I assume it happens. But the intensity is over. I am less tired now. Less strained. I still cry a lot. But perhaps it does not always have to be so intense.

Betrayal
12 September 2011

George thinks it would be a good idea if we moved to South Africa. We both loved living in Africa. That is where we met, spent the best years of our marriage, and, overall, the best years of our entire lives! It was a wonderful life. Our children spent their early childhoods in Africa, and they were idyllic. We traveled often, and life seemed serene, despite the frequent chaos of living in a charged economic and political climate. The work we did was rewarding and fulfilling. Our lives were full.

I have often said that, if I were told I had six months to live, I would immediately go to South Africa while I still had some bit of health left to enjoy my second home. During one of George's most desperate moments in his illness, while most agitated, he was plotting his escape from the hospital, saying he was going to run away to Africa.

Today, as we walked through the shady and peaceful grounds of the Indiana Veterans' Home, he suggested we move back to Africa. We loved our lives there, we would once again find meaningful work, the cost of living might be lower, and we would be happy.

I did not disagree, but I did not point out to George that the likelihood of that happening was as remote as his living another one hundred years. And I certainly did not mention that, in my mind, I was already wondering how George would manage to live out the rest of his days very likely in this nursing home.

"Is there room for me?"
13 September 2011

We have all read the articles: in a senior citizens' newsletter, in an opinion piece in the newspaper, or in a popular features magazine. A loved one in a nursing home begs to go home. I was reading one by a Sister in a progressive Catholic newspaper, writing about her aunt.

I thought it was an odd piece for a publication that focuses on how social issues in the Catholic Church impact society. But I have also long subscribed to the idea that things are put in front of you for a reason. This was not a piece I wanted to read. George had not yet even come home for his 'triumphant' return, and our goals remained walking, hunting, fishing, traveling. But this faces us all at some point. This was her aunt, cognizant of where she was and where she did not want to be. A lovely home to be sure, as many are. But not 'home.' Each visit was agony, accompanied by tears and pleas: "I'll be good," she begged. "I won't be any trouble." But in the end, we know best, right? Someone must know best, because their 'new home' is where our loved ones often stay.

George cannot remember home. He remembers our next-door neighbor. He remembers his son's home in Illinois that he has seen only twice in five years. But he cannot remember where we lived for five years. I guess in a sense that is a blessing, because he is not begging to 'come home.' No, this is his plea instead, and it is just as painful: "Where you live, is there room for me?"

I thought we could have a normal time of it.
21 September 2011

There is a lovely new state park near Lafayette – Prophetstown State Park – named for the famed Indian who had visions that eventually harmed the many Indian tribes that gallantly fought in futile battle against Benjamin Henry Harrison and his troops, whose purpose was to wipe them out of Indiana forever. It has a tranquil campsite and a winding bike trail of several miles. We packed a picnic lunch, and afterward I biked. I left George in a secure parking area, with lots of newspapers and coffee, telling him I would not be gone very long. The bike path was only 2.5 miles and I would only do a few quick loops. I really needed this exercise.

By the time I got back to the car 40 minutes later, he had begun to take his clothes off. A woman who was parked nearby was relieved

I had finally returned. He told her I had been gone a "very long time." He was frantic, repeating this over and over. She had alerted the park police to find me, and sure enough, a park police car careened up to our spot. I tried to explain to everyone what was going on. The park police looked at me very suspiciously. The woman understood. Her mother who has dementia lives with her. She cannot be gone very long either. Her mother will think it is 'hours,' when in fact only 30 minutes might have elapsed. She is very kind.

I was not as kind to George. Stupid me. I could not resist letting him know just how I felt. I could reason this out. He cannot, at this point. And I leave him feeling as though he ruined the day. And weekend. And in fact I had ruined it all by myself. I had ruined it for *him*.

'Enter at your own risk.'
22 September 2011

I read a shocking statistic the other day. A well-documented statistic. When I checked it out with a Google search, page after page of reports, articles, and other data popped up to support this comment: complications from hospitalizations (infections, errors with medications and doctors, etc.) are a leading cause of death in the United States following heart disease and cancer.

When I was growing up, hospitals were unfriendly places with dark, hushed halls, crabby nurses, and severely restricted visiting hours. Perhaps this is an exaggeration of my memory, but one could only hope that a seriously ill relative or friend could 'hang in' until visiting hours before passing.

Today, large multi-story entrances feature fountains and sculpture. The inviting aroma of lattes fills the air, and upscale gift shops are among the few places in town to purchase Vera Bradley products and Pandora jewelry. Scores of friendly volunteers – often healthy-looking senior citizens – cruise about in golf carts offering to take visitors to their destination. The places are abuzz with uplifting décor and friendly chatter. Perhaps it might be a good idea to have endless bottles of hand sanitizer everywhere, along with gloves and face masks. Perhaps security guards should ask visitors to wash their hands upon entering a hospital, and sanitize every step of the way to and from the person they are visiting: going in and out of the restrooms, stepping in and off elevators and stairwells, entering and leaving rooms. Sinks with hot water and soap should line the hallways and corridors of every floor, although this is likely to scare people, because it flies in the face of all the friendly marketing and hospitals are not likely to take this drastic step. However, it needs to be noted that MRSA, a staph infection once found only in hospitals but now in nursing homes and even fitness centers, has a frightening mortality rate! And that is only one type of virulent infection: a second and equally daunting one is cellulitis. Although not all cellulitis is a staph infection, and some cellulitis can be quickly treated, my husband's case of cellulitis had him in an acute care facility for over a month, while pumped with powerful antibiotics for hours a day via a PICC line.

This all reminds me of a movie titled 'Tucker: the Man and His Dreams,' that came out in 1988. Preston Tucker was a visionary who loved cars. Following World War II, he set out to produce beautiful models that came in stunning colors other than drab grey, had disc brakes and padded windshields that popped out on impact, and boasted seat belts. The Detroit 'Big Three' hated him. He was a threat, and they accused him of stock fraud. They challenged his idea of seat belts, which he argued would save lives in an accident. That was their point, they yelled back: We do not want to give the impression that driving cars is not safe!

Hospitals need to be honest to the public about risks and take aggressive cautionary steps, before someone hangs a sign over the doors: 'Enter at your own risk.'

It begins: "Can I come home?"
25 September 2011

George is no longer on the dementia floor. He was moved to another floor, even though he did not want to move. He found security on the 2nd floor, but the staff realizes he does not belong there. He is again reading manuscripts for possible publication. Time to move off the dementia floor! So, despite his protests, he is moved. Wait and see.

Today, he says for the first time, "I never thought I would see the day I would be living in a veterans' home." Does it finally dawn on him that he is not living in a dorm on the college campus of a "second-rate university"? Maybe not entirely. Over dinner, he tells me one of the residents he has befriended is in the history department.

And from the moment I arrived today, it was … "When can I go home with you? Is there room for me where you are living?" I was so tired this afternoon that I took a nap on the couch in the lounge while he watched TV. This would be typical if we were still living together. It gets a little crazy trying to figure out how to fill time when I'm with him. When we were home together, the routine was easy, often just doing 'our own thing.' He would be watching sports on TV. Reading emails. Buried deep in one of the endless books he stockpiled as a retiree. I would be working at the computer. Puttering in the garden. Cooking. Sending emails. In this place we both find foreign, I am running out of ideas. And this particular weekend, he is like a broken record with his displeasure. So I slept, in the lounge on the main floor, in front of the big-screen TV, where people come and go. No privacy. Just like the airports long ago during long layovers, when we were traveling halfway around the world to yet another destination for work. Only this is not adventurous. The first thing I hear when I open my eyes is, "Have you thought about how much more time I am going to stay here?" This is not adventurous for George, either.

I always thought – for years and years I thought – that, if George ever landed in a place like where he is now, he would not last. When he was in the previous facilities, home was always the goal. Now that is uncertain. He really would not be here if it were just early-onset dementia; that is not the normal procedure. But he is still in a wheelchair. And while he goes often to the toilet alone, he still has risks. Just last night the night nurse called to say he had fallen again while going to the toilet alone, losing his balance. He does not keep his legs up enough throughout the day to prevent his legs from swelling with edema, and he refuses to sleep in the bed. Flat-out refuses. So his having been here this long without serious complications is amazing.

But I think it is beginning. He said toward the end of the day, when I was not giving him the words he wanted to hear about an imminent date of departure, "If I do not leave here, I do not think I will last very long."

George is cognizant enough to know exactly where he is. And he does not like it. He cannot remember where we live. He just knows that he wants to be with me. And I want to be with him! There are wives who would do it. Despite our financial situation, I could do it. I would most certainly be living in poverty, since I could not work. But I could do it. Am I a bad wife? Am I selfish? I feel that, if our roles were reversed, he would do all he could to bring me home and be with me. I know he would. And I would trust him to do that. Am I heartless? Am I breaking a promise of trust to him ... to this good man?

The depression is getting worse.
26 September 2011

George hates the fourth floor. I figured out why he misses the 2nd floor. So do I at this point! The staff on the 4th floor seem crabby and tired, not very responsive ... just doing a job. The residents all look gloomy and sad, not willing to communicate. The people on the 2nd floor talked all the time. Most of the time, it made little sense. But they were happy! Chatting away. And the staff were saints. How can one possibly yell at these people? Sure, one loses patience. But to lose one's temper? What would that achieve? So, humoring is the order of the day. And the floor is full of joyful energy, disconnected perhaps, but fluid ... unlike the pallor of the 4th floor. Maybe I want George to return, as well.

His depression deepens again. He called tonight. He is planning to escape. He will take his money out of the trust – his memory isn't so bad after all, as I barely mentioned the trust fund kept for him at the facility – and run away. He'll visit 'my daughter' in Indianapolis (as opposed to 'our' daughter), whom he called Lydia ... which is the name of his oldest daughter in Los Angeles from his first marriage. Oh, yeah, he meant Eva. Or Doug in Illinois. Either one will let him stay because I will not, he claims. He is leaving tomorrow ... has it all planned out. I tell him he has a lot of people planning visits in the next few weeks ... coming from Ireland, North Carolina, other parts of Indiana. He does not care ... he will not be there. Then he complains that, because his legs are swollen, he cannot do much in physical therapy, and I cannot get through to him that that is half the battle. He does not keep his legs up enough throughout the day, so they are becoming seriously swollen, red, tight, and wrapped. He cannot wear ordinary shoes, and walking is difficult. He tells me he cries most of the night.

How much of this can we both bear?

I want to bring him home. Again, I know I could make him feel better. I know he would be happier. But he would not be any less 'loopy,' as the old expression goes. I would need to sleep at night, and now I know that he could be doing crazy things. I could stay in the chair, but how would I sleep with all the racket and lights and TV? That is his night now. And if I went upstairs to bed, what would he do? He did not seem to realize that when he was home last I was not going to the office. I am already worried about his nights when he comes home at Thanksgiving and Christmas, if we can make it that far. He says he is afraid he will have a complete nervous breakdown, and I am too.

God, why are you letting this happen? Why could he not have had a simple knee replacement and get on with it? What has he done in his life that deserves this? Do you have an answer? I DOUBT IT! AND, ANYWAY, IT IS NOT GOOD ENOUGH!

It was not that long ago that he said all he wanted to do was get in his truck and drive to a store. And it all was within reach, 'back then.' Just hang in there at the rehab center and it will happen. That was the plan.

A useful use of time
16 October 2011

Remember the flag? The exercise for small motor skills that involved several adults sitting around a table during occupational therapy, making an American flag out of construction paper, just in time for the Fourth of July?

I understood the point of the exercise, but that did not deflect my fury that the young occupational therapist had not considered how foolish this exercise was for a group of adults. When I complained to the administrator, I sarcastically suggested that perhaps she had grabbed the wrong age-group book off the shelf when looking for an activity for her group that day. In fairness to the facility, the administrator was not amused either.

The Indiana Veterans' Home was established in the late 1800s to provide a place for aging Civil War veterans who were either disabled or indigent and required care. This was, of course, decades before Medicare or Medicaid, Social Security, or any form of social net. As people aged, they lived with relatives. But what to do when one had no relatives or required special care? At the time, other states had established these facilities, and the original Federal building housing the commandant still sits on the grounds of 250 wooded acres, high above the Wabash River. Each county within the state took responsibility for building a cottage to house its own residents, and the streets were named for significant people or events of the Civil War, with the main avenues named Lincoln, Grant, and Sherman. One of the earliest residents amused himself by creating oil portraits of numerous US military leaders that today line the walls of the library. Walking into the front door of the library, one clearly makes out General Custer staring down at all who enter! This is quite a legacy left by one veteran, thanks to a skilled hobby he developed to alleviate his own boredom.

Nestled in the back of the library is a small room housing archives from the many decades of the Indiana Veterans' Home lifetime. Numbered yellowed pieces of paper, scotch-taped to cabinets and artifacts, reveal an attempt to inventory the archives' contents, which include books, journals, photographs, scrapbooks, military gear and uniforms, flags, and even a spike from the Death Bridge commonly known as the Bridge over the River Kwai.

As George continued to fight his deep despair, I was desperately looking for something beyond Bingo and church services. Not one for any sort of institutional church, George was attending every church service offered just to occupy his time. Given his academic background and experiences, there was surely something he could offer to these archives!

I was grateful to have been able to work closely with the main nurses on the two floors George typically occupied, including in the dementia unit. When it became known that George was reviewing a manuscript of a former student for publication by a press he continued to consult with, the medical team concluded it was time for him to leave the dementia unit. So we cooked up an idea: How long had it been since anyone had written anything about this special place that today so few knew about in Indiana, save people who lived in the immediate locale? George would be capable of leading such a project, or at least of being engaged in it. His background should surely attract the History Department at Purdue University, dementia or not. It's out there waiting for all of us! Just live long enough. This was something he could do, leaving as good a legacy as the priceless oils that graced the library of MacArthur. This would take time, but I could help. It would keep his fine mind connected to a useful task and maybe provide an example of what could happen within facilities where people feel they go to die.

What would it take to make this sort of thing work for more people, everywhere?

Some people are OK with Bingo, with attending all the church services, petting the occasional visiting dogs and cats, and listening to the endless choirs and scout troops singing songs of days gone by. Those are good! I have enjoyed Bingo too, as have our grown kids. But this gets tiresome in short order. Coming up in a few years is a generation of baby boomers who will soon enter these facilities in droves; they will not be content with sing-alongs.

I remember visiting my aunt, then in her mid-90s, when she lived in the assisted living section of a nursing home. She was in the dining room with her friends, having lunch. It was close to a national election, and I was canvassing. One of her friends commented that she should probably call Obama's local headquarters and offer her services on the telephone if they would be willing to let her call from her own room. "I have hours a day to fill," she said, and she wanted to do something useful.

To do something useful! Yes.

It doesn't matter.
14 October 2011

He cannot remember that I am coming tomorrow. As on most visits, I tell him repeatedly, within the same conversation, sometimes sentences apart, when I am coming. I am so overwhelmed. Today I was up at the usual time … early enough to get to the pool to do my laps and then get to the office at a decent hour. I also did a week's worth of laundry, some shopping, cooked my usual meal at home from scratch – never otherwise – paid bills, worked on more of his accounts, worked on the survey, made more appointments for Indy and my job search … and read the newspapers and watched TV to relax. All in a seventeen-hour day. He called a couple of times. He is still calculating how he is getting out of the VA. Last night he said his remote recliner does not work. He tried to call the floor a couple of times … no answer. I was very concerned that he would spend the night with his already swollen legs dangling down, getting worse, I finally fell asleep. Again tonight, the chair does not work. But it really does. He cannot for some reason see the remote control right next to him nor recall how it works. And in both conversations: When are you coming?"

I really should just sleep in tomorrow. Not set the alarm. Not worry about getting up and getting done whatever else I have to do (including folding the white clothes now in the dryer). I am concerned that it takes 2.5 hours to drive one way. I could just sleep in. He cannot remember when I am arriving, anyway! I could get there at any time. Any time! It will not matter to him. I know it will matter that I am there, with him. And I will be happy to be with him as well. This remains so unnatural. Yet to him, the mantra will remain the same. Whether I am there, or not there … he only wants to know when am I getting him out.

I don't know what to do anymore.
7 November 2011

It has been so long since I have written anything. This was the only therapeutic thing I was doing for me, and now I am not even paying attention to my own writing. This is how it all started. My emotions were raw when the craziness began happening. It was just supposed to be a routine knee replacement – that was all! Then it turned into something that changed George profoundly, mentally and physically. It changed our marriage. Then came the idea to start a project that would be beyond just me, just my writings, just my journal: something that could benefit others.

Meanwhile….

The idea of writing this journal is not to spend too much time catching up. This is not a novel. This is an immediate experience. When I started, the best suggestion I heard was, 'Write while the feelings are raw.' Be immediate.

So what is immediately happening? What I always knew would happen. George is a broken record. I cannot have one conversation with him on the phone or while visiting when he is not obsessing about getting out, getting out, getting out. When, when, when? What is the plan, what is the plan, what is the plan? Then he starts his stories. Doug told him he could stay with him as long as he wanted, so he is leaving tomorrow …with only the clothes on his back, since he has no other clothes. Then perhaps from there he will go on to California. He is going to run away. This is what he wants to do … like a child who hates his home and parents. He will fix them … that is for sure. He will run away. Because he can.

But he cannot. What he can do, he will not do. He has lost his really spacious room and spot next to the window, because he refused to use his 'stupid call button' to alert the medical staff when he wanted to get up. He has fallen a lot. But I would wager it is mainly because they have moved his chair and walker far enough away from him that he will be forced to use his call button ... which he will not do. And then *I* am a broken record, trying to get them to understand that he will not do it. He will not. He will not. Are they stupid? Oh, I am being ugly. But I am tired. Quit trying to pound him into your regulations. They are not working!

So they figure that by moving him right next to the nurses' station they can keep an eye on him. But he is not across from the nurses' station. Far from it. He is in a bed next to the hallway wall, with a curtain shielding him from his 'roommate.' And he hates it. No one – that I have observed – is 'keeping an eye on him.'

So now he is more obsessed than ever. There is not a breath he takes or a thought he has that is not about how to leave. How to leave. How to leave. And I am going crazy. I look at the pictures in our wedding album. He was younger and handsome, and I was so in love. We lived in Africa, and there we are next to our Land Rover. We trekked everywhere. Into the veldt and the bush, up into the mountains where the Rover's engine hummed with delight. Off to the Indian Ocean and miles off the beaten path into obscure campsites marked only by primitive fire pits. Watching schools of dolphin make their way down the shoreline. Camping above the Chobe River at sundown, having our own sundowners as we listened to the triumphant calls of the elephants deep down in the ravine and into the river for their nightly ritual. And then the fitful nights listening to the soft, elongated roar of lions, most likely farther away than my imagination was telling me.

Do I bring him home? That is the promise I made many, many years ago. Is this taking care of him? If it were not for the wretched outcome of the blood clot, he would probably not be in an institution. That is what it is: an institution. No matter how fancy … they are all institutions. I may have noticed over time something amiss: he was slowing down. That I attributed to his congestive heart failure … his heart was slowing down. He was losing concentration and focus. He would make offbeat comments at times, but Eva and I figured he was losing his hearing and was only trying to be a part of the conversation. If I had been told at some point of his 'early-onset dementia,' he would not be 'institutionalized.' That is not what usually happens.

So why now? Yeah, sure, all the other stuff. Being in a wheelchair. Being unsteady. Not making enough progress even to use a walker. Falling a lot. And being really crazy at times. It is likely that George is fighting all this. I always worried he couldn't possibly do well in such a situation. It did not take the psychologist who examined him at the rehab hospital long to figure that out.

But I cannot reach him. Keep your feet up, George, to reduce the swelling. If your leg would stop swelling, then maybe you could use that walker and get out of the wheelchair. George, use the call button! Get your old room back. George. I am trying to find a job in Indy, so that I can bring you home on the weekends! OK, not totally out of here, but wow, how wonderful … yes? George, please work on those archives in the library. You have a brilliant mind! Use it. You have manuscripts to read … I will help you with the computer. You need to contact the publisher, because you are a field editor for them. This person needs your response. Stop obsessing on what you cannot do! You are driving yourself crazy! Don't you understand?!

No.

Have I broken my promise to him?

'Find a support group.'
10 November 2001

Everyone says – the head nurses, my children, my brother, our friends – find a support group! He is going to lash out at the person closest to him … find yourself a support group. OK … you are strong. Bravo. Find a support group.

But for what? Prolonged illness? Dementia? Being in an institution? For exactly what? Because this is not exact.

So I type "support groups South Bend" into a search engine and come up with a few groups that are not confined to a specific illness or cause to which I could not relate or belong comfortably (i.e., breast cancer, AIDS). Many are largely connected to Alzheimer's and dementia and typically meet once a month.

What am I supposed to do the other 29 days?

I never thought I would see him act like this.
23 November 2011

He is my best friend. He has been my rock. While I was often the one who acted out, lost my temper, threw things about, frightened the children sometimes … he was steady. Never raised his voice. Never once used a swear word. Never lost his temper. Always knew and did the right thing. Calm. Even. Quiet and deep. Loving and kind.

And now I see him falling apart before my very eyes. He cries so much of the time. The rest of the time he acts like a petulant child. Stubborn. Angry. Saying nasty things. Last weekend he acted so horrible in a restaurant I thought he was going to throw his salad on the floor. I practically choked on my food, gobbling as fast as I could to get out before that happened.

Thanksgiving is in three days. So much has gone into preparing to bring him home for these few days. He has talked about it. Plans include a day at Mongo State Park and another day at Lake Michigan. Then Sunday at the Quaker meeting, seeing people who have missed him.

But he is angry I did not come this weekend. It was the first weekend since all this began that I have not been in Lafayette. And when he was still in facilities here in South Bend, there was not one day that went by when I did not see him.

In his anger, he is throwing tantrums. Calling every few minutes to say he is not coming. He is beyond reason ... beyond understanding the 20-pound turkey and the $100 worth of food in the fridge just for one day, not to mention the people who are coming from surrounding states. The plans everyone is making to see him and have fun. There is almost no point talking about anything with him. His reasoning seems gone, lost now in his mind. Where are you, George? What happened to you? I am still struggling to understand how this could be.

And will this happen to me as well?

Advice best given is advice asked for.
21 November 2011

When I was about to become a mother for the first time, at the age of 38, my friends who knew me only as a high-level professional career person, with also a tendency to party half the night, had lots of comments. Most doubted my capacity to 'go the distance.' I remember one person telling me that "children need routines," as I was tossing back a beer following a tennis match. Living in Africa at the time, we played tennis most late afternoons, followed by a trip to the club's bar before a late dinner. I am sure my lifestyle gave most people pause regarding whether I was up to the rigors of being a good parent who would soon realize that children needed to eat, bathe, and get ready for bed at the very time I was enjoying tennis and the social hour. Well, we had our children, we did realize they needed a routine, and we managed to create one that still allowed us to play tennis, socialize, and get the children fed and to bed at a decent time. We were all happy!

But that did not stop people from offering unsolicited advice, the most humorous of which came from friends who had never had children. I certainly did need advice – lots of advice! That was when I discovered that the best advice given was advice asked for, even from the most unusual quarters. One couple was far more conservative in almost all measures than I, but there was something about their calm approach to life that gave me confidence that they would be a great couple from whom to seek advice. She only gave when I asked. One of her best comments was to observe children I liked and did not like … in order to see a pathway from the child to a parent whose own behavior I also did, or did not, like. And she was right! What, in fact, was the parent doing that made me react a certain way to a child?

I am learning again that advice best given is advice asked for. George is coming home for Thanksgiving. When he came home the last time during that one fateful week, things turned out very badly. And now we were going to try this again. He is so desperate to get out of the 'facility,' as he calls it. And I want him to have several days at home.

The children will be home for just a few nights. The last two nights we will be alone. Alone, as we have been now for quite a while, and here I am … afraid. It seems so odd. But it's just another adjustment.

We live in a two-story townhouse, and the bedrooms are upstairs. I will need to sleep. I was a complete wreck after the one week George was last home in late July. I cannot do that again. I cannot stay up all night worrying about what George is doing 'downstairs.' I need to hire a caregiver, but one whom I can afford.

He will not require skilled nursing care. Just someone to make sure he makes it OK to the toilet without falling. To help him get snacks. He stays up most of the nights at the veterans' home. I have no doubt he will do the same here, at home. But caregivers can be expensive … one could cost upwards of $20 to $30 an hour. Plus this is an odd shift …11 p.m. to 7 a.m. … on a holiday weekend.

So I called my church … the largest parish in my diocese. They have all kinds of 'ministries.' Maybe they have one that provides this type of service, although I do not think I have read of one in the church directory. But it's worth a shot to try.

I spoke with the person who answered the phone, who put me on hold to inquire. The church did not have such a service, which did not surprise me, but she did refer me to an organization that I knew to be very reliable and resourceful, so it was a good referral. Good for them that they know of this service!

And then came the advice. I gave her the short story of my husband's illness, adding that this was his first trip home. Between the illness and the cognitive issues, I was not sure how it would go. I wanted him to be home as long as possible … to give him a holiday, a break. But how will he hold up?

She had gone through something similar with a relative, she replied. And I may come to realize that, while I dearly wanted him to be home for a longer period of time, it may not be possible. I might have to accept a shorter visit. She spoke in a tone that told me she felt she was doing me a favor with her advice.

She meant well. But I did not ask for that advice. I was asking for help.

I am being harsh, I know. It is like going to a funeral home and not knowing what to say to someone experiencing the pain of the deep loss of a loved one. So one babbles on and on, hoping words will be helpful, somehow. When all that is necessary is a squeezed hand and the words, "I am sorry, so very sorry." That completely resonates.

This woman *was* trying to help. But I was not asking for her advice. I had a specific problem and needed to solve it. It would have been better had she just said she was sorry and wished they could offer more.

As I think about it, this would indeed be a perfect ministry for a church, particularly a large one like this: a ministry of people willing to stand in as caregivers for people in circumstances like mine. And perfectly OK if they want to charge a modest fee, if one can pay. I called my church because churches always tell us they are places where we can go for help. Are they?

Thanksgiving 2011

George was amazing! Joey brought him home, and we had this big plan about how to get him to the front stoop in his wheelchair and then up over the step of the door into the house. I asked physical therapy to spend time working with him on taking these two steps. And I arranged the furniture to accommodate his wheelchair.

And then up to the front door he came in his walker!

George's wheelchair spent practically the entire visit in the trunk of my car. We used it when we took him to Lake Michigan; to a Quaker meeting so he would not have to sit in a straight-backed chair; and then back into the VA facility.

He arrived just in time for an umpteenth Republican candidate debate. He has missed all of them, and I wanted him to get some idea of what was going on. He tracked into the debate and the issues, immediately.

At some point that first evening, Joey and I agreed that it seemed nothing had happened months ago ... that it was all perfectly normal and routine, as before.

He gave us a scare, though, the second night. He commented that he thought he could make it up the stairs to the second floor, and I was firm that he was not to try. But George is stubborn. Joe was supposed to hold 'sentry,' but his bed was too tempting. I was sound asleep when I heard his walker rattling as he was obviously walking downstairs ... perhaps to the toilet? This was already a very easy thing for him to do. Then I heard him say "Joey," not in a panic, but with concern. I bolted out of bed ... had he fallen? Joey heard this as well. And what I thought was an apparition was George at the top of the stairs. He had climbed the stairs! And the excuse was that he could not get the lazy boy to move. What panic! Joey held tight to George as I got his walker, and we thought that perhaps he could sleep in our bed. But that lasted only a few minutes, and back down the stairs he went. We sat him down, and he took each step one at a time, safe enough.

He realized that was a mistake and was not likely to do that again.

And he realized a lot of things. He recognized the house. More than that … he began to call the house … 'home.' For so long he has called our home "your place" or "where you live" … and how he was embracing it simply as home.

He was as he was before … sleeping a lot during the day, which had become a pattern over the past couple of years. He has had congestive heart failure for over five years, and he is slowing down, no doubt. But mentally, everything seemed so normal. His conversations were normal. No loopiness. No crazy chatter. He was very lucid and cogent. It was remarkable. A complete transformation from how he talks and reacts in the VA facility. Is it possible he hates it so much there that this is real? Is he trying to act a certain way to convince me he should be home? Because his behavior has been bizarre enough, compounded by his physical limitations and challenges, that I have been convinced he needs to be in the VA facility.

We had a great time at Lake Michigan and Mongo State Park, and the weather was perfect. These were great outings I had hoped we could make months earlier while it was still summer. On Sunday morning we attended a Quaker meeting, which was fabulous. Everyone was thrilled to see George again. He talked a bit to the group about his slow recovery and his hope to eventually return. Perhaps some there knew about his diagnosis of dementia, but none was displayed at the meeting. It was simply fabulous.

As the weekend approached, and the returning Sunday drew nearer, he became more distressed about going back. We had to deal with some tears.

The drive back to Lafayette was largely quiet. We tried small talk and played music. He did comment that he felt he was returning to prison. We had dinner with Joey at a restaurant before returning, and again, he used only his walker … not the wheelchair.

The floor was as we had left it: lit up like a sports stadium, wheelchairs clustered around the nurses' station, with people mostly asleep. Noises and clatter everywhere, buzzes alerting anyone who might respond that a patient needed attention. It was awful. Does he really need to be here? But can I really bring him home? Is that really practical right now?

In his room, he broke down, quickly reverting to how he often behaves, saying that we all hate him, that he hates this place, that he does not need to be here, that nobody here does anything for him, that he is never coming home again unless he can stay there … he will simply stay where he is and rot. I left.

The next morning they gave him a shower, which he definitely needed … one thing for certain I cannot do at home. But why was he wearing the same shirt he had arrived in the night before? And why was he back in a wheelchair, with a strap over his waist to ensure he does not fall out? Is that necessary? They would say yes, that it is all about his safety. I agree. I am clearly not going to admit that he did have one fall while at home, but it is also all about liabilities and avoiding the possibility of being sued.

Institutionalized is what he is. I have institutionalized my husband.

Guilt! Guilt! Guilt!
Post-Thanksgiving 2011

Thanksgiving was George's first trip home since he entered the VA facility on the first of August. A lot of planning went into making this trip home – the first of hopefully many to come – and it was both good and fun for George, as uneventful and relaxing as though he had never left and it was just a regular day.

I knew to anticipate his resistance to going back. And I guess I should not be surprised that he did not wait until the end of the holiday weekend to start in.

But he also made great sense when he said that he felt he had no control anymore over his life. Others had taken over. This really is true!!

He behaved with fewer symptoms of dementia once he got home than I have witnessed since this all began. It was still sometimes hard to reason with him, as when he climbed the steps after being told not to. That was a heart stopper!! But he did not act loopy for even an instant.

So why can he not stay at home? I could make this work. Somehow. But I would have to make a lot of sacrifices … that is what I tell myself. He needs help everywhere. He cannot walk on his own, despite his advances. He sleeps in his chair all day long, and is then up all night long. How could I handle that? His leg is full of edema and is wrapped. He needs daily physical and occupational therapy. How could I possibly do all that? He falls easily. He said so himself, breaking his own fall one morning in the bathroom. He said he feels certain he will fall, break something, and then be held up "forever." He said it himself.

I get dramatic. I could give up my own desire to secure more rewarding work. I could stay with the agency I own, which has turned into work I do not like. Or how about this: since I am gone all day long, I could just give it all up. I could stay home and be a nursemaid … go on Medicaid … collect food stamps … go through my remaining funds. But he would be happy. Right? We would not go anywhere save church and the food pantry, because there would be no money. If he is home, who is going to hire an older woman who comes with the burden of taking care of someone at home? I have lots of excuses.

But, as I see his own unhappiness, like that of a caged bird once free, I am full of guilt.

Hospital Psychosis
2 December 2011

I was dumbfounded, both by George's mental transformation while home at Thanksgiving and by how quickly he reverted to negative behavior, complete with tears and guilt trips, within moments of being back in the facility.

I spoke with Carla, the nurse on the dementia unit there. She is fabulous! I told her about the weekend and my curiosity as to how he could have been so normal. Who is the real George these days?

We also talked about his condition when he first arrived. He was a complete wreck: very aggressive, hostile to everyone, often downright ugly. What was that about? She was the one who said that, when he arrived, he was "drowning," and he was. It is a wonder he survived.

She talked about *hospital psychosis*, a condition that some people develop during hospital stays. And in his case, he was in numerous hospitals. At one point he said he felt he was "going in circles." He was powerless, and he still feels powerless. He commented over Thanksgiving that he does not feel he has any control over his life ... everyone else is making decisions. And he is right! But his only decision would be to leave, immediately. He feels he is perfectly OK ... and he is not.

I realize now that, by the time we found our way to the VA facility, George was having a nervous breakdown. I am sure I sensed it all along, but I was in survival mode, putting one foot in front of the other. People are not put into waist and wrist restraints just because they are unhappy and snap at the nurses.

Hospitals are stressful for most people, especially for those who depend upon familiar surroundings for peace of mind. Hospitals (or any long-term care facilities, including nursing homes and rehab centers) are noisy and disruptive. People talk to patients in voices as though they are hard of hearing, and also often in a 'dumb downed' manner. Lights are on 24 hours a day. One of the hospitals where

George spent a week posted its daily routine of 'quiet time' each afternoon for the purpose of creating more calm for the patients. The lights were indeed dimmed (when someone remembered to do it), but I did not notice any less buzz and activity.

The fact of being in a hospital for a frightening illness is scary, and it is not uncommon with hospital psychosis for patients to hallucinate, even if they have never done this before. Hospital psychosis is not likely to be detected in patients who have brief hospital stays and are largely cogent for most of that time. And that is a goal of most hospitals (and insurance companies): get patients in and out as quickly as possible. Hospital psychosis is most likely to develop during prolonged hospitalization. And while conversations will at times be incoherent, they can also be very lucid … further adding to the confusion of a patient's family and friends.

Not all physicians are comfortable issuing a diagnosis of hospital psychosis. Some of the same symptoms may be attributed to the effects of sedatives or anesthesia. Elderly patients who do not receive the normal day/night light cues may develop another condition called *sundowner's syndrome*. They may experience hallucinations or exhibit confused speech, although this may also be early-onset dementia or Alzheimer's, rather than an actual breakdown.

Physicians may not treat this condition if it is viewed as only temporary, assuming that the patient is going home at some reasonable point in time. But it is also common to prescribe anti-depressants.

And indeed, once home, as when we brought George home at Thanksgiving, it is likely to subside, although I must say this was immediate with George. That may not always be the case.

George has been in a hospital since 10 May. I was finally told about hospital psychosis on 28 November.

The wild symptoms of this appeared when he was in the acute care facility for a month, and radically so. Everyone agreed that his first week there he was fine and appeared to be on the mend. As he succumbed deeper into the infection, his mental state changed erratically. People were all too quick to refer to his "loopy conversations" as dementia … and eventually told me I was to get used to it. Sometimes it happens that fast, 'they' said. Even the CNAs were quick to refer to his 'sundowner's syndrome' with grand authority, when all they were doing was parroting what they heard others with more professional training say.

No one talked about hospital psychosis. No one. No one. Not even his attending doctor, who should have responded to my pleas for information and my increasing panic that surely was evident in my eyes.

Thank you, Carla.

Joey is leaving
9 December 2011

We first heard about the Indiana Veterans' Home through Joey, our son. He graduated from Purdue last year as a history major and a 2nd lieutenant with the National Guard via ROTC. He has been working as a security guard here at IVH. I have been telling him he is lucky to have a job while he is looking for a job. They love him here – the vets, the nurses, the people at the switchboard. And the entire family has learned some amazing things about Joey with this job. He has incredible empathy and has matured so much. I suggested that he think about social work and even an MSW; sure enough, he snagged a new job on his first interview with Child Protective Services. It is not going to be easy. He is going to witness horrible abuse of children, which will infuriate him, and he will want to -- in his words – 'punch out' the parents, which of course he will need to avoid! But he has a new job, and he is excited. The people at IVH are not so excited. Everyone really does like Joey. One of the staff told me that she really misses him on his days off. His presence has meant a great deal to his dad, and I know that just having him around has helped calm his raging storm about being here. The nurses are worried already as to what will happen when Joey leaves. But he has to move on.

Maybe, just maybe....
13 December 2011

George's trip home at Thanksgiving was such a success I brought him home again this weekend between the two holidays. It's so important to come home during the holiday season so he can feel he really is still a part of our home. I keep talking about IVH being a place where he is getting his physical therapy and treatment. It is working a bit, but not completely. Again we went to a Quaker meeting, and Sunday evening we had friends over for dinner, just as we always used to do in the past. It was wonderful! George seemed distant, not able to keep up with the conversation. That is concerning, but he has been through so much. We also found out that there is a Quaker meeting in Lafayette, and I need to make contact. George would love to attend a local meeting, and we can do that together.

I am focusing my job search on Indianapolis with great urgency. If I can just get closer, then I can bring George home every weekend rather than my having to go to Lafayette. That way he can still be in the facility for the therapy and constant care he really needs, I can continue working, which I need to do, and he would really still be at home! I am excited about this plan and tell George to hang in: we can make this work. No one is giving up.

Rejected
15 December 2011

The first three months of George's care were paid for by Medicare, but that ended at the end of October. When I applied for Medicaid, I was assured that I would not be impacted personally in any way. But that is not what I had previously understood about Medicaid. Before the person who needs Medicaid gets assistance for long-term care, the surviving dependent spouse must reduce all assets (with the exception of the home) down to $1500-$2000, depending on the state. One can have a small term-life insurance policy with no cash value, but older people generally cannot get term insurance. One can keep a car and also earn income ... but that cannot exceed a certain amount. The family income and assets are then all weighed in this decision. My business, at one time very successful, has really taken a hit the past year. The economy has not helped, but I also have almost completely lost focus, and that has been devastating to my productivity. The facility is now getting all of George's income, so it is like before I got married. Although we are still husband and wife, I am essentially on my own financially, while still dealing with his medical bills and previous debts. A few years ago I had a comfortable and growing nest egg, which is now greatly depleted. Since I own a business, I need the cash in my remaining IRA and annuity to help with cash flow. So today's news in the mail was gravely concerning. George's application for Medicaid was turned down ... something about insufficient income information, although they do have our tax returns. The letter also mentioned what I expected about our resources exceeding what is allowed.

So what are my choices? 'Spin down' my remaining assets until I have only $1500 left? Wow, at my age (63), that is a recipe for disaster, as I march into my own aging, facing eventual poverty. I could end all this by bringing George home, which he would certainly love. But I really cannot take care of him by myself. Maybe I could do it if I stayed with my business, which I do not want to do. Given my background, it was a mistake to think I could be happy in this line of work. I am miserable and have been taking very aggressive steps to find something in my old field again. Before all this happened, I was engaged in a national search I was certain was going to be successful, and then everything blew up. I am happy to stay in my state capital; it is a very neat city. But I would have to give that up to basically stay home and take care of George. Owning my business would give me the independence to do that, but, if I don't pay attention to the business, it will eventually deplete all my resources and I will not have the cash flow to keep things going. I could hope that his older children from his first marriage would help pay for the remaining bills not covered by his income, but they may see this as my problem and my responsibility, not theirs. Our own children from our marriage are just out of college and could be of almost no help financially.

So this is it. I almost feel this is where my life ends – maybe not physically, but in almost every other sense of the word. I look and act far younger than my age and had hoped to live a very long, active, healthy life. But that is very likely to change if I become a full-time caretaker. It was exhausting when George was home just for one week this past summer. We will continue to do things as we can, going to the Lake and having people over for dinner, but how long will that last against his dementia? Almost on a daily basis there is some health issue: chronic urinary tract infections, falls, banging his arms and bleeding profusely, wrapping his legs so that he can only walk short distances with the walker, and so on. He cannot change his clothes or get his own food. Everything must be done for him. And can I really go swimming or biking or cross-country skiing, hoping he is OK in the lodge, or in another part of the park, or even home in his secure chair? This past summer I was gone only about 40 minutes at the state park, biking, when he became almost hysterical, seeking help from those nearby, who alerted the park police.

This will read like a very selfish entry … unless, of course, you have walked in my shoes.

Guardian Angel
16 December 2011

I had the worst night I have had during this whole journey, with the exception of when George was so horribly sick with the infection. I was wondering how it could all come to this. Living the wonderful life I have had, enjoying the adventurous marriage we have shared … what went wrong? I am feeling very vulnerable financially, and the great success I had hoped for with the business has eluded me. I was going to correct this while I still could by getting back into a job in a field where I belong, so that I could begin making money again, paying off bills, and saving once more. But that now seems out of my reach. So much for an adventurous life: I am now facing a wall I cannot climb. If George had had long-term care insurance, that would have helped. I have it, and when I made the purchase I told the children I had gotten them a gift that day – one that would spare them any financial burden and help keep me at home, rather than in a nursing home. George would be home now if he had a long-term care policy, but too often people think of this too late to afford it, or no longer have the ability to secure one because of existing health issues.

An email arrived from the Veterans' Home. It was too bad our application for Medicaid was turned down. They understood I was going to appeal. In the meantime, George would not be asked to leave. In almost every other facility I can think of – private or non-profit, even faith-based – someone has to pay: the patient, the family, the government. Someone. But George would not be asked to leave. Yes, a debt would be accruing on a monthly basis. All they asked was that all of George's income go to the facility, and that was already in place. And the debt? What happens with that? Well, when George leaves the facility – and that could be in a casket, I imagine – the debt is turned over to the state Attorney General and it is written off. Somewhere in the history of this facility, the state decided that this is what they would do for the veterans of Indiana. I could not believe what I was reading. The email ended with this: Please do not worry.

There *are* guardian angels.

Christmas 2011

I brought him home a couple of days before Christmas, with the plan that he would stay until New Year's Day. Both Eva and Joey were also home, and my brother Art came for a few days. We all really did have a good time, and the weather – while there was no Christmas snow – was very accommodating. I took him to the YMCA to use the handicap shower facilities, which worked out very well, but it would have been challenging if Joey had not helped. George also came home with a urinary tract infection and a horrible rash that have been treated now for a couple of weeks, and he did not, after all, make it all the way to New Year's Day. We had to take him back early. He was also wheezing so badly we all feared he was getting ready to have a congestive heart failure episode. It turned out it was an allergic reaction to the antibiotic for his rash. Eva had already left, so it was up to Joey and me to get him out of the house and into the car – all this at about 5 a.m. Friday morning. He did not want to go back. He had it in his mind that he was going to stay; he did not have to go back; he was perfectly fine; he could take care of himself; he did not need to be in 'that facility,' which he hated. When it was becoming clear to him that we were taking him back, he, of course, hated all of us. He said I should never come to visit him. Then he would not get out of his chair. He weighs 225 pounds, and he would not get out of his chair. Somehow we got him to get up, but then he balked about moving forward. I was not at all convinced we were going to get him into the car. We told him he was sick and needed immediate attention, which he did. He wanted to go to a local hospital and see his local doctors, whose names he remembered. He said he had no confidence in the people in Lafayette whom he considered incompetent. He was not moving.

But out the door we got him. I fully expected him to fall on the ground at any moment in protest, and possibly also to hurt himself, forcing us to take him to a local hospital. That would have been so easy. It made no sense to him whatsoever when I told him that I could not take care of him. His right leg remains wrapped, and he cannot wear a regular shoe. Now his left foot was festering and required attention. I knew that it, too, would soon be wrapped. I reminded him that, when we went to the Lebanese restaurant the other day, it took all four of us to get him in and out of the restaurant, a place that, while delicious, was not handicap-friendly. It took two of us to give him a shower, still with some difficulty. But none of this mattered to him.

He made it into Joey's car, and down the road he went. I walked back into our home where, just moments before, as days before, he was happy and at rest. I proceeded to take down all the decorations. Christmas was over.

For the sake of Auld Lang Syne
1 January 2012

George and I have rung in the New Year all over the world: in Lesotho, Swaziland, South Africa, Zimbabwe, Kyrgyzstan, Lebanon, even over the Atlantic Ocean and in many parts of the US. We have lived, worked, and traveled a 'boatload' of other places ... but these are just our New Year's Eve haunts.

This year is a bit different, for sure. It is not to our liking, but I made it as good as possible. I grilled T-bones on a portable grill, working behind the small unit where I stay so the security guard would not ruin our fun. I am sure there is an ordinance against open fires such as the one caused by this little grill! Joey made our onion rings in his home oven, and I bought one of those Caesar salads in a bag. I had wanted to make all this at home, but I know it will work out. We watched an upbeat movie. I am not sure how much George was able to track with it all, but at least we were together. He was supposed to spend the night with me. He has been wanting to do that. The place is pretty basic, but easy enough for him to get around. I might not get much sleep, but that is OK. If he gets up, which I am sure he will, I will hear him. But at some point, he really is not comfortable with this. Innately, he already feels more secure in 'the facility' that he hates so much. So, well after midnight, two dark figures slog through the snow-covered sidewalks back up to his building. It was OK ... that is all I can say. Just OK. I cannot help but think about New Year's Eves past.

I am getting tired.
3 January 2012

My life continues to race ahead. My business has lost money, and a good chunk of my savings is now lost as well. The stock market decline has not helped. I am definitely part of the group that will work until age 70, and I have no problem with that. But I cannot slow down, that is for sure. Nor I do want to!

I swim a mile most mornings of the week and am generally passed in the pool by women older than I am, which is encouraging. I bike long distances. I kayak. I cross-country ski. I hike. I am told I have more energy than people far younger. And I do not look my age.

But I am getting tired. I have to keep going. Someday I would like a normal life again! Forgive me, George, but one with romance again. I am young enough! I feel as if my entire life is nothing but work and putting one foot in front of the other – coping. Listening to one unsteady health report after the other. I rarely go out. I have so little time, and besides … not much money. I am looking for a new job in Indianapolis to be closer to George and hoping that my professional background, experiences, sparkle, and energy come through over age. But I do want to be closer, so that I can continue taking care of you.

I am getting tired. No doubt this has aged me too. And I am not ready to be old. Or even old*er*, for that matter!

I feel selfish.

"I was working on a project."
4 January 2012

George did not sleep last night. He said he was up all night long. This is not unusual. But I ask him what is wrong. It is just something to keep the conversation going. It is getting harder these days, as we have less and less to talk about.

He says: "Well, I was up all night working on a project with the staff."

And perhaps this is why we have so little now to talk about. He is clearly cogent on many occasions. No doubt. He vacillates back and forth between being very grounded, sensible, and intelligent, and his emerging world of make-believe.

Noise Noise Noise Noise Noise Noise!
7 January 2012

I am with George this weekend. I am also trying to work. I am in his room, and I have my laptop. We did not go to the library today, as we have been doing these winter weekend days. I thought I could get some work done in his room before we went out to dinner. Despite the size of this building, there are few places one can go to get away from people. For the moment, he has his own room, since he has a contagious urinary tract infection. So at least I would not hear a roommate's loud TV blaring some obnoxious program. But his room is across from the nurses' station, and there is noise, constantly. A call is forever beeping loudly indicating that someone needs help in a toilet. Every time someone who requires assistance leaves a wheelchair, an alarm sends the staff scurrying to find the potential fall victim. And, just for the heck of it, there seems to be a beep that is constant regardless of the necessity. I cannot stand it! When I asked George about this, he initially responded, "What noise?" I guess one gets used to it … and then he commented, "This goes on all the time. All the time …," with the knowledge one can only acquire by living in such a facility. And again, like a nail pounding into my heart, I am reminded that I have institutionalized my husband.

Steps
8 January 2012

We were excited about finally getting to a Quaker meeting, but, when we arrived, the steps going up to the house were impossible for George to manage. We were really disappointed, but had enough time to race over to the Unitarian Church, which is handicapped-accessible. The first time we attended Unitarian services here in Lafayette, we joined people for coffee afterward, and George had the minister and others captivated as he talked about his dissertation on Theodore Parker, an American Transcendentalist and formative minister of the Unitarian church. George tends to sleep through the services, but I doubt anyone has noticed much. I am sure they must wonder – given his still fine mind and ability to remember such scholarly detail – why on earth I have him in the veterans' home! I often wonder as well.

I spoke with the clerk of the local Quaker meeting, expressing our disappointment that we could not attend because of the steps, which did not feel very 'welcoming.' She agreed. What a nice woman she is … she said they knew this was a barrier. Perhaps this was the push they needed to put in the ramp that had been talked about in too many previous meetings. She also wants to visit George. He would love that!

We then went to the local library, which has become a regular Sunday outing, when we can manage it. There is an Indiana document room in the rear of the library intended for serious research. It is a comfortable room, with plenty of outlets for laptops. George says he wants to do research on the Underground Railroad movement in Indiana, and each time we are there, I pull the same book off the shelf and he does 'research,' which primarily means he is only copying what he is reading off the page. But he is happy. This is just another stab at trying to make things as palatable as possible, although the first time we went he stressed that he could do so much more of this type of research if he were home. I did not want to ask George how he intended to get to the library each day for this purpose, or say that just dropping him off on my way to work would not work either. But it was just his continual, gentle way of saying that he wants to get out of his prison.

Nature Reserve
11 January 2012

We finally got snow. I tell people that we live in a tundra. South Bend is famous for getting what is called 'lake-effect snow.' Everyone in the area loves Lake Michigan. It is what keeps me here in the region. I have lived near several oceans and seas around the world, yet love this lake with a passion. And the lake has been gentle with us so far this season ... so far!

We have a lovely patio that in the summer is overflowing with plants and herbs. In the winter, it looks bare and lonely, save for the feeder that continues to provide sustenance to hungry birds throughout the season. We have a bird feeder out the front window as well. George and I used to joke that, if we forgot to fill the front feeder, the birds would peck on the window!

We also have a bevy of squirrels and rabbits which we feed with husks of corn for much of the year. In the early spring, we have a male and female duck that wander in and fight with the squirrels and rabbits over the corn. Occasionally at night we see the large, dark body of a possum passing through. We even have an occasional hawk that will perch on our fence, scaring everyone away. I wish we had an owl ... that would make it all complete. We call this our own personal nature reserve.

George used to call me during the day to give me reports on animal antics. He always reminded me to feed the rabbits at night. If I put corn out at night, that gave the rabbits a fighting chance to get something to eat, as the squirrels – whom we see only during the day – are very aggressive.

I have been so busy lately, and falling asleep in the large La-Z-Boy most nights, I have forgotten to put corn out at night. I looked out tonight to see if it was still snowing and saw the rabbit tracks. I so dearly missed George. When was the last time I put corn out? Was it last spring? Amazingly, I still had corn left. But George was not around to remind me to do this. He was not around to call me to tell me what was going on in the backyard, and to remind me of my duty to our 'reserve' … just one of our special rituals that, while quiet, made for a loving relationship.

I opened the door and threw out a couple of pieces, hoping the rabbits would come back. It did not feel the same. I was not sharing this with anyone. I was reminded again … now, why do I have him in an institution? Why?

He keeps falling.
17 January 2012

George has fallen twice in the last 24 hours. They are literally begging him to use his call light. I, too, beg him to use his call light. He says he will. Then, moments later, he is up. He has not fallen in about a month, and they were about to move him into a more pleasant room away from the noise of the nurses' station. But now he has fallen twice, and both times he had not used his call light. They are afraid he will break a bone, and that would be a disaster. It goes beyond just a liability issue … I know they care. I never did tell them that, while home at Thanksgiving, he fell with us as well. As a last resort, they may have to restrain him in a chair, which will force him to use a call light. And that will push him only further into despair. It will also impinge on his independence. He is used now to going all over the place, and, since he must use the toilet often, he uses it alone. That might change as well.

I guess this tells me why he is not home.

Is it ever going to get better?
31 January 2012

We had plans that George would come home this weekend. He is hanging in there, holding onto the promises I am having him about come home as often as we can arrange it. This is Super Bowl weekend, and I want him in front of his own TV, whether he recognizes it as his, or not. I am not interested in watching it, but he would enjoy it … sitting in his own chair, munching on popcorn, a fire roaring in the fireplace, rooting for whomever. But his wrapped legs, which a few days ago were looking great, now have several open 'weeping' ulcers, and one foot is discolored. Angela tells me that the wounds have a strong odor that indicates it could be MRSA. As it is, since his visit to the dermatologist last week, now the wraps on his legs are changed twice a day with fresh medication. I can do this! They know I can do this. But if he has MRSA, that is likely to be more than I can handle. And it is probable that he would not be able to come home. Sure, I can always go 'down there' again, but we both were looking forward to his being home. I do not think at this point that George is ever going to be as he was before all this happened. He probably has the same doubts. We do not talk about it. It is too depressing. But all we want at this point is some simple joy. Now even that is beginning to elude us.

Now, a possible blood clot!
1 February 2012

Welcome, February. Remember George's discolored foot? It seems that the doctors and nurses cannot hear a beat. Tests will be ordered. This is clearly a circulation issue. It is possible that George has blood clots in his foot. He is already on blood thinners. If there are clots, they will have to be removed. Worst case scenario? Amputation. This is getting beyond words.

As the day wears on and this new 'news' sinks in, I become increasingly depressed. Again, I cannot stop crying. I am not home. I have a full day, out in the public. 'Keep busy,' I tell myself, but I am choking back tears. My eyes are red and look sunken in a grey, drawn face that spells sorrow. 'Keep busy, keep distracted,' I repeat over and over. But I worry. How much can *I* take before a toll is manifested in my own health and mind? How much of this could I have prevented? If, in the very beginning, I had brought him home … I would have made sure his legs were up and there would never have been that devastating blood clot! That is how all this started. If he had been home, he would never have fallen into such a deep abyss. I would have managed his pain medications. He might never have become depressed and so compromised. He certainly would not have gotten the bacterial infection – the cellulitis – and now possibly MRSA. He would be moving more. He would have reason to move more. He would have better circulation.

Super Bowl Reprieve!
6 February 2012

I did bring George home, and it was so nice. The nurses and doctors were not crazy about this, but he so looked forward to watching the Super Bowl at home. If the worst happened, at least he is home. I am willing to take all chances. Again, it made a big difference in his attitude. We went to another Quaker meeting, where he acknowledged that he was facing bigger problems than he had initially understood, but was hopeful about coming home in the spring. I could not face the group … everyone by now knows the profound struggle this has been. His legs are swollen, and just for these few days, at least, we can get by in our home. He came home Friday evening, and the initial plan was to take him back on Tuesday, keeping him home as long as I could. I am now facing Medicaid regulations. He can be out overnight only 30 nights a year, and we really do want to save them for major holidays. It would even be nice to think about a little vacation this summer … maybe a quick swing up to Wisconsin or over to Iowa. That will be a hard choice! He thinks he should stay until Tuesday. He feels "pretty good right now" and does not know how he will feel come Easter, when we have plans for him to come for, hopefully, a longer stay. I am torn. And what does he mean by this? George has always been optimistic about how he felt against whatever the future might hold. Is he becoming fatalistic as a result of all this?

But I remember that Doug has plans to take him to his home in Illinois in a couple of weeks. He was there in January, and had a terrific time. When he called me on the phone, I missed his call but saved his message. His voice sounded like the old George completely! Gone was the stress in his voice and tone. Just that wonderful, soft, deep voice I fell in love with. I listen often to the message … I cannot take it off my phone.

So we will go back on Monday, once again with heavy hearts. It is SO nice having him home. I am picking up speed to find a job in the Indy metro area! The sooner I can make this happen, the better. If I cannot bring him home every weekend because of the dumb Medicaid regulations, then at least I will be close enough to drive him back and forth …. each day of the weekend, if necessary, from early morning till late at night, in time for night meds, slipping in like Cinderella before my car turns back into a pumpkin. I will stay the night, and bring him back home the next day. We will make this work! My prince is worth it. Hang in there, George!!

"I want to go home."
22 February 2012

Again, George moved through the last potential crisis. How does he do this? Where does he get the reserves? But this time, he is not so lucky. His weight has skyrocketed the past couple of weeks. He had been holding steady at 225, but then he soared to almost 270. Now he is in the hospital with acute kidney failure (as opposed to simply chronic renal failure, which is part of CHF and years of strong diuretics). This is his first episode since the one six years ago, and the first time he has been on oxygen. He is in the hospital because his numbers are so seriously bad, and the fluid needs to be drained quickly from his body, far more quickly than IVH can do this. I should have stayed on top of this better than I did. They have been so focused on the swelling in his legs, full of edema. His weight on 8 February was 243, already up. Then George panicked yesterday. When he tried to walk, he could not breathe. They brought him back to the room, and there was panic in his eyes. He knew he was in trouble. All he said was, "I want to go home." Terrified, he still thinks that is the best place for him, and that I will save him. It's where he feels safest and most secure.

I so wish that were true, George. I so wish.

Like old times
24 February 2012

I am on my way to an interview! To head up an organization that is connected to the Quakers and involves offering micro-grants to women's groups in parts of Africa and India. It will involve considerable fundraising and international travel. It speaks to my background, my passions and interests, my skills and abilities, and my heart. I am excited! Since it is based near Indianapolis, I am very close to achieving also my goal of moving closer to the Indiana Veterans' Home and hopefully bringing George home more often. Yes! But I am worried. I am not a Quaker and do not have a Quaker personality by a long shot. George is a Quaker, and that, along with my background, has gotten me this far in the interview process. I am very familiar with Quaker faith and practice … plus my Ph.D. study was on Quakers in South Africa and their social witness against apartheid. My friends say I am perfect for this! Yet I am worried. Quakers are often quiet. Decisions are made after much 'discerning.' I am comfortable with the use of consensus and use it as a business tool in making decisions ... but working as a 'Quaker' means much more than that. I might be too strong for the Quakers. My Catholic personality is robust, ribald; we swear too much and can drink too hard. We have huge hearts, which may be our saving grace. I call George. I tell him my concerns. I can see him on the other end of the phone, just listening. "I am afraid I am going to be too strong for them!" I can see him with the expression on his face of not quite understanding this, as he sweetly replies "You were not too strong for me!" suggesting that when we met, I did not scare him off. Oh, my sweet George. I hope there is someone like you on the search committee! It is so easy to see why people have always loved this nice man. As we carry on with our conversation, he is full of support and questions. Just like old times. We have a conversation just like old times. He is so excited and happy for this hopeful opportunity, and my being closer. Old times.

DNR
26 February 2012

More than ten years ago, George and I both signed living wills stating basically that we would refuse the application of any extraordinary life-saving measures to our lives if recovery would not lead to a decent quality of life. This is easy enough to do when one is young and still vigorous, envisioning what a severely diminished life could mean: life in a wheelchair, unable to perform many simply daily functions, mind fading as well. Sure ... pull the plug!! Until you are actually there.

George is now there. He is approaching his late 70s. His health has been challenged for years. He had a routine knee replacement so that he could walk better again, keeping his congestive heart failure at bay. He still wanted to fish and hunt and camp. He wanted romance! And now that is gone. But he still wants to live!

He is still in the hospital. He has been there now for three days. He is not losing fluids ... only one pound in all this time, and he has gained almost 40! I told the nurse soon after he was admitted that he was DNR ... Do Not Resuscitate. This was not in his chart. Then, last night I got a call from an attending physician. He was confused. When talking with my husband, George told him that he wanted "full code." Should he stop breathing, he wanted all that could be done to revive him. Was that true? The nurses told the doctor about my statement, and he needed clarification. I felt like God. Do I have that right? Although he has dementia, he remains very cogent. He has feelings, he is a fighter. He wants to live! What right do I have to deny him this? Can you imagine if he knew what his wife was telling the hospital – the woman he trusts more than anyone else, the woman he thinks can still save him – can you imagine his incredible fury, his pain?

No, I said softly. He is DNR.

The doctor told me that, even if he remained full code, given his condition, there would be little chance he would survive resuscitation. And, if he did, the quality of life would be minimal, if any. I am sure the doctor was telling me this to help me feel better.

I did not.

They are not all hard of hearing.
1 March 2012

It has always amazed me that, often, when people are talking with children (or 'to' children), they feel they must raise their voices as though the child is hard of hearing. Picture it ... **"Tommy (or Mary), how are you?"** in decibels that encourage the child to either respond loudly or shrink back. We do the same thing with older people. OK, some truly are deaf. But not all. And not everyone's name is 'cutie' or 'honey.' I acquiesce to the intended endearment, but when I hear it so much from too many medical staff, it grates. I have wondered if it is really a term of endearment, or just for my benefit when I am there: 'See, we just adore your husband.'

How about the first name, or better yet ... the last name? This is still a generation that expected people 60 years their junior to respect them by calling them by their last name. I know that sounds old-fashioned. How about real conversations? I hear such silly nonsense and superficial comments in nursing homes, as though the residents are children. Sit down with these people, talk with them about who they are and their interests. Find some time to do that every day. Help take away their despair. Remind them they still have fine minds.

But there is no time for that. Long-term care facilities are chronically understaffed and the demands are constant. I understand. Just wait until the tsunami of baby boomers hits the system.

Fluids
2 March 2012

George was in the hospital for a week, weighing in at 270 pounds. He lost only about five pounds ... this after a week of aggressive treatment to flush the build-up of fluids from his body. When he had his first congestive heart failure episode six years ago, he lost 30 pounds. This is not a good sign.

Who were they before they came here?
3 March 2012

There are a few women, but it is mostly men. They are all veterans. The women could be veterans as well, or the spouses of veterans. But it is mostly men at the Indiana Veterans' Home. Most of them wear a cap that signifies their branch of service. George has never done this, and I do not know why.

Sixty percent of people in nursing homes have dementia, and IVH is no exception. Some look too young to be here ... they are possibly veterans of the Vietnam War. One is easy to spot ... he sports a ponytail and looks like an 'aging hippie.' I guess we all are, those of us from that era.

It surprises me that several of the patients do not ever seem to interact with people outside the facility. They will talk with each other – those who still can – but seem cautious with outsiders. And that I clearly am … an outsider. I can leave at any time. I can get in my car and return to my freedom while they stay, wishing they could leave.

I wonder what they were like before they came here with whatever illness – physical or mental – that made it impossible for them to live on their own. Today they wait out the hours between meals, the days between Bingo … sitting in the hallway or clustered close to the nurses' station, waiting, with nowhere to go and life's purpose gone. Pictures on the stands next to their beds reveal that, before the days of absent staring, they were alive and lively. A few are in the uniforms of their youth, but mostly there are pictures taken with family and friends, while fishing or hunting, at a backyard BBQ. I wonder if they ever thought they would end up in the 'old soldiers' home.' I imagine their youth and vigor, when they still flirted, drank beer, smoked cigarettes, cruised around town, worked at a job while anticipating retirement – a stage of life that almost certainly did not include a nursing home.

Thank you, soldier.

He finally breaks a bone.
13 March 2012

George still refuses to use his call light when he needs to get out of his wheelchair or use the toilet. He has fallen at least twelve times since he arrived in early August. He fell again this week. The nurses have been concerned that he will eventually break a bone, and he finally did. Thankfully, it was nothing as significant as feared, like a broken hip or arm. Just a couple of fractured toes. But this means that now, in addition to his growing girth, he cannot put any weight on his foot. I do not know what this means in terms of getting George away from the veterans' home for a weekend visit, or even for the day.

What does freedom look like?
18 March 2012

I was hoping finally to take George to a Quaker meeting today. They built a ramp so that he could get inside the house … this for a man they had hardly met. I was going to take him last weekend, but I forgot his toilet riser and their toilet does not have handicap bars. And now he has two fractured toes. I watched yesterday as it took two aides to help get him in and out of his wheelchair. How was I going to be able to handle him by myself? I found out today. I could not help him get from the wheelchair into the car. He tried and tried. He was convinced he could do it. But there was no way. He just stared into the car as though it were the last vestige of freedom in his life. We turned back.

How will I get him home for Easter?

The hospital, again
25 March 2012

George is back in the hospital with another congestive heart failure episode. But this time is radically different from a month ago. Yesterday he was so tired that he was actually willing to get into bed. Today, when I arrived, he was shaking and said he felt miserable. And he has been in bed all day. As the hours passed, he became increasingly incognizant. Doug arrived from Bloomington for just a friendly visit, and that was a good thing. The IVH doctor told us he was again filling up with fluids, and we had a choice. If we did nothing, they would do everything possible to make George comfortable, and he would likely die. Or, we could again take him to the hospital where they would run every possible test to see what was going on. My mind raced. Is this it? This suddenly?!

George has never wanted to talk about the 'what if' questions related to the end of life.

This was a difficult conversation. We need to know what he wants to do. But what do we say? "George, if you stay here at the Veterans' Home, you are likely to die sometime in the next few days ... or we can take you to the hospital and see what happens. What would you like to do, sweetie?" I really do not know how to do this. The living will we both signed over ten years ago covered the 'big stuff,' like DNR; this is very gray ... we are at a wall. I really struggle. Holding his hands tightly, I try, but am no good at this. George says only once, "I think I am dying," and I cannot lie. He crunches up his face.

George also continues to drift. We wonder if he is truly aware of what is going on, and I ask him if he knows who I am. He gets that playful grin that people love and says, "My wonderful wife." You bet I am, is what I say. We all laugh. "I love you, George. We have been married 28 years ... a long time." And George says that he hopes we are married another 28. At this very serious juncture, we have this tender moment. So many marriages will come to this when the end of someone's life is at hand. All privacy is gone for intimate moments ... but they happen anyway, with abandon. There is little privacy when we enter the world, and likely very little when we leave.

Finally, Doug finds the right words. "Dad, what do you want to do?" George quietly replies: "I want to feel better." And we know what to do. Call an ambulance, we tell the nurse. He will go to the hospital. And yes, we will see what happens.

Before the ambulance arrived, Eva came up from Indianapolis. As we were asking George what he wanted to do, he kept asking us, "What does Eva think?" I saw this as a message that she had better come. She arrived well before the ambulance did and just held his hand for the longest time; when he finally left, she cried and cried. Later we realized what was going on. She had visited with her dad earlier in the week and he kept introducing her to everyone as his daughter who was going to medical school. We realized that he thinks she is a doctor ... which she is going to be at some point, but a Ph.D. doctor – like George and me! – not a medical doctor. It was so cute! He simply wanted to know what his 'medical doctor' daughter thought ... losing confidence, perhaps, in the other doctors treating him.

By the time we got to the Emergency Room, Joey had arrived from his weekend Guard training. Several hours later, George was finally admitted, and it was time for us to find a restaurant still open late on a Sunday night. Among all the chaos, everyone remembered it was my birthday. The kids treated me! They are still broke for the most part ... but growing up and with a few more dollars in their pockets. It was my birthday, and it needed a bit of celebration.

We are missing you, George. You should have been here with us. We have celebrated Joey's, Eva's, and George's birthdays here at the Veterans' Home or nearby at the state park. So many people have come to visit and help George cope with all this, including a friend from Ireland and a student from his teaching days who now lives in North Carolina, nearing his own retirement. People have called from across the U.S. who are concerned and simply want to cheer him up ... perhaps looking also for traces of the 'old George.' We celebrated our wedding anniversary ... not ideally, but still together, out and about town. We have tried so hard to make this work. And now it is my birthday. I am so grateful I am with the kids. And they are treating me!

Incognizant ... again
26 March 2012

For whatever reason, George is again not cognizant. No one can explain why. This seems an odd congestive heart failure episode. Is that all it is? Is there more? Is this a new routine? Something we can expect? And why are there so few answers or explanations? Now hospice would like to talk with me.

The Quakers are coming!
27 March 2012

I got an email from the clerk of the local Quaker meeting who said that they would not be meeting at the house for a couple of weeks, just in case we came and no one was there. I explained that George was in the hospital again, hopefully briefly … and would they be interested in meeting either at the Veterans' Home or at the hospital? George would love this if it could be arranged … and yes, they can do it!

I asked the nurses if a quiet room could be found for a few hours Sunday morning, as the Quakers are coming! They are really nice in this hospital. They make arrangements also to use the library at the Veterans' Home just in case George is discharged before Sunday.

Alert once more … sort of
28 March 2012

I am home packing … I got the job! I also found a condo to purchase … and am on my way, as promised. I have a storage locker to clear out, items to separate to keep, sell, or give away. I am selling George's truck. I do not need two cars, and he will not be driving again, I am sure. Closing with a mortgage company is taking lots of time, and I am racing about town trying to find as many free boxes as I can muster. I need also to clean out closets and begin packing. I own a business, and that must be settled. I wish I had time to race up to the lake, if for no other reason than to spend a much needed quiet day … the weather has been unseasonably warm. But there is no time. Later. All George has to do is hang in … but, given all that is happening, I am really worried about bringing him home. His previous visits were easy. Getting him in and out of the wheelchair is now very difficult, and, as yet, he has not been out of bed in the hospital. This will only set back his ability to use the walker. And what about his toes? Is anyone paying attention to his fractured toes? Surely they have not healed. Has that been noted in the chart?

The good news is that George is alert again. Doug is visiting and will stay for a few days, until I can get back on the weekend. I have been talking with George every day, and his spirits are high. He knows the Quakers are coming on Sunday, and he is excited.

And about that room ... they moved George from the ICU to a suite. So now he has two rooms! Incredible.

Maybe George is going to pull this off again. I do hope so! But Doug is concerned that he is not sleeping and is becoming slightly more agitated ... asking lots of questions, wanting to know every little move that is going on about him. This is really odd for George.

Kidney Dialysis?
29 March 2012

When George was in the hospital in February and was losing a little urine, I asked about kidney dialysis. This was discussed as a possibility at the Veterans' Home, but the cardiologist with whom I spoke questioned whether his heart could handle dialysis. Today a kidney specialist mentioned the possibility of dialysis to Doug, saying also that he could possibly live another two to three years with dialysis. Really? With what quality of life? Did she talk about that? Look at him! He has not been out of bed since he arrived several days ago. Kidney dialysis three times a week ... and in between that he does what? Does he fish? Joey and I have some fishing forays planned if he gets through this. Does he go out to dinner with me at local restaurants? Do we go to the library for research? We have been doing that all winter. Does he come home for visits that mean the world to him ... and to me? Does he even play Bingo? Or does he lie in bed feeling miserable between dialysis sessions ... because the medical world can make this happen? The medical staff at the Veterans' Home tell me that several residents are on dialysis; for some, it is working just fine, and for others, not so. We may have to make this decision soon. I so very badly want him to live longer, but with a quality of life. Would this be OK for George? As we have with everything else this year, if we do this – if he wants it – we will make it work for him. We will not give up on George.

Meanwhile, hospice talks with Doug. Is this happening? Is this for real?

George is not ready.
30 March 2012

We are very deep in the gray area of all this, bouncing between specialists who tell us that machines can keep him going and hospice that want to know what we want to do. What does *George* want to do? One of our closest friends is a Catholic priest who, in his mid-80s, has traveled from South Bend to Lafayette a few times to visit his "good friend." I have known Ed since college, and he is one of the people responsible for the development of my views and commitment to social justice and action. He has called often, and I share with him my concerns that George does not seem to understand he may be dying; he still wants to be resuscitated if he stops breathing … although the DNR remains firmly in his chart. Ed visits with George today, and they have a great time. George is so happy to see Ed, but he does not tell me all about their discussion. Ed does.

Ed told George that he needed to let "Betty and the kids" know what his wishes were regarding end-of-life decisions, and George agreed. He needed to do that, but did not feel "it was necessary at this time." In his mind, he is not going to die just yet. He is doing just fine.

So George goes merrily back to the imaginary world where, for months now, he has lived. He is really looking forward to the Quakers!

Stop being silly!
31 March 2012

George is a playful person. There is, indeed, his serious side, the academic, the quiet nature, the profound and thoughtful comments. But he is also playful ... always has been. He has an endearing chuckle that people love and that makes him very approachable. But today he is just silly, almost annoying. He will not stop talking and making dumb comments. We had such nice conversations on the phone all week that I was looking forward to seeing him, hoping we would have some good chats. But this is strange. I reminded him that the Quakers were coming tomorrow and asked if he was going to be able to be quiet and still for an hour of silent worship. He said he could, but not very convincingly. I am doubtful. And for whatever reason, he could not feed himself! There is nothing wrong with his arms. He is not shaking. He is not incognizant. But he could not and would not feed himself. Not very amusing. He is also fidgeting a lot, and I am not very patient with this. The nurses probably think I am a grump. Right before I left, George decided that he had a major pain in his "rumpus." He wanted a nurse, and right away. He was in pain, he said ... a lot of pain. I went to the nurses and they were all busy. George was not happy. He wanted a nurse right away; he was in a lot of pain and started moaning more and more. I told him that they were probably busy handling emergencies far more grave than the pain in his 'rumpus,' which he was bemoaning. So he moaned some more.

Finally, a nurse came, appearing to be in no hurry. Despite his crazy behavior, George was in no danger. It was time for me to go. This was quite a day. "You're going?" he said, "when I am in all this pain?!" The nurse and I exchanged glances. I smiled, and told him he was in good hands. He was angry, but I was leaving.

This is not George!
1 April 2012

I heard it before I even got to his room. Someone was talking non-stop, and not making sense. This is a hospital ... one can expect to hear and see anything odd. But as I got closer, I realized it was coming from George's room. There was no shouting, just endless calling out and senseless talking. When I walked into the room, a nurse's aide was sitting up close to his bed. He had no clothes on ... she said he had taken them all off. For the sake of his dignity, they had laid a sheet over his midriff. He was reaching out, trying to grab things in the air, pulling at his tubes, swinging his legs over the side of the bed. He had been like this since about 1 a.m., said the nurse, and someone had been by his side ever since. So, why hadn't someone called me? Or any member of the family?

I stood by the side of the bed, staring in disbelief. What was going on? It was apparent she did not know. She was an aide. But would the nurses know any more? So far, much of this has been a mystery. "This is not George," I explained to her. Surely she would realize no one normally acts like this.

I leaned over and called his name, softly, and told him I was here. It is Betty, and I am here. He pulled down my hand and held it tight, kissing the back of my hand. Eyes shut tight, he was not cognizant of anything or anyone else, but he knew I was there. And again, my heart leaped. This entire experience has been full of grace ... the grace of sorrow and joy. And in this awful craziness, he still knew me. I could take no more.

At 10 a.m., the Quakers came ... several of them, anticipating a supportive service with and for George. I quickly shuttled them into the adjoining room and explained what was happening, or did so at least to the best of my ability. Some of them did not know a thing about George, and I was asked to give a brief update, starting with the knee replacement and infection that led to all this. They wanted to know if they should stay ... would I be more comfortable if they left? George's anguish is evident, as he continues calling out for names and things I do not recognize, saying over and over, 'I have to get up, I have to get up.' No, please stay. I feel I need your support right now. They all find chairs, center themselves, and begin their meeting for worship, in silence.

After a few moments, one of the Quakers leaves the room. I am uncomfortable. This really is too much for people. The clerk of the meeting has been to the Veterans' Home and met with George a few times. She knows him under very different circumstances, and has really enjoyed their visits. But to the rest, he is a complete stranger, and one in some sort of pain – possibly physical, mental, or both. The walls only soften the anguish that does not stop. This cannot be easy for them to hear. He is in profound need. I also leave the room and there she is … sitting next to George's bed, holding his hand.

I return to the other room and try to center my own thoughts, listening still to George's constant call. Another Quaker leaves, and I am not sure what she is going to do. But then … in a few minutes, I find out. One of the Quakers is singing softly to him, while the second one who joined her is now also holding his hand. He is not a stranger to them.

Before they leave, they call others to come and pray with George.

I am thinking that George is exhausted. His unwillingness to sleep has led to this agitation. When he was in the hospital just before coming to the Veterans' Home, he was in a similar state of high agitation. They gave him something that literally 'knocked' him out. It also came with wrist restraints. I do *not* want restraints, but can't he be given something to make him sleep? I am told they are giving him all kinds of medications, and nothing seems to be calming this behavior. Finally, a doctor arrives and tells me that, even if they are able to get him to sleep – which in my naïve world I have always found to be a panacea – he might wake up and continue acting like this. I ask him why and get no answer … just another distant look.

And again, hospice visits. What am I supposed to be talking with them about? I feel I am not getting any straight answers … so what can I say to hospice? Is anyone here going to tell me he is dying? Or are we still talking treatment?

When the night shift arrives, I recognize a nurse I have worked with earlier. I want to talk with her about kidney dialysis, and she tells me that his 'numbers' for BUN and creatine are just fine ... in fact, better than they have been in a very long time. The issue is not his kidneys ... he now seems to be in some kind of respiratory danger. His heart levels are weakening, and she thinks he may be struggling and in pain and needing relief. Morphine helps bring relief. I also know that morphine is used at the end of life to bring comfort until someone dies. I ask the nurse if this is what she is suggesting. She says that, once they start the drip, they are not likely to stop, and that it is possible that someone can go to sleep and not wake up.

This feels so sudden. I am alone. Eva is off to a long-awaited conference in Chicago; Doug is back in Bloomington; Joey is with friends. Everyone should just stay where they are. I will stay here until Monday, and then Joey will be in charge. Who knows what will happen? In fact, nothing may happen.

But the doctors again have different plans that do not include morphine. They will allow an injection only for pain relief, but not a drip. They want to do yet more tests. It's something about his lungs. What could they possibly be looking for now? And to what end? Should I step in and say, 'Stop! This man is dying. Let him be!'? But I am not ready to let him die. Go ahead: run the tests. Maybe there is something 'out there.' And the machines arrive in his room.

No change
2 April 2012

George shows no change. He does not even seem to be calmer, despite the morphine injection and all the drugs in his system. He still has not slept. He is still calling out names and asking for things I do not understand. When I whisper that I am here ... there is no reaction. He is now fully in his own world. In my world, the movers are coming. The drive home is lonely.

'Help me! Help me!'
3 April 2012

Doug came back early today and will stay the week. He holds the phone close so that I can hear what is going on. George is now pleading for help, but we are told he is not in any real physical pain that can be determined. No one since Day One has had any definitive answers on any part of this wretched journey, so how can I believe now that he is in no pain? I am being cynical. But this is too much to bear. By tomorrow, if this does not stop ... we start the morphine drip. Doug agrees. This is no longer up to George. George is no longer with us.

Doug did some research on delirium and found that it is not uncommon among people very close to death. I quickly went to the internet and found several medical citations that matched George's high agitation and senseless delirium linked to the end-of-life experience. So, when I asked the doctor on Sunday what was going on ... and hospice ... why could we not have been told this? I called the hospital and told them I was tired of 'hospital speak.' I was aware that hospitals need to be careful with families, and caution also stems from attention to potential liability. But I made it clear from the beginning I wanted straight answers and had not been getting any. No one disputed that what I found on the medical web sites was accurate. Doug is like his dad: patient, quiet, he listens, he does not argue. I am sure the medical staff at the hospital prefer having him around to the difficult wife.

Last day
4 April 2012

The call came at 5:30 a.m. George's agitation had stopped. He was no longer delirious. His breathing had changed radically and had become shallower. "You need to know."

OK. This means what? This is not the usual report that I have been getting all year from every place he has been. George would stumble in the bathroom, cut his arm and need a band-aid, and I got a call. I know the night staff is following protocol, but these reports could have waited until later in the morning.

This was not a 'protocol' report. I asked the nurse if she had experience with people who were dying … her voice sounded very young. She said that yes, she did. OK then, how much time do we have? To which she replied, "That is between him and God." At which point the 'difficult wife' told this young nurse I had not asked her views on religion. I was the wife and had family to call. Should we come right away? Some of us were hours away. Yes, we need to come, right away. I told her she had years ahead of her in her career as a nurse. When a family asks a question, be straightforward.

We were all there by 10 a.m. Eva from Chicago. I from South Bend, praying all the way that he just hold on. Joey and Doug were already in Lafayette. Right after I arrived, they finally started the drip. They were waiting for me, and now this is it.

George still had his 'suite.' This was incredible. Down the hallway was a large family waiting area with several TVs and lounge chairs that could be used for sleeping. The room was full. And our family had the privacy of this suite. The children went to a store to get fruit, yogurt, sandwiches, snacks … we would now all stay here in one place, and wait. Hospice said death could come in a day, or not for 2-3 days. The doctors concurred. All we knew was that George was sleeping. No more agitation. No delirium. But also, no more taking my hand, recognizing me or anyone. And he would not wake up again.

At one point in the late afternoon, he started to become more agitated, pulling off his covers, making sounds, reaching out again at things. The nurses had been increasing his morphine drip throughout the day. Was he still not ready? Was George going to rally again? It would have come as no surprise to any of us.

The hospice nurse said that sometimes people wait until everyone leaves the room before they die. There is perhaps a subconscious level at which they know everyone is around, but they want to die alone. That felt sad, if George wanted that … but we decided to leave for dinner and see what happened while we were gone.

When we returned, George was still with us! Hanging in. We were told that his temperature and blood pressure had dropped. These were clear signs of impending death. Each of us quietly commented that we were ready to spend the night. Days before we had all agreed that it was OK if we were not present when George died. We told Joey that, if he was alone in Lafayette, it was OK not to put his dad on a ventilator to keep him alive until we were able to gather. We would not put him through any more pain. But now we *were* all together. And we were prepared to be with George till whenever. We would be by his side. He had waited for us to return from dinner … not wanting ever to leave, I guess. But this was now beyond even his reserves and control.

Joey started talking with his dad. He thanked him for all the fishing trips and conversations they had over the years … all the support. He told his dad he loved him. He was a great dad. Joey was not the least self-conscious doing this in front of all of us.

I dozed off in the recliner next to George's bed. Eva woke me about 10:40. 'Dad' had stopped breathing. Two nurses confirmed that, yes, there was no heartbeat. He is gone. We stayed for two more hours, until it was clear that we did not want to see the changes that were going to take place in his now lifeless body. His face was calm, sweet, and handsome. He was still warm, but his fingers, while still in the same position they had been all day, were now turning blue and his cheeks were beginning to sink in. We could wait, but we could not turn back the clock. The day was done.

I heard an owl call my name
And I knew my human journey was over.
I heard an eagle call my name
And I knew my journey would continue.
I heard a dove call my name
And I knew I would have peace.[2]

The Final Salute
12 April 2012

The service takes 90 minutes. We are in no hurry. There's a flag-draped casket that we chose to have closed. It's a beautiful warm spring day. We're in a sweet chapel that was perfect for the service we all wanted to have. People are gathering while spirit flute music plays in the background in tribute to George's native American heritage. We have 15 minutes of silent Quaker worship, so still that we can hear the birds chirp happily outside the windows. Doug's words bring us to tears. We have a Catholic mass for me, led by our good friend Ed, sharing words and the Eucharist with all present. It's a beautiful eulogy. A bagpipe player leads the pallbearers with *Amazing Grace* … the year *was* full of grace – full of sorrow and joy, but always full of grace. The bagpiper then leads the procession, as we walk to the adjoining military cemetery, playing *Scotland the Brave!* Doug carries a bowl of burning sage, an Indian purifying rite held during funerals. Everyone along the way stops, as we process by. White-gloved soldiers are waiting at his gravesite. A bugler plays *Taps*. The soldiers fold his flag tightly. With an arm and voice shaking, one of them salutes as he gives me the flag. This is not an easy ritual, no matter the resting soldier's age. Joey, in his dress uniform, places a dog tag on the cross he had made for his dad. A simple marker will come later. Just as George had given Joey his first salute when he became an officer, Joey then gives his dad the final salute.

---

[2]   Poem by Carmen Carter, George's first wife…..Native American poet.

Day is done, gone the sun.
From the lake, from the hills, from the sky.
All is well, safely rest, God is nigh.

The box
18 April 2012

It was going to happen sooner or later. The box. I was completing a form for health insurance with my new job today, and there was the box. What was my marital status? I looked at the 'single' box and was going to check it. And then, there it was … the box for 'widows.'

Long after others move on
2 May 2012

Long after others move on, you will remain in your emptiness. During the high drama of George's illness, I could call at any time with the latest news. I wish I could still call, just to talk about what happened. It remains so fresh. I know that everyone misses George. But everyone is moving on. I see it on Facebook. Gone are the daily postings, except mine. I am trying to post other things, and I do. But I am not moving on very well, or very fast.

"I ache for him to be back as him."
6 May 2012

The *New York Times* had an interesting article on a rare form of dementia called frontotemporal dementia, which can strike people younger than the normal onset age and is often evidenced by bizarre, uncharacteristic behavior. George's dementia was just your normal, run-of-the-mill kind, but the wife's comments struck my heart. When his behavior became bizarre and difficult to deal with, she became frustrated and angry with him. His behavior became so strange, she considered divorce. I can picture her shouting as him, as I often did at George. We would be at the dinner table trying to have a conversation, and he would not track. He would say things completely different from what I was talking about, as if he wasn't even listening. I would get angry and say something like, "I cannot wait for you to have that operation and stop taking those dope pills," the pain medication he seemed to be constantly taking. And he would just look at me as though nothing was the matter, nothing was wrong … indicating, 'What is she saying?' When the woman interviewed in the article was told of her husband's condition, she said she cried for days. The realization of this dreaded illness I am sure terrified her: it is a death sentence. But she cried also because of her own behavior: "I apologized to him for every perceived wrong or misunderstanding." I knew exactly what she was talking about. Eventually, he was unable to read, speak, write, or talk, and she had to put him in a long-term care facility … and again, she cried. She said she ached for him to be back home, but "for him to be back as him."

Sometimes she still crawls into his tiny bed to cuddle him. That was the picture that accompanied the story; don't we all do that as couples? Just cuddle? It is so comforting. I miss that as well. She worried if he still remembered her, and a doctor assured her that yes, he most likely did. It may not be apparent, he said, but deep down … yes, he remembers you. One of the times she crawled into bed to nap with him, she asked him a question based on an e. e. cummings poem they both loved: "Where do you carry my heart?" And he smiled and patted his chest. He did remember her.

The last Sunday of George's life, the day the Quakers came and the day I walked in to see my beloved prince in an agitated state of incredible delirium … I had walked up to his bed and called out his name. "George, George … it's me … Betty." He grabbed my hand to pull it down. I thought he was grabbing it just as he was grabbing at everything else. But he kissed my hand. He just wanted to kiss my hand. And that was his last display of acknowledging or recognizing anyone. Me. He knew me. He knew I was there. And my heart leaped.

They were never mine to begin with.
10 May 2012

George never made me feel as though his first marriage was in any way better than being married to me. Never. I know he missed Carmen. I expect that someday I will have romance again ... but no one will ever replace George. And I did not replace Carmen. In his bureau, George kept a few things. Unlike me, George was not a collector. He had the original birth certificates for each of his children; a medical record for one of his sons from when they were living in Canada; Carmen's death certificates and letters from the City of Hope where Carmen died; a few pictures; and a beautifully framed wedding picture of George and Carmen with their wedding party. He did not look at them very often ... or at least while I was around. But I always knew they were there, in his chest of drawers, which sat next to mine, in our bedroom, in our home. When he died, I knew they had to go back to his kids. They were never mine ... these had nothing to do with me, our marriage, our own children. This made perfect sense, and Doug was thrilled to see these for the first time. Yet it still felt strange giving them back. While never mine, they were still a part of me, as George was a part of me. Now I had to let them go. Even this makes me feel so very sad. George, just a short while ago you were still a part of my life and you belonged to me. Now I have to let you go in ways I did not imagine, and things that make perfect sense I do not want to do. Now I want to hold on to everything.

Grief Counseling
Mother's Day 2012

I need grief counseling. I cried so hard last night that I woke up this morning with a headache. I seem to be crying most nights. It starts to happen when I am eating dinner, which is usually late. I have had some wine, the day is done ... and I sit down alone for dinner. I think of George, who used to sit with me, and our traditions, which I still keep: candles, cloth napkins, music. The house is empty. Of course, it is a new house. Two days after George was buried, I moved into a new home ... one purchased with him in mind. So I really am alone ... there is no lingering presence of him here, which in a way is even sadder. I am so glad that I have a job that I love and that keeps me well occupied. Otherwise, I am sure I would cry throughout the day.

One foot in front of the other
5 June 2012

Just a year ago, it all happened. First, it was just routine surgery. Then it was a recovery, which became a serious recovery, but a recovery with hope. Then it was a recovery with grave concerns ... recovering to what? Then it was a determined attempt to change everything, to make it work, to bring him home and make him well. I was going to do that ... I *could* do that. I was going to show all the naysayers who were trying to convince me he needed 24/7 help. That got squashed rather dramatically, when it became an issue of adapting to a 'new normal': coping with his deepening despair; doing all we could to make things happier, if at all possible, when we were ourselves so frustrated and sad. And throughout it all – through his anger, depression, demands, and craziness – I was putting one foot in front of the other. Every so often the wonderful, sweet, intelligent, and reasonable George would peer through ... but only every so often. Only now that it is over do I realize that I was in remote control, putting one foot in front of the other, doing what it took to survive and make it all bearable and sensible for him and for me. What do I do now?

I keep forgetting....
15 June 2012

It happens so often. I will think of someone we both knew, or a place where we lived, an event we shared. Someone will send me an update, and I catch myself thinking that I must tell this to George. He will want to know. I must remember to tell him ... then I remember. He is gone. I keep forgetting that. And there really is no one else to share this story with, this funny little anecdote, this bit of gossip couples thrive on between themselves. No one. And I stare off into the middle distance, feeling lost and clearly alone. And then sadness hits. Not his death, but the illness. If he were still alive, given his cognitive state, would he have connected, in any event? Would I have had to explain it all to him, hoping to jog his memory that seemed to have left so swiftly, leaving behind his still brilliant mind and lots of new stories only he seemed to understand or recognize? Oh, he would have nodded and forced a wan smile, wanting so badly to connect ... and likely make no comment. Conversations like this ended fairly quickly after the infection took over. I just missed talking with him. I never realized how much it meant, and now I cannot take back the time.

Empty pockets
22 June 2012

I remember months ago finding slips of paper in George's pockets with grocery lists and receipts from the post office and Starbucks. I am so lonely tonight. I want so badly something that tells me he is here, in this place he never lived. Maybe if I search his pockets I will find something. I did this months ago. But maybe I missed something! Maybe something is buried deep in the corners. Something. Anything! But nothing.

Final entry
8 July 2012

I feel that this journal is now finished. I crafted the last interview the night before I got the job offer. Then the days were filled with looking for a new home, packing, unpacking, ordering new utilities and internet service ... and George coming to the point of his final days, which brought us all together.

I am in a new and very amazing stage of this journey. I am swallowed up in a very deep sadness of missing him. I cry almost every night. I must find a grief support group. They are harder to find than I imagined. So many meet only once a month, and I feel I need more than that. I do not want individual counseling ... I really do want to hear other people's stories. I will share my own in due time.

There are plenty of groups for widows, but when I call, I hear a voice that sounds elderly. I am clearly not ready for that! And I am not looking for a mate ... I am told that happens with some of these groups.

Someone else said that there was a great group in her community. They talked for a time about their loss, and then moved on to great friendship, laughing, drinking wine, playing cards and golf. Good for them. My grief is way too deep to think it can be wrapped up in an afternoon of chatter followed by golf.

I will find a group; but the bigger challenge seems to find the time to find a group ... my new position is very rewarding, but also very demanding of my time.

So much of the past year keeps flooding back. The images of George in all the horrible and vulnerable positions he never wanted to be in: wearing bibs and diapers, sitting in one wheelchair after another, trapped, going up and down institutional hallways with noise and racket that never ended; his mind wandering about, thinking fellow residents were colleagues in the 'history' department, and CNAs the deans. And always trying to figure out where he would live once the 'semester' was over, asking if my home had space for him. Wondering also why he was where he was, and why I allowed it. That was my greatest pain.

In all this, I fell in love all over again. I looked at this man, becoming more fragile, and saw on the one hand what others saw ... indeed, an ailing and aging man in a wheelchair. But increasingly, I saw another image that over time grew stronger and stronger; that of a much younger man from 28 years ago who shook my earth. I had fallen in love with all the emotions one can imagine. I would remember all the frolicking we did in our eleven years in Africa, in one game park after another. There were endless weeks driving across the isolated reserves of Botswana, watching scores of lions and elephants up close and personal, yet driven also by fear of the lions' soft roar each night at our campsite, I always ended up sleeping in the Land Rover. Fishing in the high mountains of Lesotho and swimming on isolated beaches of the Indian Ocean. An audience of two watching a school of dolphins making their way down the coast. Dinner parties well into the night with friends from all over the world. We came back to the States for a few years, until our international wanderlust drove us overseas once again. New adventures included hiking the ancient mountains of Central Asia that formed the Silk Road, and the following year roaming the Roman ruins and the pyramids of the Middle East. We lived a life others only dream of. We vowed to spend every New Year's Eve in a new country, and, since we lived overseas for so long ... that was possible for quite some time. Paramount to our marriage was the joy of our children. George was a widower when we met; he had four grown children, with the youngest 18 years old. Few would have been willing to begin parenting all over again, but he was happy to do so. I saw also a man who was a Fulbright Scholar and Senior Fulbright Specialist. An editor of the Daniel Webster papers at Dartmouth. A fellow at Yale, and Lambeth Palace in London. A scholar in residence at UCLA.

And I saw also a man who I so wished would be sitting in his chair once again, watching sports on TV. Our sharing laughs at British comedy. Absorbed in news. And golf. Phoning to tell me what was going on in our 'nature reserve'. Calling from the bottom of the stairs: "Betty. I'm going to the store. Do you need anything?" As he did just days before his operation.

So beloved was this man by his former students and colleagues that many visited or called to cheer him up, knowing that this could also be their final goodbye. And then, in his final chapter of life, while many who worked in these facilities saw just another 'loopy' old man sitting in a wheelchair that was on the floor and part of the equipment before he got there, and that would be used by someone else after he left ….. all I saw was my handsome prince. And I fell in love again, this man with an endearing 'chuckle,' impish grin, and deep blue eyes, who never, ever, lost his temper or raised his voice. And I was so happy to fight and be by the side of this gentle, quiet, and unique man, who raised the bar on the measure of love that will never leave me.

The Survey

In order for this issue to be taken seriously and to demonstrate that I was not alone with either my anxiety or my anger – I had talked with too many others to know that was not true – I felt it was important to include a survey in my project. This was also critical to give voice to those who are also patient advocates, but feel they as well are either alone, or no one will listen: "The issue is not all that serious…… The 'system' will take care of everything". As it is, the 'system' needs patient advocates……each and every one of us.

I compiled a list of questions I felt were common to us all, and left plenty of space for personal comment and additional narrative. The survey was reviewed by a committee of advisors who are health and medical professionals, educators and researchers, and social service providers, all of whom are compassionate about how individuals are treated and cared for in our current health care system. The survey was distributed widely over social media and select national patient advocacy organizations. Over 250 people responded to this appeal:

> *My husband had a routine operation in early May. All faculties were intact going into the operation. A blood clot shortly after prompted a second trip to the hospital where he contracted an infection. Since then he has been in a series of hospitals, rehab centers and long term care facilities. He remains in a wheelchair with serious cognitive issues. And I became an advocate. Advocates are often critical to a patient's recovery, if not their very life. Sometimes we are welcome, and sometimes not. I am writing a book*

about this critical piece of our health care system. I have a survey on Survey Monkey. If you have been an advocate, or know of someone who has been, will you please take or share this survey. Will you please repost this survey link. Will you please help me reach out to a wide geographic and demographic diversity of people whose voices need to be heard at the table of health care reform.

I have included the **exact wording** of those who provided fuller answers, or narrative. I did not want to change the tone or 'voice' of those who responded: in their voice is captured their anger, fear, sadness, concerns, hope and sometimes joy.

Survey Results

Some of the responses will equal greater than 100%. This would be in cases where people advocated for more than one person and did not fill out two surveys. The percentages are not extreme so as to skew the outcomes.

1. ***Are you a male or female?***
   - Female   78%
   - Male   22%

2. ***Was the person for whom you advocated a:***
   - Female   60%
   - Male   50%

While this equals 110%, the response suggests that some people who responded took care of both a female and male

3. ***Did you advocate for yourself?***
   - Yes   15%
   - No   85%

4. ***What is the highest level of education you have completed or the highest degree you have received?***
   - Less than high school   .05%
   - High school/GED   4%
   - Some college/no degree   11%
   - Associate degree   11%

- Bachelor degree   36%
- Graduate degree   38%

What does this data suggest? The survey was widely distributed through numerous sources, including Facebook. While several sites were web sites and organizations, the largest response came from Facebook, and from people willing to share and thus allow the survey to go 'viral' which would mean it would reach a diverse demographic group. Are people with higher levels of education more likely to be in the role of an advocate? Are people with higher levels of education more able or willing to challenge a health system that previous generations have entrusted and responded with silent consent, even when dissatisfied or angry?

5. *Which of the following categories describes your employment status?*

- Working less than 40 hours/week   17%
- Working at least 40 hours/week   46%
- Self employed   15%
- Not employed/looking for work   3%
- Not employed/not looking for work   4%
- Retired   13%
- Student   1%
- Disabled/not able to work   4%

6. *What is your race/ethnicity?*

- White   93%
- Hispanic   .05%
- African-American   .03%
- Asian American   1%
- American Indian   0%
- Native Hawaiian   0%
- Pacific Islander   0%

7. **Where were you an advocate?**
   - Rural community less than 10,000   8%
   - Small town less than 50,000   17%
   - Mid-size city less than 100,000   21%
   - City less than 250,000   17%
   - City 250,000-500,000   16%
   - City 500,000 – one million   10%
   - Metropolitan area more than one million   16%

8. **As an advocate, how close did you live to the person for whom you advocated?**
   - In the same community   51%
   - Within 5-20 miles   21%
   - Within 20-50 miles   5%
   - Within 50-100 miles   4%
   - Within 100-250 miles   6%
   - Within 250-500 miles   3%
   - Over 500 miles   14%

9. **In what region of the United States were you an advocate?**
   - NE/New England   9%
   - Mid Atlantic   9%
   - SE   5%
   - SW/Lower Southern Region   4%
   - Rocky Mountain/Western Region   2%
   - West Coast   6%
   - NW   1%
   - Upper Midwest   12%
   - Midwest   56%
   - Hawaii   1%
   - Alaska   0%

10. *Was the person for whom you advocated a:*

- Spouse — 19%
- Partner — 3%
- Child — 8%
- Parent — 50%
- Sibling — 4%
- Other relative — 11%
- Friend — 7%
- I was a self-advocate — 5%

11. *What was the age of the person for whom you advocated?*

- Infant to age 10 — 3%
- Age 11 to 20 — 4%
- Age 21 to 30 — 5%
- Age 31 to 40 — 4%
- Age 41 to 50 — 10%
- Age 51 to 60 — 16%
- Age 61 to 70 — 16%
- Age 71 to 80 — 16%
- Age 81 to 90 — 34%
- Over age 90 — 12%

12. *What was your age when you advocated for this person? Or self-advocated?*

- Age 15 to 20 — 2%
- Age 21 to 30 — 9%
- Age 31 to 40 — 14%
- Age 41 to 50 — 26%
- Age 51 to 60 — 45%
- Age 61 to 70 — 10%
- Age 71 to 80 — 2%
- Age 81 to 90 — 0%
- Over age 90 — 0%

13. Was the advocacy a result of:

- Injury   12%
- Surgery   23%
- Illness   67%
- Accident   4%
- Nursing home care   26%
- Rehabilitative care   12%

The overall percentage is 144%. This would suggest that several cases, advocates were needed in more than one instance for the same person; i.e., a surgery may have led to rehabilitative or nursing home care and the advocate wanted to include all places. Compounded medical experiences or maladies are not unusual.

14. Did you have medical or health power of attorney from the person for whom you advocated (this would include durable power of attorney, advance directive for health, and/or guardianship. This would have been asked when the person for whom you advocated was admitted in the facility):

- Yes   60%
- No   36%
- n/a   4%

15. Did the person for whom you advocated have a living will? If you self-advocated, did you have a living will?

- Yes   67%
- No   33%

16. The question was asked "for how long you were an advocate?" and the choices were in weeks, months and years. The following are the averages for those who responded thus:

- Weeks: an average of 111
- Months: an average of 13
- Years: almost 5.5 years

17. *The question was also asked in what year the advocacy took place. The overwhelming majority of those who responded were advocates within the past ten years, and the majority of those since 2006. In many cases, advocacy is on-going.*

18. *Was the person for whom you advocated aware of your role as an advocate?*
- Yes, a great deal   55%
- Yes, to some degree due to illness   28%
- No, was not aware due to illness   15%
- n/a   5%

19. *The question was asked: What is the first word that comes to mind when you think about your experience as an advocate for this person. I have grouped similar words together to keep the list short:*
- Essential, imperative, need, everyone needs an advocate, relief I was there. (given my conversations with people, I assumed this one would have received a far greater response, but people were focusing on their own emotions which is understandable)   20
- Frustrating, trying, challenging, difficult, demanding, intense, tough, complicated, stressful, overwhelming, exhausting, tired, painstaking   42
- Anger   2
- Terrifying, horror   7
- Demoralizing   1
- Confusing   3
- Sad   3
- Love him with all my heart, love   3
- Rewarding, an honor, happy, worth it, satisfied, lucky, thankful, Grateful, fulfilling   11
- Helpless, powerless   9
- Understaffed   1
- Protect, protection   3

- Enlightening, learning experience, educational, valuable   4
- Gut wrenching, heart breaking, heart wrenching   4
- Persistence   3
- Ridiculous   1
- Tenacity, responsibility   4
- Quality of life versus just existing   1
- I understand the health system and knew what to ask   1
- Unappreciated, invisible   2
- Information, not informative   2
- Speaking for those who can no longer speak for themselves, communication   2
- Thankful, grateful   2
- Time consuming, burdensome   4
- Life changing   1
- Compassion, respect, caring   4
- Negotiator, 'adversarial', cooperation   3
- Help   1
- Whew!!   1
- Persuasion   1
- OK   1
- Border Personality Disorder   1
- Chaotic, roller coaster   2
- Courage on her part   1
- Knowledge   1
- Translator   1
- 'think'   1
- Pain, pain management   2
- Expected   1

20. *Please describe the facility:*
- Public hospital   54%
- Private hospital   18%
- Public specialty hospital (LTAC)   4%

- Private specialty hospital (LTAC)   1%
- Government/VA hospital   5%
- Private nursing home   25%
- Non-profit nursing home   6%
- Faith-based nursing home   6%
- Private rehabilitative facility   10%
- Public rehabilitative facility   5%

There were 44 comments. It was not unusual for a patient to be in a variety of facilities either over the course of their illness, or toward the end of their life, and prior to dying. Several who answered stated that overall they preferred smaller facilities over large chains or even large non-profit or faith based facilities….they felt confident the person for whom they advocated got better attention and care. A few people expressed concern or annoyance over poor communication and some wished that the health facility or doctors were willing to use email and found resistance to this suggestion. The health care professionals may already feel too overwhelmed to deal with responding to emails, or possibly view this as a potential liability issue.

21. In your opinion, did you feel that the medical staff taking care of the person for whom you advocated supported and respected your role as an advocate?

- A great deal   24%
- To a large degree   26%
- To some degree   32%
- There was mild resistance   11%
- There was moderate resistance   7%
- There was complete resistance   6%

There were 108 comments. Several comments had great praise for the entire medical staff and administrators. On the contrary, and in general, there were more negative comments about the "arrogance" of doctors than the nursing staff. Others commented that they were health professionals – i.e., RNs, dentists, social workers – and felt this afforded them greater respect and attention than they would have received otherwise. Several comments focused on their upset or concern that the person for whom they advocated – while very lucid and lacking signs of dementia – would be ignored while medical comments were directed to others in the room. They saw this as disrespectful, rude and lacking dignity. In a few instances, concern was expressed that medical staff dealt directly with a patient who indeed had cognitive disorder and ignored the advocates. A few tried to understand how being understaffed strained the system, and that being understaffed was not the fault of the staff but the administrators, or if a private or for profit facility, the fault of the owners. The following is a selection of comments:

1. They liked me there to be able to help with care but some were a little resentful of the watchful eye I was portraying and of my vigilant documenting of everything that took place.
2. I always attended monthly care plan meetings
3. It wasn't that simple. When I finally spoke up, I think they were cowed by the degree of emotion I expressed. At first I was clueless about advocacy. The staff humored me. But then it was a staff member who finally thrust Ombudsman brochures into my hand saying, "You have rights!" After that, I hammered home my concerns until the facility responded. I can't say that I ever felt respected.
4. I think that the resistance was greater in my case because I live 150 miles away and was not able to develop a regular presence in the facility
5. In the beginning when my friend moved into the nursing home due to advanced PPMS the staff was incapable of providing adequate care for her. My co-trustee and I never let up, never gave up. We attended quarterly care conferences, called, wrote letters, contacted the state, the ombudsman, spent 12 - 15 hours a day with her, pleaded her case, insisted the staff be trained in her special needs, brought their attention to every major infraction and now, after eight years she is finally getting the care she needs. Her needs are even

higher now than in the beginning but the staff responds to her increased level of care willingly. They finally 'get it'. They now call us to report any event, any change in medication or any concern they have for her welfare. I also want to add that my friend has also developed a volunteer base who help her with tasks enabling her to be a mother to her two teen-aged daughters, do her laundry, help her into her standing frame, play music, bring special food, help feed her, hold a book for her to read, clean and straighten her room, give her cold water showers daily, open her mail and hold it for her to read, answer mail, help make phone calls, etc. This strong base of about 30 people makes her life bearable, relieves the staff, and is our eyes and ears for changes or concerns and the staff knows it.

6. Many of the hospital staff, physicians especially, felt threatened by the fact we questioned some decisions and presented viable alternatives. The nursing staff often encouraged our resistance, which was very encouraging, but most of the physicians refused to listen to me and my family, in spite of the fact that I am a doctor. The hospital administration was also no help at all in providing access to medical records to my father's wife, which is, quite frankly, illegal.

7. It is critical and necessary that absolutely every patient have an advocate, no matter their situation or condition. There should be an organization, company, or association, that could provide advocates in hospitals and facilities. I would certainly be interested in being an advocate.

8. Everyone seemed to think they knew my mother better than I did and of course, knew medicine better than I did so my opinions didn't carry much weight. I had to really fight for some of the things she needed and for some of the things she didn't need. Several times I just went ahead and did things and didn't ask anyone for help or their opinions. I got tired of others telling me what was best for my mom when they had only known her for a year or so and in her present condition.

I remember the woman who raised me, who talked with me about her feelings and fears. I knew what she had been through over her lifetime, who her parents and family were and how they had formed who she was. I knew the kind of deep love she and my dad had for each other for over 50 years. My only sibling, my sister, moved to Arizona the year I got married so I was the one who was there for my mom and for my dad for almost 40 years. I was not an absentee child. I was very involved in their lives, taking care of them, helping them until their care was beyond what I could give. I didn't feel any validation or respect or understanding about that. In some instances, I got the feeling that I was just in the way and that they could do a much better job with my mom if I wasn't there so much.

9. I had to be pushy when I knew I was right. I found out where all the supplies were and just did things.

10. I believe I received a supporting response from the nursing home staff because the facility itself encouraged advocacy and because I was a son assisting his mother. They told me they usually deal with daughters.

11. The best thing a person can do is to have a Health Resume that details all the problems and surgeries from the past. This resume needs to be kept updated and it also needs to accompany you to every doctor's appointment.

12. Had to tell the story over and over again.

13. Grandmother was in a nursing home, a non-special unit nursing home. She kept taking things that belonged to other residents because of her disease process. She was 'kicked out' of the nursing home and it took [six] months to find a nursing home that would take Grandma and they were equally unable to meet her behavioral needs. Grandmother died [six] weeks after moving into the last nursing home and I fully believe all her behaviors were not behaviors but rather symptoms of the disease process that are manageable by trained staff.

14. I was acknowledged as the partner and included in all decisions. I thought there would be difficulties because we were a same sex couple, but there were no problems.

15. I was the advocate for my son and the medical staff knew it. I questioned each and everything they did for my son. There was a family member with him 24/7 from the first day of the accident. We spent [four] months in the hospital. After the first month I was at the hospital every other week. The weeks I was not there I called everyday to see what was changed and why. I never asked more of the hospital than I would expect out of myself being a nursing professional. I was active in his daily care when he was in ICU and remained active in his rehab.

16. We choose places that were aligned with our thinking and would welcome our daily visits. They knew this was a family affair and we would be very involved with the care of our parents.

17. My father had had a heart attack, then…..a stroke. After a couple of months in a nursing home he went into heart failure. He was hooked up to oxygen, feeding tube, monitors. He removed all the tubes and lines. The nurse wanted to put him in restraints. I objected. She called the doctors. I explained my father's wish to die, promised no legal action, asked them to look the other way and let him be. The doctors acceded to my request. My father died the following morning, after waiting until I came to his room.

18. Mother and Dad were in and out of Hospital as well as Rehab centers. Mother was KILLED in a facility when she was there for Respite Care, it was a for profit facility. The hospital appreciated my advocate role and enjoyed the three ring binder I gave them when they needed information or past history. I was frustrated with the lack of Social Work help and advice. I made a lot of "left" turns when I should have turned "right" because no one ever educated me on how the "system" works. Found out after parents were passed about the VA Aid Benefit, I could have used that. I lost my corporate job after

20 years there due to caring for my parents. Now I am in Home Health Care field because "I am that family member" that has no clue where to go for help or resources.

19. An occurrence in an emergency room was frustrating because when I explained my husband's illness (Alzheimer's Disease) the staff seemed unprepared as to how to handle him. They expected me to find a way to get him to fulfill their test requirements rather than adapting the requirements to his abilities.

20. I am a registered nurse and certified case manager. Almost all hospitals now have case managers on site - but you have to know to ask, many insurance companies have RN case managers as well - but again you have to ask and there are many independent RN case managers out there as well - again you have to know about them to hire one. This is one of the issues with case management - underutilized and not well marketed. Being in the health arena all I can say is stay well - I know too much and it is not pretty. I would be scared to death to be in a hospital now and cannot imagine going in not knowing what I do. You have to ask questions and keep asking questions and demanding - nicely, to know more and expect answers. I recommend staying out of hospitals with medical schools - the MDs there are still learning!!

22. **Who gave you the greatest support in your role as advocate?**
    (Some people checked more than one)
    - Dietitians   2%
    - Speech therapists   4%
    - Occupational therapists   4%
    - Nursing staff   50%
    - CNAs   11%
    - Administration   9%
    - Physical therapists   8%
    - Social workers   21%
    - Doctors   31%

23. Who gave you the greatest resistance in your role as advocate?

- Dietitians 4%
- Speech therapists 2%
- Occupational therapists 2%
- Nursing staff 28%
- CNAs 5%
- Administration 29%
- Physical therapists 5%
- Social workers 41%
- Doctors 41%

There were 103 comments to the two previous questions, and people checked more than one. Again, there was either praise or scorn, and those who are medical professionals often stated that once this was either revealed or understood, they got cooperation. The following is a selection:

1. Admin did not care to hear any problems
2. I advocate on behalf of the elderly every day as an elder care lawyer and I speak all over the country and train other lawyers about Medicare, nursing home Medicaid and related topics, and it was intensely frustrating to watch my mother lose a great deal of weight and meet with great resistance from doctors and administrators and to a lesser extent, aides, when I sought to impose calorie counts and other measures designed to improve her condition. Eventually it worked but I'm certain she never would have left if I and my siblings had not pushed so hard. We ended up flying in to take shifts to stay and ensure her needs were met.
3. Doctors were always very supportive of my wife's support unless they assumed she was a retarded welfare patient. We corrected the doctors as soon as we recognized the problem, and once they knew they were going to be paid by my insurance, they gave great care. Toward the end of her life, my [mother-in-law] was in severe chronic agony with lower-limb neuropathy. When she was receiving 600mg of methadone for

the pain, nursing home administrators looked at her insurance first, and then decided that she could receive better care in their facility than we could provide. When she went from a hospital to a nursing home, she was back in the hospital in about a week each time as the care facility could not or would not dispense the near-lethal dose of methadone required to kill the pain. My [mother-in-laws] screaming was disruptive to other residents, so she was shipped back to the hospital, from which we would then take her home.

4. There is a personality/culture in each facility and it changes shift to shift and has so much to do with patient load, management and trust/respect of the workers by admins., MDs and clients.

5. Advocating is a full time job. It really takes time and effort to balance the needs of whom you are advocating for with your own family and personal life. I've been done a couple of years now and find myself still recuperating from the ordeal. However, I have great satisfaction in knowing that my mother lived a quality life and this message was strong and ongoing.

6. I had to almost beg the hospital to have a nutritionist come in to give my mother counseling on how to eat right to control her diabetes. And, then it was more like she was being lectured at, instead of how could she incorporate the components of a healthy diet into her lifestyle, and why diet was so important to her quality of life. I felt like they were treating her illness, but not really focusing holistically on her overall health and quality of life.

7. It took a while for the doctor to realize how important our role was and that we were an asset to her. Then she became our best advocate to the nursing home for their recognition of our authority. The staff turnover on the administration level has resulted in improvements that we could not have anticipated.

8. My mother had a quadruple bypass within a few days of having a carotid artery surgery. Communication amongst

the medical team seemed poor and each handled things very differently. For example, we were told the nursing staff (whether it be CNA's, nurse's, whomever) would walk her several times daily once the doctor gave the go ahead to do so...he gave the go ahead, however if I (or a family member) didn't walk her it did not get done. There were many, many personal care issues that would not have been done had I (or other family members) not requested or pointed them out to the staff. It was very frustrating and opened my eyes to how important it is for someone to be there round the clock so even the simplest needs were met. You wouldn't think that family members would literally have to "staff" their loved ones stay, but it seemed imperative here!

9. You can tell the nursing staff and therapists what the patient needs, but you have to work through the administration to get the benefits approval (eg, VA benefits) ---- this is extremely difficult at times.

10. My role as an advocate continued in the second nursing home, where I had to file for Medicaid fraud (it was never followed up) involving hospice care and the physician ordering bone density scans for the residents (he owned the scanning facility); and I ended up getting the administrator fired for yelling at me for not using the facility's pharmacy and I also reported him to the [Attorney General] for practicing medicine without a license. In this second facility a 20% weight loss went unnoted and unaddressed until I pointed it out at a quarterly care conference. I should mention that the second facility was originally a faith based one that was bought out by a rapidly expanding chain; as a faith based facility, I felt she got good care.

11. Some administrative staff members do not take the time to get totally involved with the resident or person. The attitude is their "too busy" running the facility which separates them from understanding fully the needs of their patients or residents. Decisions and policies are made without the input

from families or residents as to how those decisions may affect them on a long term, or for that matter, a short term basis.

12. I only had one real issue with a doctor. In ICU after my son was extubated, his vitals were better than they had been since admission. His oxygen sats were slightly low but livable. His lungs were clear and he was on 2L of oxygen. The intern came in, listened to my sons lungs and responded to me, "I will have the surgery consent ready for you to sign in a few minutes". I was shocked. I said to him, "What for?". He told me for a tracheostomy to be placed. I informed him in very firm terms that there would be no insertion of a trach at this time. I explained that my son was NOT in respiratory distress, his lungs were clear, and he was only on 2L of oxygen. I told him if, and only if, my son went into respiratory distress we would address it then. The intern was upset and said, "I guess you no longer need my services". I told him, "I guess not." My son to this day has had no respiratory distress and never needed the tracheostomy. [*This person identified herself as an experienced RN who had knowledge she exercised with the medical staff.*]

13. Hospice has a whole team of support for the patient and their families. We felt they were angles on earth, whereas the CNAs and some nurses it seemed that this was only a job. In all fairness, perhaps there was some burn out for them.

14. Doctor was sister...not a good thing

15. Administrators at first wanted me to spend less time with my husband. They eventually came to seek my involvement.

16. Administrators were reluctant to allow me to make medical decisions for my partner. I think they were concerned with liability.

17. No one resisted exactly, especially when I was physically present, advocating face-to-face. But trying to advocate long distance is much more difficult, and I rely on friends who visit to keep me informed. My mother is no longer able to communicate consistently and effectively, and I am in the process of trying to find an appropriate nursing facility locally.

We had a place, but as soon as the new facility communicated with the current facility, they decided they could not handle her. If this happens again, I'm wondering if there is a recourse similar to when someone gets a bad job recommendation?? If the current facility is deliberately trying to prevent us moving her by reporting that she is difficult to manage, what recourse do we have? My mother has private insurance, not Medicaid.

18. My husband was gravely ill. It seemed to me that the social worker assigned to him was more interested in his moving on (to another facility) than in his care at the hospital. When he ultimately get released to another facility, the social worker left the information on my home voice mail, even though every other conversation we had had, she had contacted me on my cell phone, and had implicit instructions to only contact me that way, as I was seldom home due to my time spent at the hospital with my husband.

19. Our doctor was over 100% supportive. Maybe it helped that he was also personal friend

20. Just takes guts to stand up to a doctor and other nurses sometimes

21. A good physician-patient/advocate team is unbeatable. A bad one is a real struggle. I have participated in both.

22. None of his real doctors could even get anything from this place. I had to fax everything to his MD and Cardiologist. They all were doing everything they could to get him out of there. The staff and social worker at this place lied when they said they sent the clinicals to the places I found to have him transferred to. The night before he left they called the police and made me leave against his wishes and tried to get him to sign something that said he was leaving against doctor's orders. I had to have his daughter come to stay with him the next day so they couldn't make him do anything against his will.

23. The doctor on call was seldom visible.

24. I did not feel resistance in any way from anyone. I know from my experience that staff really appreciates family assistance from knowledgeable family members.

25. Administration (mostly billing and financial aspects) felt like a merry-go-round in a bad way. And insurance was often a nightmare, especially when it came to medication.

26. In general the nursing and CNA or aides vary all over the map. Much turnover in Aides; you get comfortable with a few, they can relate to my husband and then the shift changes and they are sent to another floor. Some can barely enunciate the English language. Higher speech requirements would help, as people with wounded brains, as it is my husband can't always pick up or understand when they do not speak slowly and clearly. Some don't want me there to observe their care methods.

27. I went to the admin office to lodge a complaint and was basically told to get lost. It was because I had a personal relationship with ONE board member that I was able to advocate to the entire board on this one issue.

28. All but one Doctor were fantastic. We had one Doctor removed from the care team due to his arrogant, dictatorial nature.

24. *As an advocate, did you feel your opinions and concerns were heard and valued?*
- Yes   77%
- No   28%

There were 109 comments, and the following is a selection:

1. I think that the participants in the system have their own routine but have been met with more cooperation from registered nursing staff, who would seek to improve their patients' health as well.

2. When I ask the [nurse practitioner] to look into something for my father he will do so eventually, but only if I make a point of asking.

3. Everyone assumed that Dad was getting appropriate care and that my stepmother was tracking his meds and his doctor's appointments, making sure he got to therapy, got appropriate nourishment, etc. She did not and no one on the medical staff could/would contact his children about this. I know this is separate from purely medical, but it's an important issue, too. Who protects the elderly spouse of an abuser? Apparently no one.

4. Many times there seem to be confusion on what services could be provided or which individual at the facility was responsible. Would have been nice to have had some type of chart of the organization to follow.

5. I have received great cooperation from the staffs of the hospital, the rehab facility, and the assisted living facility. Apparently there are a lot of us middle-aged people out there, caring for our parents, on very shaky legal grounds.

6. Doctors were almost always open to my input. When we learned my [mother-in-law] was not eligible for Oregon's Death With Dignity Act, a doctor in a hospital with a church implied in its name pulled me into a janitor's closet, turned on the water to defeat eavesdroppers and told me about Compassion & Choices, an organization devoted to end-of-life dignity. The doctor was violating both hospital policy and church doctrine by assisting us in finding a legal suicide option. Nursing homes were consistently more interested in boosting their cash flow at my [mother-in-laws] expense if they could pursue that option ethically. They brought in Human Services to try to force my mother into nursing care that would have drained her estate and left her in the facility on Medicaid. My [mother-in-law] chose to die by VSED [Voluntary Stopped Eating and Drinking] rather than surrender to the health care bureaucracy.

7. At first I had some push back by the health care providers because I alway was focused on the goal of a quality life. But once they saw that I stuck to my guns then little by little they started coming on board. I think it was a new way of looking at things for some of the healthcare professionals. Especially when she entered a nursing home.

8. In retrospect, I should have been more adamant about testing and using other methods to determine my father's condition. For the most part, I went along with the doctor's recommendations because of their expertise and being able to understand their logic/approach to the situation.

9. Changes were made as a result of care plan meeting

10. There were times when care givers were not informed by previous staff (shift changes for example) and so care was not as fluid as it should have been. Things that may have helped my mother's disease management were missed.

11. It has been a long and hard battle to get to the point where we feel the nursing home is providing exceptional care, with occasional setbacks mostly due to new aides, and that we are all part of the same team.

12. I think they are heard but I'm not sure they are really taken seriously because we are not seen as medical personnel and therefore they feel we are not "educated" in the needs of a patient.

13. One nurse seemed to "hear" and value my questions/concerns; most other team members seemed oblivious to Mom's presence most of the time. I probably would have thought differently had this been a "simpler" surgery but this was her HEART and I was well aware how critical the first 24-48 hours were but it seemed no one else did. They rarely came into her room, oftentimes when they did they didn't check all of the monitors; in fact, I had to point out that one wasn't even plugged in and that particular staff member was like "oh, wow, it should be, that's important..." but acted as if it weren't a big deal. HELLO...this is my mother, her life is in

your hands! There were important things not passed on at shift change (I learned to listen closely and was appalled at things that were left out). I was told several times that "we're shorthanded today"...really? and that's just supposed to be ok? Wow!

14. Able to come and go as needed. Staff was open to phone calls to receive updates throughout the day.

15. Heard, not always valued!

16. Fighting for her to have quality care was worse than having to fight the disease process.

17. One observation I walked away with was that the older nurses knew how to handle my mother better and she responded better to them. Their bedside manner was more respectful.

18. Once it was established that I had a legal role in advocating, then my concerns and opinions were valued.

19. Doctors often have the opinion that they know everything about the patient. Very seldom do they have any information regarding the personality or character of the person. This lack of knowledge can often impede or detract from patient care.

20. Heard doesn't mean respected or understood.

21. Yes, heard and "valued" -- but not always acted on!

22. Wouldn't trade it for anything!

23. People assume that as a self advocate, you are being difficult. However, I was educated about safety, outcomes, and regulations before being in that situation. I was educated, not difficult - there is a difference.

24. Most of the time. During one extended stay in the hospital, I made every doctor and every nurse repeat reports to me so I could track them in a notebook. It started as a way to inform her partner what had happened during the day (we changed shifts after his work day ended), but it quickly became a very valuable tool to ask questions throughout the stay. Yes, they maintain charts--but you don't get to see those, so having your own notes in your own words--and a place to jot down questions as they come up became a very useful tool. Do

NOT have surgery or a major illness without a notebook/notepad to record this info!!

25. Only sometimes really -- I was very young, so not taken all that seriously by the hospital staff.

26. The hospital staffs are still adjusting to the idea that relationships exist that do not fit the label of "husband and wife" and "parent/child." HIPPA also seems to interfere: "Are you allowed to know this information?" Huh? I wanted to say!

27. Yes but had I know been there God knows what would have happened. It makes me wonder what happens to all those who do not know to ask. I am embarrassed for the nursing profession.

25. What was the cognitive ability of the person for whom you advocated. By this is meant: mental ability, alertness, ability to understand surroundings and people, memory of current conditions and events, familiarity of friends and relatives:

- Very cognitive   32%
- Moderately cognitive   26%
- Somewhat cognitive   18%
- Not very cognitive   15%
- Very impaired   19%

26. Was the cognitive ability of the person for whom you advocated impacted by their illness, accident, etc.:

- Yes   76%
- No   24%

There were 133 comments. Many responded that either the severity of the illness, surgery, medications and a combination of all three created cognitive disorder. For some, following a prolonged hospitalization and rehab, a return to a home environment over time significantly reduced or altered the cognitive disorder. In others, this caused a form of vascular dementia that while later reduced, never reversed course or was simply accepted as onset of dementia. Perhaps there were previous signs of this ignored previously, but not visible, and accepted. Others reported that during prolonged illness and hospitalization, 'mini' strokes and similar TIAs were discovered, and among yet others, 'hospital psychosis' with symptoms of high anxiety, paranoia, hallucinations and depression. For many, a urinary tract infection (UTI) often created serious disorientation. Regardless, few were prepared for this sudden change in cognitive ability which for some, also impacted physical recovery. The following is a selection of comments:

1. Had no memory of illness
2. Chemotherapy dulls everything as well as tires you out.
3. Mom had two falls. One put her into rehab for three months with extreme hallucinations. Her second put her again in rehab for a couple of months, again with periods of hallucination. She had chronic [urinary tract infections] and would have short flirtations with delusion when the infection was active. It took two years for them to get the UTI's under control.
4. Because of Dad's intelligence we did not know before the illness how far along the dementia was. The drugs and shock not only made it much worse at the time, he never fully recovered after. He definitely lost the ability to hide the fact his mental abilities were failing.
5. Primary Progressive Multiple Sclerosis affects the brain because of damage to nerves and plaque deposits. My friend's long term planning, seeing the whole picture, and short term memory have all been affected. She decided to go off of a medication with disastrous results. We were notified only after the situation was beyond repair. Had we been notified as POA's [Power of Attorney] should, we would have discussed with our friend the consequences of a sudden stop in that medication. We would have consulted with her doctor, suggested a slow taper, etc. It was because of this incident that both the doctor and the staff realized the important role we serve in helping our friend process information and reach reasonable decisions. It is the very reason we are her POA'S.

6. Medications first gave her a flattened affect and then made her confused, mostly sleepy and then mostly unresponsive. This was not what we expected based on the literature and when queried, staff avoided discussion, or passed this off as a natural progression. While this I believe to be partially true, there was not enough time given to discussing the changes or our expectations.

7. My brother was very much aware of what was happening till they silenced him with drugs due to the terrible pain he was in.

8. Parkinson's added problems to memory

9. He has Lewy Body Dementia.

10. Became more distant due to dementia.

11. Frances' stroke left her with short term memory problems and she also often lived in denial of the restrictions of her diabetic diet. Example: She would "reason" that if the item was "sugar-free" it was okay to eat as much as she wanted without affecting her blood sugar level, even if the item was very high in natural sugar such as peach pie.

12. He lost his ability to read and write and think logically; he cannot remember the details of his former profession--a food chemist and technical consultant. He was a Bible scholar and adult teacher at our church. He can participate in church services, but cannot discuss any issues. He can give short opinions for simple things, but not much. But he knows the foundations of his faith as a Christian and has deeply held beliefs that have not changed. But he can speak, show courtesy in social situations; remembers friends and relatives; loves to have people share what they are doing in life. Enjoys being read to and seems to follow the content somewhat. He can still speak his second language--Finnish.

13. Coming out of surgery, you are in no position to be making big decisions without help. There are also the emotional factors involved if it is a serious, life-threatening illness or

procedure. So even though my sister was very cognitive, there were moments when she needed an advocate.

14. When a bladder infection was active then mom could not think or respond clearly.

27. *What was your greatest concern as an advocate?*
Check all that apply:
- Medical incompetence on the part of the doctors: 37%
- Medical incompetence on the part of the nursing staff: 41%
- Lack of compassion   38%
- Physical environment   22%
- Physical therapy   12%
- Occupational therapy   6%
- Other therapy   4%
- Use of medications   58%
- Bureaucracy of facility   29%
- Language barriers   6%
- Cultural barriers   4%
- Cleanliness of facility   10%
- Poor technology   3%
- Indifference   33%
- Insurance deductibles, copays and restrictions   21%
- Personal financial situation   18%
- Inability to pay medical bills   10%

There were 69 comments and the following is a selection:

1. My greatest concern was that all the staff heard the patient's voice and that her rights and dignity were upheld. At times, she was told she "had" to do something that she really felt uncomfortable doing. For example, she did not like to sleep without a pad in her undergarments because of night time

incontinence issues. She was in rehab for a broken hip. The staff insisted she not use one at night. She revealed to me that she had to "sneak" it into her underwear after they put her to bed and were out of the room. This was embarrassing for her and a personal affront to her dignity. I intervened at her request because the nursing staff did not seem to care that this really bothered her. Once I spoke up on her behalf, things changed. She was a very compliant patient and didn't want to say anything that would upset anyone. However, she expressed to me how this upset her. Sometimes, advocates are necessary to help the vulnerable patient express things that he/she are afraid to say as was the case for her.

2. What if someone finds out I don't have POA? or any of the other legal papers that should be assigned to me?

3. I worked nights so that I was available during the day for doctor's trips and caregiving for my two ladies. [Caregiving] doesn't pay that well, and has poor benefits. I took one job as a caregiver in a foster home, but differences between personal and professional caregiving caused problems. Family caregivers work from the heart, but a professional caregiver needs first to do what's required to hang onto the job, then care for the resident.

4. Constant turnover of aides who do not receive any education or training for residents who are not elderly but are there because of their special circumstances.

5. Failure to provide adequate supervision to a patient who had lost bladder control and cognition. Nursing staff said "extra care" included checking on my father once hourly. That is not acceptable for a patient who is unable to perform basic body functions, press the call button, or take drinks of water without assistance. My father fell out of bed and suffered severe hematomas as a result of the lack of monitoring.

6. Inability of doctors to work together. One doctor prescribed this, the other changed it, back and forth. This happens frequently in the hospital and can be a big problem for the

patient and family. Being an advocate and working with multiple doctors is hard. What does the patient do that doesn't have an advocate? Or a patient that the doctors don't listen to? Who orchestrates their care?

7. What would happen when I wasn't present.

8. Keeping her positive. Not letting depression sink in and telling her that it would be better.

9. We were fortunate that my husband had brought home information on cancer insurance many years before. [One] out of [two] men and [one] out of [three] women get cancer in their lifetimes, but few have cancer insurance. Otherwise we would have been financially devastated.

10. In regards to my personal advocacy I was able to do some extensive research of doctors, hospital and staff prior to choosing where my surgery would take place, but not when I advocated for my aunt. When my aunt became ill and I was rushed to research doctors, possible treatments for her condition, medication that would be necessary. I was however, not concerned about her financial situation. My aunt's financial outlook was in great shape and she was set with Medicare and excellent secondary insurance. However, financial concerns were high for myself. I was a single mother of two daughters at the time and have also been financial responsible for my mother for the last 22 years.

11. My greatest concern is to try to find the best nursing home facility for an Alzheimer's patient that my parents can afford.

12. Coordination of care. I kept things going in the right direction and without me being concerned and being there constantly my father would have been at the mercy of poor communication and it would have further prolonged his stay or it would have killed him.

13. Unfortunately, I was dealing with the devastating diagnosis given to my spouse at the same time as trying to be his advocate. My emotional state was just a mess.

14. Lack of Information. My mother went into the hospital with one thing and left after contracting a life threatening bacteria. I was not advised of the probability of contracting this (which is high) and did not know it existed. It seemed routine to them but little information was provided to me or my family about this. Upon more research I found that the only way to stop the spread of this bacteria was to wash your hands under hot water and soap. It does not get killed with hand gel. Every sink I used in the hospital required about 60 seconds or more for the water to get hot. The rate at which the nurses and doctors moved in and out of the room I am sure they would have found it highly disruptive to their busy day to have to stand there and wait for hot water. Much more information needs to be made available to patients and families at the beginning of any hospital of nursing home stay on the probability of contracting one of these secondary life threatening conditions. The hospital and nursing home or whatever facility should state the steps they are taking to reduce the risk of this type of infection and what the family can do - rather than wait for it to happen, act rather matter of fact that it did, treat it with highly expensive medication, and leave the real healing to the family to contend with after the initial diagnosed reason for being in the hospital has been addressed and the patient is released. This is not health care.

15. Poor dementia education of all staff at every nursing home that Grandma lived in

16. Finding an appropriate and clean facility took weeks. He was a relatively young man in an environment with mostly elderly patients.

17. [They encouraged] her to stop walking and stay in a wheelchair facilitating her rapid decline instead of encouraging her to help herself as much as possible parking her in front of a TV, instead of encouraging her to take part in activities and conversations

18. I encountered the most problems when dealing with my insurance company and the hospital billing department. People get to hide behind a phone and pass the buck because they are not face-to-face and really listening to the client. When I had questions or needed specifics on "what department/person" handles a certain area, I would get the runaround. I wrote down names and took tons of notes because I had to repeat things often.

19. We were fortunate enough to have long term care insurance so that is really a blessing and helping me to stay in the black financially. But when that ends, and with the current upheaval in the medical system, who knows if we will be able to get any state aid when the resources run out. I will still have to live, and I am healthy so could live a long time with no resources for myself.

20. He had kidney and liver failure and they did not do regular blood tests nor give him potassium while on diuretics. The doctor argued with him when he should have stayed calm and several nurses bragged about having "Hep C" and curing themselves by some medication they got from a hospital. One even said how he liked working intensive care the best, because you had patients unconsious and was very little work with IV's and breathing machines. The 1st morning he was there, the patient in his room was so heavily sedated from the sleeping pills they gave the patients that he couldn't even wake up to eat breakfast and the OT argued with him about taking his shower before he had his breakfast once he was awake b/c it was her scheduled time. The "doctor" said they didn't have to follow the instructions from Northwestern, that they were only suggestions. He was only allowed to take a shower every other day, and I had to help him do it. The PT would not do appropriate therapy with him and he had to demand that he get out of his wheelchair and get on the table to do stretches. He was supposed to follow cardiac precautions and they did not do that either, nor empty his bedside urine. His records

were changed, especially when they were forced to send them to other facilities and insurance when I demanded it. It was very frustrating to find that so few of the medical staff seem to actually read the charts and take proactive action.

21. In the hospital, I got so tired of explaining things over and over to the nursing staff. They would write things in the file, their shifts would be over and the new nurses never read a damn thing. I had to just stand there and repeat and repeat. They were careless with medications and insisted that my mother, who had difficulty swallowing, take a fistful of pills all at once.

People were given an opportunity to offer more comment, and this is a selection:

1. I am deeply perturbed and alarmed by the real lack of knowledge when it comes to elder patients in terms of recognizing, diagnosing and treating delirium, UTI's, dehydration and overmedication appropriately. There is not enough training on elder issues and this is a crisis starting to bloom. I am greatly concerned by the use of antipsychotic meds with elderly folks as a way to "manage" behaviors that may be delirium, not psychosis. The long term effect can be devastating.

2. The staff seemed to have no understanding of my mother. She was a PhD being pressured to play bingo. She loved Brahms and Placido Domingo.

3. Involved several specialists. They all seemed focused on their particular specialties and didn't acknowledge how all symptoms/issues were related. Didn't view the patient as a whole. Very frustrating.

4. If a patient breaks a leg and can't be weight bearing, they can't do physical therapy. If they can't do physical therapy, then due to Medicare restrictions, the facility forces the patient to discharge (or private pay). Then there is no coverage for

physical therapy after the patient is weight bearing. It is a recipe often leading to permanent disability, permanent home care or institutional care and, therefore, a much greater chance the patient will end up in Medicaid due to impoverishment.

5. There were so many drugs involved in the treatment, that keeping a list of the medications was very important.

6. My mother's (former) doctor prescribed a medication that I fortunately investigated before getting the prescription filled. The drug had the highest alert warning possible. Several elderly women who took it had severe mental complications that are NOT reversible. Some even committed suicide. I feel very blessed that I looked up the drug - something I used to do only rarely. Now I am more regular about checking new meds.

7. Insurance concerns took too much attention from physical conditions

8. The person for whom I was an advocate was in a private nursing home located in one state while her personal physician was located less than five miles in another state. He was unable to assist her because she was in another state (federal or state law); thus, she was provided with another doctor who did not know her condition and whose workload was over-extended.

9. It is my policy that no one in my family will spend time alone in a hospital until they are able to advocate for themselves.

10. We just found out my husband's cancer is showing activity again and he will be on chemo very shortly. In a month and a half, we will be on a new insurance plan and I'm dreading the complications this will cause. Although my husband is not happy about having to go through treatment again, he is relieved he will be doing the same therapy and not something "stronger." I think once we get to the even more serious treatments down the road is where I will encounter more issues as an advocate.

11. Hard to afford that time out.

12. The fact that nursing homes are understaffed and underpaid led to my problems as an advocate. I shudder to think what it will be like when we "babyboomers" hit the nursing home scene. I advise anyone who is an advocate for their loved one, make your presence known at all different times of the day so you can observe the different shifts of staff. Once they know you and know you are there for your loved one, they tend to be more attentive and helpful than to those who have no visitors or anyone looking out for them. You know, people tend to slide when they can and I saw that with those patients who had no one looking out for them.

28. Did you feel you were prepared to be an advocate?
- Yes   55%
- No   47%

29. In addition to being an advocate, were you also the primary care giver?
- Yes   51%
- No   44%
- n/a   8%

30. Was your health and/or mental well being impacted in any way as a result of your experience?
- Yes   73%
- No   25%
- n/a   2%

31. If yes to question #30, what was the impact? Choose all the apply:
- I lost my job as a result of time spent being an advocate and/or caregiver   8%
- I experienced great mental stress   71%
- I experienced increased illness (i.e., colds, headaches, stomach upsets, etc.)   26%

- I had a hard time sleeping   57%
- I was tired much of the time   68%
- I found less time to do things important to me
  (i.e., shopping, being with friends, church,
  social activities, etc.)   60%
- I became resentful as a result of the
  time this took   19%

There were 64 comments. Everyone who shared a comment felt stress and it manifested itself in various ways. Depression and isolation were often cited. Some people gained weight while others lost weight. Some felt restricted by time and were not able to shop and prepare healthy meals as was their habit, often grabbing fast food just to stave off hunger and get sleep. For those who once maintained active and routine workouts, this also became restricted. Several people became ill during their advocacy, most especially if the illness and/or recovery of the person they cared and advocated for was prolonged. This is well documented -- that caretakers often become ill, and some quite ill, in the process of caretaking. Adult children taking care of gravely ill parents found they were often ignoring their own children, performing perfunctory duties. Some owned a business and while they did not risk being fired, their businesses suffered because they were paying less attention to their business and experienced loss of income while at the same time financial debt increased. Those employed felt incredible pressure to keep up a productive work load and struggled to keep their advocacy from being either noticeable or interfering to the point of jeopardizing their jobs. A few were concerned that they were not able to advance their careers and thus the repercussions of this period left them vulnerable for years to come, long after the advocacy passed. There was resentment toward other members of the family who did not appear to be offering much help. Others stated that although the advocacy was strenuous, it brought them closer to the person when before there might have been a strained relationship. Others felt increased love, and to take care of this person was a special honor.....to be their advocate and caretaker. The following is a selection:

1. I was more emotional and cried easily...... misunderstood people.
2. Resentful of family not helping or offering to help.
3. When it is not rewarding, it is very isolating and stressful.
4. Many jobs require a person to put their job first. Those that don't, pay poorly. Giving care to my wife is my first priority. Her mother's care ran a close second, leaving my employer at best third on my list of priorities. Few of them were happy with my choices, so employment was always poor-paying and under-enthused. Working nights is a recognized carcinogen by the ACS. I found cancer after a double-hernia operation, and that left me with 20% of two $30,000 surgeries, or $12,000 on my credit cards. Wheelchairs are paid at 80/20 also, and they aren't cheap. Co-pays and deductibles killed us because my medically fragile wife needs consistent medical and dental care. My mother in law, toward the end of her life, needed intimate care roughly every [four] hours around the clock. We had compassionate neighbors who came in when called at night while I was at work. At $10 a visit, they were both cheap and expensive. During my off hours, I got up every [four] hours or when called. That represents a hard time sleeping.
5. I was tired to the point of exhaustion most of the time. My life outside the family evaporated.
6. It was impacted in an amazing positive way! The whole situation brought me closer to my mother and family. While I worked very long hours on tasks related to my mother's care, it was some of the most meaningful work I had ever done. I also found much solace and gratitude in friends, neighbors, church family responding positively when I asked them for help. The crisis happened in such a small window of time that I was surprised by the "web of support" that quickly emerged.
7. Resentful at times as I have no life now and no friends cause they all seem to drop you when you can't do anything anymore. Almost like retiring and everyone else is still working and

you feel left out. Weight gain [because] there is no time for exercise.

8. My entire family to this day is paranoid and afraid of going to a doctor or hospital. We all needed therapy. My parent's marriage was almost terminated. My middle brother attempted suicide and as a result his marriage ended. I completely left the medical field in the traditional sense and left teaching

9. Felt incompetent, helpless.

10. My ability to be a good mother to my son was greatly impacted.

11. I have had a heart attack (due mostly to stress) and have developed arthritis

12. I stayed with him as many hours as possible. His family did not provide the support expected, but actually sapped us of time and money and complicated the experience. I went on sabbatical from the university due to the exacerbation of my fibromyalgia and chronic fatigue. I eventually had to quit due to their lack of compassion.

13. I did quit my job as an ICR RN - could not deal with the additional stresses.

14. I have experienced a lot of stress and don't feel able to take time for myself. When I do I feel guilty.

15. Basically, I feel as if I have not been able to protect this person from the vagaries of the health care system. I feel as though I have let her down, despite all efforts. I am seriously exploring legal alternatives since I feel that the doctors' decision to keep her on steroids for over six years (medications intended for short term use only) have suppressed her adrenals to the extent that a 4 mm malignancy that was not detectable at the end of January 2011 suddenly appeared at the beginning of September.

16. I lost a summer with my two grandsons and my youngest daughter's wedding was impacted by my new role.

17. The emotional impact of virtually losing my partner and husband of ......48 years is great. Underlying every aspect

of my life is a deep sadness at the loss of what will never be again--our life together. Also, so many things that my husband handled, I now am responsible for: our car upkeep, etc., the financial things are difficult. Our papers were not all in order, and I am struggling with preparing for end of life issues, alone.

18. Since I had a lifetime of nursing this came as a natural response to caring for someone. I also had a great deal of family support. People not familiar or used to caring for individuals both physically and mentally are not prepared for the amount of time an energy one person's medical needs can place on the caregiver. That being said, people should be aware that creating an environment for the patient to improve is imperative. Encouraging independence as much as possible helps the person recuperate much faster and relieves the burden on the caregiver.

19. I barely kept our company going, and ended up hospitalized myself a year later with life threatening illness made worse by previous year's stress, less than optimal nutrition, loss of sleep and physical fitness. Was worth it, and we are both fine now, but it took SO MUCH mental energy to keep having to insert myself into the treatment process as an advocate, when they should have welcomed me as an asset!

32. *Did you have support from others? Choose all that apply:*
- Yes, from my children   28%
- Yes, from my spouse   46%
- Yes, from my partner   6%
- Yes, from my siblings   37%
- Yes, from other relatives   39%
- Yes, from friends   48%
- No   7%

33. What resources did you use to help you in your role as advocate? Check all that apply:

• The web/Google searches	62%
• Public library	10%
• Support group	11%
• Other health professionals	47%
• Social service workers	23%
• Friends	58%
• Relatives	44%

Most people recognized their friends and family, but people still need resources beyond such a support base, which is indeed a critical emotional support. Also, several people mentioned faith and prayer. We all need the resources of groups and organizations that have already done the research and 'walked the path' to share vital information quickly when advocates are caught up in the daily frenzy of care, often putting one foot in front of the other. Several mentioned groups such as the Alzheimer's Association and hospice as well as local support groups and resource centers. Several who responded are health professionals, and felt this reduced significant tension that comes with struggling for accurate information or dealing with barriers to get such. Local senior/community centers were also of great help, as were the local VA help centers. Many suggested contacting an ombudsman, either one connected to a facility – although there was some cynicism that if there was an issue with a facility how open an ombudsmen might be who was 'on the payroll' – or from within the wider community, from an unbiased source or group. People who had been advocates previously drew from their knowledge. Often within a family, people lean on people who have already advocated for another relative, although this expectation of knowledge and ability carries also stress and burden and some feel that too much then is expected of them. Almost all would agree that no one can 'go it alone'. The following is a selection of comments:

1. There was no one close by us at the time. We were geographically far from our home and community. My parents didn't want anyone to know--so our family talked

to no one about this until I wrote the book this year. It took its' toll on all of us.

2. I prayed a lot. My faith in God helped me through most of it. My sister was supportive of the decisions that I made and I kept her abreast almost daily of what was going on. But with her being in Phoenix, her support was limited to listening to me over the phone or email. A lot of times I just felt so alone and I did resent the fact that once she would get off the phone my mom and my problems were gone whereas I had to live with it 24/7. My husband didn't know how to be supportive of me in the way that I needed, my children were having babies, going to school and just getting their adult lives going. Many, many times I would drive home from visiting my mom in tears knowing there was no one I could talk to about how I was feeling.

3. Medical research. This may be covered under web/Google - but it goes beyond the searching typically done. I regularly read and understand articles in the applicable medical journals which is a distinction many physicians do not appreciate when they make comments like "stay away from the internet."

4. Used everything at my disposal. Trying to find out 'when' is the right time to just let a person die, and when to hold out. I held out and have no regrets on my decisions. I let the doctors guide me, but not control me.

5. I took classes in mediation.

6. I did not feel that the social workers were much help for me, or our side. They were concerned about following all the rules and getting out what the facility needed; little compassion. I could not find a support group that met my needs. The few meetings I went to had such a diverse group that it was a waste of my time, which was in short supply. I am still looking for a group; there are so many things to be talked over and helped with decisions, but I have to be careful to whom I reveal some things. So don't feel well supported. I don't know

how to be an advocate. Just take it one day at a time. If there are books on the subject, I haven't found them.

7. Need to have some help for advocacy in the legislature to protect elderly from spousal abuse and not just assume the spouse has rights to the whole estate just because of marriage... especially when said spouse is doing so much that is obviously wrong, immoral, and unethical, but apparently still legal.

8. It can be an impossible position, and what I need most is having time off and getting to take care of my own needs. Family comes to town, stays in your home and the last thing I need is company. They don't get that. They come in and expect me to change to fit their needs.

9. Family were quite clueless about how to help. One sister ran in the other direction and was a major source of stress for me.

10. Google was my best friend.

11. HIPAA was created to protect patients, not to deny access to medical records to their spouses when permission has been granted.

12. If you have a loved one that is having an elective surgery, designate one or two family members to be available round the clock the first 72 hours after the surgery. I think it's imperative that there are eyes/ears around during these critical hours. Do not be afraid to ask questions of the medical team and if you aren't satisfied with an answer, ask the next person "up" until you are satisfied! Be cognizant of medications, be cognizant of the doctor's orders for follow-up care that is SUPPOSED to occur by the medical team for the entire length of stay. Keep calm, show respect...you get better results and it tends to be reciprocated. All of the above should apply for any family emergency...few of us plan for such events, but we should! Communication amongst family members should occur RIGHT NOW, plans should be laid out for "if this happens, this is who will do what...", write it down and share it with all involved (type it up/print it out/give copies!).

13. Spouse was supportive but I know it was a difficult time for him as my focus was my daughter, work, and then him.

14. Many people who act as advocates don't even know where to start or what questions to ask. Our health care system is overwhelming and difficult to navigate even when you do not have the knowledge.

15. If you think of what you are doing as a marathon, not a sprint, it goes much better.

16. My daughters live on opposite sides of the country, and my husband was essentially too busy with his career; it was MY mother, not his.

17. Every time you are switched to a different facility, you are assigned a new doctor, and you have to furnish all recent medical records and history. Some facilities will not share their records with other facilities. It's like starting over again with each facility. My husband was moved from a nursing facility to a psychiatric facility to a hospice and back to another nursing home within [one] month. The caregiver is already under stress from care, concern, traveling, and sleepless nights, then they have to be constantly dealing with answering questions.

18. Our husbands were very supported and never complained of the impact our care of our parents had on them. One brother helped by doing the financial portion of the care. He handled all the money and paid the bills with my parents bank account. He issued credit cards to my two sisters so that they wouldn't spend their own money. That was a big help. My other brother still had small children at home and could only come occasionally. It should be noted that when the brothers did come they would treat it as a vacation and stay with my sisters and do other activities, it wasn't a break for my sisters, but maybe even more work for them. I made sure that I would get a rented car and truly give them a break when I came to town. I wanted them to have a real break.

19. Information from other friends who had experienced much of what we were going through was helpful in determining where to have therapy and the nursing home that was best suited to our needs.

20. Being a medical advocate can be exhausting and stressful. You feel you must learn everything you can medically and about available services. You must have the confidence to monitor care and to persist to have concerns met. We are not medical people and yet you feel you must monitor medical care as well as being a support for your loved one. Advocacy is not for sissies! Too often the medical community wants to dismiss you and your loved ones. You must work to keep everyone focused on your loved one's needs.

21. I documented my feelings and links by learning to blog. This led to other media projects that connected me to a community media center. I help produce programming for many aspects of advocacy in volunteer support roles... cmcm.tv

22. Someone had told me early into this medical crisis that we would find it very interesting who would be at our sides every step of the way and that we would find out who we really could count on. It was so true! We have large extended families and an awesome circle of friends, but there were some surprises as to who really kept close and checked in on us. My husband tried not to take it personally when certain people did not come through for him. I think the seriousness of his illness scared some people.

34. If there was something that could have helped you during your role as an advocate, what is it? For example, the hospital or nursing home offering support groups, literature specific to advocates, etc.

This was a most helpful question, and 105 people responded. Many stated that more support groups and those specific to an illness or disease would be of great help. Others mentioned mental health counseling, advocates for the advocates and classes on how to be an effective advocate. One person suggested professional therapy and I am assuming this would be due to all the compounding stress advocates and caregivers experience. More focused literature on advocacy -- documents to have on hand, what is legal and what is not, rights and responsibilities, etc. – and better informed hospital social workers on local rehab and long term care options. Advocates do not need brochures as this is considered paid advertising....advocates expect social workers to have informed opinion and knowledge -- good and bad -- about the facilities. Several mentioned scheduling more care meetings, and ones that accommodate people who work during the day rather than the staff. The following is a selection from the comments:

1. I have learned that the assisted living facility where my mother lives has a support group. I will attend my first meeting in a couple weeks. before I learned about this group, I was very close to 'divorcing' my mother, and having the court appoint an advocate for her.
2. Support for a family dialogue. Instead the family is now split on what Mom needs.
3. Transitions and support regarding discharges, home care, what to expect. Better prep. info in terms of insurance/ options/benefits help. A comfortable room to be warm, quiet and nap in peace without TV blaring.
4. More agencies in rural communities are very limited and I would have had to move her to a bigger community to get them....taking her away from supportive friends.
5. Yes, a support group at the nursing home would have given me a way to articulate what was difficult. A sit-down with the social worker, introducing me to my new role would have helped. A sit-down with the head of nursing explaining what I could expect and how I could best work with the staff would have helped.
6. The biggest thing that would have helped me was to be able to speak to another advocate who had recently been through the whole experience. I didn't have time for a support group, but

if the hospital social worker or discharge planner could have given me a list of a few people willing to be called and share their experience. FYI, I know this is done with transplant patients. My friend just gave her kidney to her 30 year old daughter last year, and now that they are fully recovered, they serve as "peer mentors" to other families facing a transplant. This is "one on one" and very meaningful support.

7. The hospital held a case meeting due to so many issues that developed with my father's care. The doctors who were the biggest problems failed to come to the meeting. When my son was severely injured, the hospital he was in had DAILY case meetings with ALL physicians and family members. I wish my father's hospital had done the same.

8. I believe the facility is not motivated to get my father back in his apartment. Why would they? They have a paying bed. They are giving him speech therapy when he is rehabbing for a broken hip. Although he has some dementia and is extremely hard of hearing, it is ridiculous to be giving him speech therapy, and I'm sure charging Medicare. Aids allow him to do things he should not be doing by himself and yet they refuse to move him in that direction by getting him walking. They are allowing him to lie in bed all day long with one physical therapy session per day. They are not trying to get him up and around the rest of the day. We want him out and eating with everyone else and working with a walker. The list goes on. We are not happy with the treatment and will address it in our case meeting scheduled for next week.

9. More information on protecting assets and whether if the time comes and mom has to be in a nursing home and runs out of money and goes on the state whether they will come after me, especially if I sell my home. Will they come after our income?

10. We, as a family, would have planned our vigilance much more thoroughly. We didn't anticipate having to be there 24/7 but ended up doing so just because our overall impression was if

we weren't there, what REALLY is and more importantly what really IS NOT happening. Again, you wouldn't think you would need to "staff" your own families hospital stays but it's imperative that you do. And then, if you are fortunate enough to have an incredible medical team that does give exemplary care, you can back off and perhaps even just be there during "visiting hours"...the way it should be!

11. Someone who was or had been through what I was going through to just sit and listen and put an arm around me to give me comfort. I just needed some comfort and peace and understanding. I needed someone to validate my decisions, to tell me I was doing the right thing, the best thing for my mom. To give me strength when mine was waning. Someone with the medical knowledge to help me know these decisions were right, what the choices were, what the results would be or wouldn't be, what would help, what wouldn't help. I remember I kept asking the doctors, 'think about your mother; if she was your mother, what would you do?'

12. More hospitals and nursing homes need to make Internet access easily attainable. Wi-Fi is good for those who have laptops, but making public computers available for patients and/or their immediate caregiver on each floor would be great!

13. I just needed someone else my age to talk to and offer advice about Alzheimer's Disease and to understand what I was going through. My situation is totally different than someone trying to take care of an older adult. I had to still be a mother at the same time that I had to take over all of the household responsibilities and work full time and keep my husband's affairs in order (work, short term/long term disability, social security, etc.) -- it was so stressful.

14. I found that the most important thing in a continued role as a care giver is to find time to spend with others in a completely different atmosphere…. to relax and reenergize physically and mentally.

15. Whether someone has full mental capacity or not - a hospital stay is overwhelming - and you are by definition not at your best. Either advocates need to be more routine - or hospitals need to go back to basics and learn that a patient needs to be treated with a viewpoint wider than a diagnosis. Hospitals and nursing homes need to seek ways to promote the fact that they are in the business of life, not just illness and death. There was not one health care worker at the hospital that thought my mother would live after she contracted the bacteria. They spoke frequently to me of the downward spiral of life - to prepare me.........I wonder how many people expire out of this expectation.

16. I think it is unrealistic to expect hospitals, nursing homes, assisted living facilities and the like to create and support groups whose primary function is to help members assume a near adversary role toward the institution. At the same time, the need for support groups and literature is acute. A better solution might be for the various organizations which support and advocate for segments of the institutional population (Alzheimer's Association, e.g.) to come together jointly develop resources and literature that can be made available within the institutions and through the organizations.

17. I wished I would have known about the Alzheimer's Association and the Long Term Care Ombudsman at the time. I also wish I would have known a resident's rights. I would have known that Grandma could not have just been 'kicked out' of her home.

18. I feel that if a person suffering from dementia or Alzheimer's could have some kind of physicians letter on file with utility and phone companies then they should NEVER have their utilities or phone turned off and that POA's should be held more accountable.

35. Is there a statement you want to make that was not addressed in the survey?

Several people thanked me for putting together the survey and making this attempt to create an awareness of the problems people encounter in a health care crisis. Sadly, too many did not start out as a crisis. My husband started out with a successful and routine knee replacement when a secondary infection two weeks later turned everything into a very serious and tragic crisis. Several people who commented are health professionals and despite this experience, found caring for and advocating on behalf of someone very close to them was exhausting, and at times, even they felt powerless. While most people who took the survey had an issue of great concern, that is not to suggest that people used this forum only to complain. I have included comments from people who also understood the limitations of institutional care and were grateful for the care their loved ones received. The following is a selection from the comments:

1. There is definitely a need for older people to have younger people in their life!
2. Although I had training earlier as an ombudsman, I was not prepared for the attitudes from admin. and some nursing staff. I think they should have been more interested in trying to improve things, instead of complaining they were too busy, underpaid, etc.
3. I am a health care professional but during this time I wanted only to be family.
4. This is a very important project and very much needed. Everyone should have a medical care advocate! I would not let my loved ones go to the hospital without one! As the senior population grows the need is just going to explode.
5. Caregiving is expensive. Advocating for a disabled loved one by acquiring medical and financial POA is a great way to alienate family and start a war with some private or government lawyer. There are people who have given up great

jobs to share a one-bedroom apartment and a welfare check with an aging disabled relative.

6. I have shared caregiving for my mother in law, my father, shared with my mother, and now my mother. It's been quite a ride since 2007. I've transitioned mom into a senior living complex as of August, and I can see her aging before my eyes as she grieves the loss of my father. She has a mass in her pancreas so I know it's a matter of time. I'm filled with guilt over moving my mom out of her house. There are so many things I wish I could change and control. But I can't. Thankfully I have a very supportive spouse to support me and two grown kids to help.

7. It is so much harder to do than anyone thinks. My two sisters take care of my mother. There are always issues no matter the amount being done. I will say this. The child doing the least is usually the perfect one to the one needing care. My Mom thinks I am so perfect only because I am not there dealing with the day to day problems. I am not the one saying what day the doctor's appt. must be because of that is when my sisters can take her. I am not the one saying you must have a nurse set up your pills. I am not the one limiting my Mom's choices. Thus I am the perfect one. It was the same with Dave's family. The son in Florida who shows up [four] days a year is the perfect one. The children need to understand this and support each other. I try to let my sisters know how much I appreciate what they do for me. And I thank them daily for being there when I can't.

8. I cannot begin to tell you how strange it is/was going through her house finding "easter eggs"-- jewelry in a toaster in the oven [yes, you read correctly], antique guns in stored handbags... jewelry in mugs in the pantry, rings in medicine bottles. The deed to the house in her under-wear drawer... the will is in her safety deposit box! To which, of course, I don't have a key!

9. Hospital care has deteriorated to the point that it is essential for every inpatient to have a family member present 24/7 to ensure the correct medication is being administered (my father was also given an incorrect medication more than once), to protect the rights of the patient, and to ensure the patient is receiving the level of care that is required. Patients whose families cannot provide an advocate/monitor 24/7 often suffer as a result.

10. No one knows till they go through it how stressful it is on the caregiver and her immediate family. I have no kids home now but do have grandkids and I don't get to see them or spend much time with them. Mom....gets jealous when I give attention to someone else and not her. Hard to even get house work done. There needs to be more programs to help the caregivers and give them someone to talk to and help out when a break is needed and not have to pay 100's of dollars for it. Most people don't have that kind of money when they get to that age, even though they think they have planned well.

11. I am thankful that, for the most part, all of the caregivers and medical personnel who have interacted with my family member have been wonderful. We have a fabulous in-home care giver who truly cares for our family member and even requested to be assigned to our case. I wish we could get these care givers the proper amount of pay for the work and care they give to people.

12. I once heard, and am starting to think it not a bad idea... when I get to the point that I need long term care...I would prefer life in prison...I'll get three meals a day, showers 3x a week, cable TV, scheduled visits, healthcare (medication, infirmary), "yard time", pen pals, religion...and the taxpayers will pay for it ~ seems much more reasonable than my family losing everything they have for less than equal the care/provisions I'd get in a healthcare facility! Can someone justify $6 for ONE Tylenol pill? How is that even possible? Yet I've seen it, and even more ridiculous, on itemized bills from

hospitals! Yes, there is definitely something wrong with the entire healthcare system.

13. I came away from this feeling that every person who goes into the hospital needs a pushy, knowledgeable advocate if they are going to have a successful experience.

14. As a care giver/advocate of a spouse with children, it was very difficult dealing with their anger at me for putting their father in a nursing home, etc. This stress on top of dealing with a spouse with Alzheimer's was very difficult. My children supported me in every way possible, but that did not help the hurt and stress of dealing with the anger and resentment from his children. We had been married for 36 years. This is an issue that I would like to see literature, etc. about. A care giver/advocate has so much to deal with without dealing with this type of issue. The children would not listen to the nursing staff/Drs. and were constantly questioning every decision made. The nursing staff finally got to the point where they were going to the children instead of the spouse to discuss issues and/or give updates. I spoke with the administrators and they discussed this with the nursing staff, but it did not change much. In such situations you hate to threaten anything legal when you know the children want what's best for their father, but at the same time they were causing extra expense insisting that extra tests, etc. be done that the Dr. said were unnecessary, but you were told to pick your battles. I have a new sympathy for care givers/advocates that I never had before. No one knows until they go through this type of situation just how hard it is on both the patient and care giver/advocate.

15. It might be important to say that at all the places my parents lived the workers would comment on how involved we were with my parents care. They would say they wished all families would be like ours. I truly believe more would be if they were in our place. My sisters were retired school teachers with all their children grown and doing well. The impact on

their lives was less than if they had jobs and small children at home. I could fly for free and my parents would pay for the rented cars. I was substitute school teacher and could be flexible with my jobs. My parents raised us to be positive and look for the best in everything, and I think that is why we saw these last few years as gifts. We had a tremendous relationship with my dad the years before he passed. My mom's story is sad because she doesn't know us anymore and it's been a long goodbye. She has us to visit her every day and feed her lunch and know we love her. Our visits are no longer a huge chunk of the day like they use to be because it's only my mom now and she sleeps most of the time. We love the private home she is in and are thankful for the nurses there and caregivers.

16. I believe that some sort of meditation, (or prayer in my case) helped immensely in acquiring patience, courage and understanding of the patient's disability.

17. I am shocked and appalled at the influence corporate America (the insurance industry) wields in healthcare, especially in determining protocol. I am equally disappointed that the AMA, like labor unions in the 1960's, seemingly exists to protect its weakest members. Barring law suits, there is little recourse for addressing medical incompetence or dishonesty.

18. This is an important topic as you know. As an advocate and a nurse I know that every hospitalized patient needs at least one visit a day from a caring competent friend or family member. I suggest that we form groups to agree to visit friends and family in the hospital especially for elderly people who do not have family in town.

19. Since Dad's passing, I am continuing my advocacy in general through my work in chaplaincy, in the same hospital where he was in and out over the final 20 months of his life. My experiences then inform my practices now.

20. Choosing a nursing home was a most painful process for me. My husband has been in three; each time the search did not get any easier.

21. After and during the period of time I was acting as an advocate for my mother she said many times - What would I have done if you were not here? - Thankfully, I was here and in retrospect I wish that in a few situations I had been more aggressive and demanding with the health care system. My mother's generation has an unquestioning respect for medical doctors and health care institutions - she did not want me to push harder - but in the end it is possible that she would have suffered less if I had intervened more!

22. The care my mom received in a nursing home was so dependent upon who was working that day. It was sad that some days she did not even get her teeth brushed. It was sad that many a meeting [was held] and all we asked is that someone help her brush her teeth every day. Yet, it still did not happen. I really took a stand when she was not gotten out of bed for days because her wheelchair needed a tire repaired. No calls were made to her family. She just was left in bed. This is what happens when nursing homes are for profit businesses. Thank you!

The Interviews

Of those that took the survey, many wanted to be interviewed. Twenty interviews were chosen for this book. Patient advocates all, with the exception of one who was his own advocate. He came to realize how he could have benefitted having an advocate by his side; everyone who goes to a hospital for whatever reason and whatever procedure needs an advocate.

What is remarkable is that while each of the people I interviewed had a unique story, each of us also had much in common. The people I interviewed had stories from hospitals and nursing homes; issues with diet and medications; doctors and nurses; health administrators and insurance companies; pharmacies and pharmaceuticals. Some of the people had expressions I thought of using as a title for my book: "Where is the outrage?!" and "I am an advocate: I put on armor and fight."

I am sure that you will see yourself in one of these stories. I am also sure that you have, as well, a story of your own. Everyone I talk to has a story. Are the hospitals and nursing homes listening?

Stand Strong!
Patients

Speak Out!
Advocates

Listen Up!
Medical Community

3

---

3   Design by Paula Lambo.

Up Against the Insurance Companies

Fiercely independent, Leslie's mother lived on the family farm in southern Indiana until she was 87 years old. In 1980, she was diagnosed with *idiopathic thrombocytopeni purpura*, or ITP. The cause of the condition is unknown, but it means that the blood does not have enough platelets (also called thrombocytes) and the skin is prone to excessive bruising (thus the word, 'purpura'). For people who have ITP, all the blood cells are normal except for the platelets, which are tiny cells that form blood clots to seal minor cuts and wounds. A person who has too few platelets bruises very easily and can bleed for a long time after being injured. For example, a nosebleed may be hard to stop, or one might have bleeding in the intestines, or even bleeding in the brain as the result of ordinarily minor trauma. Obviously, falls and fractures are of extreme concern with ITP, and most especially as one ages. Leslie's mother was treated with steroids, standard operating procedure at that period, and in very high doses for weeks at a time. The harmful side effects of long-term use of steroids are well documented. In addition, her spleen was removed, although one of the functions of the spleen is the storage of platelets; thus, whatever little defense Leslie's mother had was removed.

A prudent woman, in 1991 Leslie's mother purchased 'nursing home insurance.' Today it would be called a 'long-term care policy,' which people commonly associate with financial payment for a nursing home when they are no longer able to live independently. Long-term care policies can also be used, however, for residential rehabilitation for medical issues such as fractures and joint replacements, as well as to allow people whose 'activities of daily living' (ADLs) have declined to stay in their homes with nursing services plus additional funds to purchase equipment for the home such as hospital beds and the like. The policy Leslie's mother purchased in 1991 was strictly for nursing home services in a long-term care facility. The criteria according to which Leslie's mother would be able to use her policy were set forth in the contract, which stated that "medically necessary care ... certified by YOUR physician as part of a treatment plan and standards of medical practice" could be exercised in a nursing home facility.

Over time, Leslie's mother had two hip replacements (on the same side) and replacement of both knee joints as a result of the steroids. Additionally, she developed osteoporosis, which led to six spinal fractures of which three were treated with surgery and three with medication and braces. She also became 'hard of hearing.' Each hospitalization for the fractures meant dealing with a new host of doctors; meanwhile, it became increasingly difficult in her small rural community to find specialists who knew how to treat her increasing health risks when combined with ITP. To complicate matters, Leslie's mother also developed congestive heart failure, which may have had its roots in the steroids, or may have been simply a result of aging. Yet she continued to live on the family farm, holding onto her independence.

In time, the combination of bone fragility, the heart condition, and the hearing deterioration prompted Leslie's mother to consider a change, perhaps to assisted living. Her children were already sufficiently alarmed. It was time to finally use that 'nursing home' insurance purchased almost twenty years previously.

The original insurance company that issued the policy had gone through change of ownership, but the terms of the contract had not been amended since 1992. Leslie's mother's family physician agreed that it was "medically necessary" that her "treatment plan and standards of medical practice" be met in a nursing home facility, so the family began to make these arrangements, requesting a claim form from the insurance company so that payment could be directed to the facility. The company did not provide a claim form; instead, they said they were going to have a nurse meet with Leslie's mother to determine her level of need, a service that would be paid for by the insurance company.

The nurse met with Leslie's mother at the family farm. Leslie's mother was able haltingly to walk very short distances (e.g., from her chair to the bathroom or kitchen) with a walker. She could eat only if someone prepared her meals, which had been arranged by the family. She had not taken a tub bath in "at least a year," since she was physically unable to get into a tub ... so she gave herself sponge baths out of the kitchen sink. She was at 'fall risk' and her hearing problem made it difficult to use a phone, which meant further danger to her daily living. Despite all of these factors, the company-paid nurse determined that she did not need to move to an assisted living facility.

The family, eager to get their mother moved into an already identified facility before any serious harm happened, now waited for a determination from the insurance company. According to Leslie, Indiana law states that such determinations must be issued within 30 days; 60 days had passed. Indiana law also states that insurance companies must issue claim forms when requested, but the family still had not received one. The family complained to the CEO of the insurance company as well as to the Indiana Department of Insurance. Each state has such a department, and they carry considerable weight over the policies and practices of insurance companies in their individual states; in this case, the insurance company "backed down" and agreed to submit a claim. Departments of Insurance, however, cannot litigate; that is not their purpose. Once an insurance company responds to a complaint, it is up to the original 'injured' party to pursue further action.

The insurance company then stated they wanted to send a request to the family physician who had declared Leslie's mother a candidate for a nursing home facility, requesting a "certificate of medical necessity." Leslie stepped in to say 'No.' Just as the company-paid nurse found Leslie's mother competent to continue living in her home despite her inability to perform even perfunctory 'activities of daily living,' the form sent by the insurance company could be "twisted" in such a way as to continue denying the claim. Leslie said that the family would deal directly with the family physician.

Meanwhile, the family moved their mother into an assisted living facility where she lived until her death in 2012. They were fortunate to have sold the family farm, which helped pay the bills, along with their mother's Social Security benefits and small pension from her late husband. The family continues to fight the insurance company to get them to comply with the stated terms of the contract, which, they argue, are being violated.

It is important to note that Leslie is an attorney who specializes in health care. She knows how to read health contracts. She knows how to fight insurance companies when the contract terms are being ignored. She has been doing this for quite some time. "What do people do without this ability?" Leslie asks; obviously, advocates need a "medical legal understanding to deal with insurance companies." Most people lack this. One can consult an attorney, but that is expensive. For many families, by the time this may be necessary, the medical issues have likely already been costly to the family; hiring an attorney adds to the family's financial burden. It is unwise to live without insurance, to drive down a road, to own a home, to hope we do not get ill or hit by a 'Mack truck.' Insurance covers risks and accidents. Insurance companies also have their own bevy of attorneys to protect them against insurance fraud, and these attorneys may be used to win cases. But there is a reason why insurance companies leave a bad feeling with people: not all companies are noble. They are accused of greed and felt to exercise too much control in the healthcare industry through their highly paid lobbyists. They also know that most people do not have the ability to read the fine print in insurance contracts, policies bought in the 'good faith' that was advertised in the first place.

Having long-term care insurance can both offer an affordable choice for a long-term care facility and help protect family assets, most particularly if there is a dependent spouse in good health who anticipates living an independent life for years to come. Caution is encouraged; people should purchase a policy from an established company with a high rating and experience with selling this type of insurance. A company's financial stability can be checked at rating agencies such as A.M. Best as well as with individual state insurance commissions. Each state has such a commission, which holds powerful sway over insurance companies.[4] Once you have a policy, read it! As with any insurance, you want to know in advance what you have – or do *not* have – before you need it.

---

[4] Andrews, Michelle, "Seven tips for buying long term care insurance," *US News and World Report*, March 2009, p. 11.

"Follow the Dollar"

Mary Ann and her sister, both of whom are RNs, have the advantage of being more aware and knowledgeable medically than the average consumer – even a well-educated one – as well as being less cowed by the medical industry and the accompanying titles of professionals. Mary Ann's father was 84 when he developed severe abdominal pain; it was linked to his gall bladder, which was surgically removed. His hospitalization had no crises, but he was so weak and in so much pain that he relied on bed assistance, and even that was a chore. He was taking three different antibiotics, which "wreaked havoc on his GI system," including instigating diarrhea. Because of his weakened condition and his confusion about how to use the call light, it was not unusual for her father to lie in his own feces for hours at a time. Mary Ann blames much of this on the hospital's being "short-staffed." But that is not shocking news to anyone, most especially to those who have experienced even the briefest of stays in a hospital in recent years. There is so much more, however, that is not immediately transparent.

"Each floor used to have someone whose purpose was to answer the phone, so that the nurses could focus on patient care. Today, that person has been replaced with telephones. Nurses are given cell phones and can be reached directly by anyone who has their number, for any purpose or demand." Mary Ann witnessed this personally, while a nurse was attempting to change her father's IV. When the phone rang, she answered, carrying on a conversation which sounded to Mary Ann to be of a medical nature, all the while attending to her father's medication and IV. Do we think a mistake could not be made?

This is all about "cost containment," said Mary Ann, and every health facility has to watch its costs. This is not a bad thing; after all, families watch their costs too. We all want to stay out of debt. But how are decisions made relative to patient care? "Follow the dollar," said Mary Ann: "I would argue that we do not have a healthcare system as much as we have a sick care system."

In the United States, starting with physicians and moving on to include practitioners and nurses, medical professionals are trained to diagnose and treat symptoms. Prevention is not necessarily ignored; for example, the government has pressured the cigarette industry and the health industry since the 1960s to magnify the dreaded message of the harmful effects of smoking on each and every packet of cigarettes sold to the public. But the message in medical school is loud and clear: pharmacology is powerful! Drug companies "feed money into medical schools to help fund programs," in the meantime "getting to promote their own drugs." There is no money made in touting the virtues of healthy eating and alternatives to drugs. "I argue that food *is* medicine," said Mary Ann. "Look what happens to bodies when people eat unhealthy versus healthy foods. The facts are well documented. Yet doctors receive very little training on nutrition in medical school." Sometimes this training may come in a very quick course, which may or may not be optional ... if it is optional, it is generally ignored. Med students are too busy. And then they become too busy as doctors, because they are really overwhelmed ... treating symptoms, rather than causes. "Med students are trained to 'fix things.' They expect to see sick people. They know all about prevention. They practice prevention in their personal lives. But every appointment has a billable purpose. 'What are you doing here?' they ask. If you are fine, they do not have anything to fix and the appointment is over."

Mary Ann talked about the experience of a friend of hers who lived in Japan. "A friend told me that Japanese doctors were offended if their patients got sick. They took great care promoting healthy living and it was a failure to them if a patient's illness was linked to unhealthy living." Mary Ann commented also on countries in Western Europe that put more emphasis on doctors being general practitioners than specialists ... learning how to treat a person holistically rather than by specialty. The general practitioners might have a specific area or sub-specialty that held their interest, but being a GP meant that they were considered "better grounded"; it was not uncommon for a well-established GP to make more money than a novice specialist. In the United States, medical students learn early on that there is more money in being a specialist than a GP or family doctor.

But is this what Mary Ann meant by 'follow the dollar'? "I also worked for an insurance company for thirteen years," she said, "a large, well-known non-profit." In the 1980s, insurance companies began to require utilization reviews conducted by nurses, social workers, and doctors, which helped determine the medical necessity of a procedure; all this became part of 'managed care.' The California-based Kaiser Permanente was founded in 1947 and credited with being the first major managed care facility dependent on patient choice, known also as an HMO or health management organization. The purpose of the HMO was to improve health and lower costs, focusing on prevention as well as treatment. The popularity of HMOs, however, did not spread across the country until years later, culminating in the HMO Act of 1973. This act lifted barriers to HMO development and, among other things, required businesses with more than 25 employees to offer an HMO as an insurance option if one was available in the community. The act also provided for grant assistance to develop new HMOs.[5] Outside California, HMOs were not popular among consumers. They were cynically referred to as 'managed cost facilities' rather than 'managed care,' and people were convinced they would not get a choice of doctors or not be granted needed treatment if 'whoever' managed the costs in the home office – likely a pencil-pushing accountant lacking empathy – denied such.

"The idea was to make hospitals more efficient," said Mary Ann, "and to follow the dollar. Who is responsible for using insurance in

---

5   Fershein, Janet, and Lewis Sandy, "The Changing Approach to Managed Care," *To Improve Health and Health Care, Vol. IV*, Robert Wood Johnson Foundation Anthology, 2000.

excess compared to other people? Who is responsible for driving up the costs, eventually, for everyone else? And how can these costs be contained?" Chronic illness and disease such as congestive heart failure and diabetes were major factors, as were premature babies. The cost to the employer was rising and still is, but, in recent years, the increase in cost has been generally passed off to the employee. Rather than loyally staying with the same insurance company, as might have been the practice in the past, employers began to shop frequently, perhaps annually, as premium renewals came due. Insurance companies had to respond, and wellness programs became the vogue. If employees lost weight, quit smoking, or joined a gym, they could reduce their insurance costs by paying a lower premium. "Wellness Baby programs were very popular," said Mary Ann; "they included home visits and lots of education on the benefits of breast feeding and nutrition ... all to keep the babies healthy now, and hopefully in the longer term." All this makes insurance companies sound like the 'good guys' when in fact we would really like to bash insurance companies. But few people would be comfortable driving a car, owning or renting a home, or enjoying their boat without insurance. Insurance is about risk: a policy protects consumers against high risks – i.e., automobile accidents, house fires – but also assumes those risks. If a consumer is 'too' risky – too many auto accidents, sick too often – a company is likely to drop the consumer. And if consumers have no stake in the risk, they are likely to act with even further abandon. Mary Ann argued that this is why some politicians want to change Medicare: If people are fully covered, then why act with responsibility or with prevention? A trip to a doctor ready to dispense drugs and 'fix things' is all too easy when a consumer has little financial risk in the process.

"I would suggest people look for an insurance company that is non-profit rather than for-profit," said Mary Ann. A non-profit or mutual company might return an investment to a consumer either through dividends or through lower premiums. A for-profit company is by the very nature of its business structure intent on realizing a return of investment to its stakeholders, and according to Mary Ann, "likelier to be stingier in its practices in order to pay dividends to investors." But every company has a bottom line, whether for-profit or not-for-profit: "If a charge for a medical treatment is $140, yet it is costing $190 to perform the service, the insurance company is going to demand a more efficient delivery of service."

What about that nurse with the cell phone? Is that just another example of 'managed care'? Not according to how it is defined in this profile. But, clearly, attention to 'managed costs' has to take account of the fact that it is cheaper to equip nurses with cell phones than to employ 'switchboard' operators on each floor. What next? During a trip to the Emergency Room with my husband, the ER nurses were all racing about with small notebooks strapped to one hand. This was their first day of integrating ER records through individual computer input; the nurse working with us admitted that she was 'learning' the process, and it seemed that she was very likely distracted as a result. All the while she was asking my husband critical questions as to why he was in the Emergency Room, she was trying to figure out how to use her new notebook and where to store the data so that everyone could see it. Integrated record systems are a good idea. But having the ER nurses do this 'on the spot' is yet another distraction from old-fashioned eye contact and careful listening for what the patient is *not* saying. Mary Ann called it 'touch.' "I was helping a new nurse bathe my father, and each time I put his bottle of lotion into the hot water, she would take it out. In nursing school, in addition to anatomy and pharmacology, we were taught basic human care. The lotion was going to be cold. My dad is elderly. Putting it in the hot water was just a simple way of warming it up. The nurse had never heard of such an idea, yet this is what we talked about frequently in our classes on direct patient care and how much a nurse mattered." Patient care ... how old-fashioned.

Insurance companies could make it easier.

Holly and her husband, Pat, were married less than two years when a malignant tumor was found in his brain. He owned a franchised and popular sandwich shop, but soon had to abandon the long hours required to make it a success. After several months of treatment, the malignancy seemed resolved, only to return two years later. In the meantime, the publishing company where Holly had worked for eleven years shut down, and the couple struggled. She was able to work in a restaurant owned by one of her brothers, but at far less than her previous earnings. Her current wages were now the only family income. "Overall, we had a great experience with our medical team, and our friends and family were fabulous," said Holly; "I think we are incredibly lucky." Because so many of their friends were also young, some had a difficult time relating to her husband's potentially fatal illness and backed away, but most were very supportive: "We have awesome friends and relatives."

Holly had the option to go on COBRA, which she did. There would have been no other health insurance. But the cost was staggering, and some of the policies, she felt, were inflexible. "My husband's chemo treatments had to be timely, and the drug had to be fresh and refrigerated. I would come home and there it sat … in the mailbox. If I did not use the in-network mail-order drug company, I would have been forced to purchase Pat's chemo on the open market at a much higher price; as it was, we could barely afford the insurance.

192 | *Betty Tonsing*

We *had* to use their drug system." There were times when Holly did have to purchase her husband's drug at a local pharmacy, to avoid having it arrive too late, jeopardizing her husband's treatment.[6]

The mail-order drug company advertised that people could save money by ordering drugs in two- to three-month supplies, but her husband's drugs could not be 'stockpiled.' "I was always on the phone with this company – every month there was a new issue – and rarely talked to the same person more than once, and rarely got any real satisfaction." Holly would ask for a supervisor, and then spend -- or waste – even more time working her way 'up the ladder.'

Is this really necessary? How could this be handled differently?

---

[6]   Pat died in May, 2013

"Where is the outrage?"

Jeri's next door neighbor – Mary -- was 81 years old; although diagnosed with dementia and COPD (chronic obstructive pulmonary disease), she was still driving and living independently. She had no living relatives, so "I had the Power of Attorney," said Jeri. Mary developed a urinary tract infection severe enough to have her admitted to a hospital for treatment. The hospital kept Mary the requisite three days, so that she could then admitted into a facility for rehabilitation. I asked Jeri what rehabilitation her neighbor needed, and Jeri replied "None." However, before she was sent to the rehab facility, Mary contracted a bacterial infection called *clostridium difficile* (commonly referred to as 'c-diff,' or acute diarrhea) that further complicated her recovery from the UTI. This is a bacterium that is slow to grow and difficult to culture, and usually manifests itself by diarrhea. It is not uncommon to get this bacterium if taking antibiotics …. as Mary was doing for her UTI. If possible, the antibiotic originally prescribed needs to be stopped and a new series of antibiotics prescribed, such as *metronidazole* or Flagyl, which is affordable. If that is not effective, then a more expensive drug may be necessary, such as Vancomycin, also considered a very powerful antibiotic.

Like so many who enter a nursing facility at an advanced age as a result of an illness or a broken bone – initially for rehabilitation and eventually for returning home – there is a likelihood they will not recover. They become permanent residents. Mary was already in a compromised medical state when she entered the nursing facility, and her health never recovered to the point where she could again

193

live an independent life. This is a very painful process to watch and accept. We feel powerless.

Mary was in the nursing facility for six and half years. While there, she was hospitalized several times, fell several more, and never left her wheelchair. Jeri had just enough knowledge that she felt confident questioning some of Mary's treatment; as her POA, she also felt obligated and responsible to do so for her friend. During this time, Mary's weight dropped to 90 pounds, and Jeri felt she was continually given drugs that compromised her system. "Rather than the standard drugs, tried and true and some of which Mary had been taking, she was often given those demanded by the insurance and drug companies; doctors have no leeway in prescribing treatment or drugs, if they want to be reimbursed ... I believe this to be true." Jeri also called this "greed' on the part of drug companies and accused the Food and Drug Administration (FDA) of being full of 'industry insiders.' These are very strong statements; Jeri really has no proof, and she is not a doctor. Some would say that she is simply 'spouting' out of anger. Yet, as I interviewed her, I remember when my mother entered a nursing facility for rehab after breaking a wrist bone. It became quickly and sadly apparent that, at 87, she really could not go home to live an independent life again. Mom had had a massive heart attack when she was 62, surviving because of a new surgical technique called 'balloon surgery,' a coronary angioplasty that reopened her arteries and allowed her again to live a full life. A change in her diet and exercise made that a healthy life. On a regimen of drugs that did not cost more than $35 a month, including vitamins, my mother was the heart surgeon's oldest surviving patient when she died. We received a bill for $1,000 bill from this facility, after one month, for prescriptions. When we inquired about this, we were told they were looking for 'new drugs' to 'improve her life.' We asked if these drugs had been prescribed by the best heart surgeon in the region – who was her doctor – and of course we knew the answer. We refused to pay this bill, and to this day, it remains in my brother's bedroom bureau, unpaid.

Because Jeri was not a relative, she felt her POA was largely ignored by the doctors. When Mary was hospitalized, she was often sent to the same hospital. One of the doctors from this hospital would visit Mary at the nursing home and then file "fraudulent claims with Medicare" that these were visits in hospice, but Mary was not in hospice at that time. Medicare would reject the claims, but he could continue to file more claims. More outrageous is that no one in any facility seemed to challenge this doctor. The nurses might grumble, but they were in no position to object: "99% of the nurses were wonderful," said Jeri.

Jeri realized that the doctors might have paid more attention to her if, as her POA, she had Mary "declared incompetent," but "I would never [have] put Mary through that embarrassment." Jeri asked a question that could literally be the title of this book: "Where is the outrage?"

Are small residences a good alternative to nursing homes?

Marti's mother needed nursing home care. She was 89 and still living alone, but very quickly the family realized that she could not even get along in an assisted living facility. She was going to require closer supervision and care. They first went to a local, well-respected facility, but it was expensive. The difference between her mother's income and the real cost of the facility would have to be borne by the family. Also, Marti's mother was still using her husband's old GM pharmacy plan, which was saving considerable money on a monthly basis, but the nursing home insisted they had to use their own pharmacy, which was very expensive. Marti found a private residence operated by a woman and her daughter; the woman, she felt was a person of "deep faith," and Marti was confident that this would a good alternative. The woman operated two homes on either side of the city, which appeared to be more personable than the corporate facility and at one-third the cost. Marti's mother would have her own bedroom, which was also appealing. There were only a few people who lived in each of the homes, and Marti was sure her mother would receive more attentive care and stimulation. An RN came once a week to fill weekly medication needs, which were then dispensed by the operator or her staff, called 'helpers.' Some of these people worked also at other nearby nursing home facilities.

Marti was almost immediately concerned when the owner of the home indicated that, in her opinion, Marti's mother was not "going to last very long." Marti was very angry at the woman for making this assessment so readily. Her mother was very quiet and did not speak up in her own defense, so Marti felt that she was the 'voice' for her mother and spoke up often.

Marti was also concerned that her mother was not getting enough exercise. She was still ambulatory, and Marti felt that she needed assistance with walking as much as possible, even though she was using her walker: "The TV was on all day, and she would sit there after walking from her room to the chair. Why was she not walked more?" Marti expected more stimulation than a TV, and also "there was not enough interaction." Marti felt that some of the 'helpers' really did care: one of the staff was a young woman attending nursing school and "she cared about the people the most." Others, however, were busy on their cell phones or doing as little as possible, lacking compassion overall. This would be most noticeable when the operator of the facility was not present, so accountability was a serious issue. Meanwhile, the operator remained "insistent that my mother was dying."

At one point, Marti noticed that her mother, becoming increasingly quiet, would not open her hands. For whatever reason, her hands were curling up. Marti brought a ball in for her mother to squeeze, in order to exercise her hands. But this was going to require the staff's help, reminding her mother – when Marti was not there – to use the ball. Marti spent much of her visit time thereafter trying to find the ball; it was obvious to her that this routine was being ignored by the staff. Eventually, her mother's hands began to smell and her nails were digging into her skin. Since she required immediate care, Marti's requests became demands. One of the 'helpers' told Marti this task "was not her job." "There is an economic factor to all this," said Marti. "I realized most of the staff were not paid well and, therefore, they were not going to do very much. The negative economics of being poorly paid leads to neglect."

Marti also felt that, despite the small size of the facility, the attendants knew very little about her mother; several seemed not to care much at all. To them, this was a job, and apparently not one they enjoyed very much. People in nursing homes often have pictures of themselves in their younger days, visible so that people – including staff – can see that they were once young and vibrant, not always slumped over asleep in a wheelchair. They were likely placed there by caring family members who wanted people to see this side of the ones they loved. Marti wondered if this was enough. "What is their story?" she asked; "Everyone has a story. For each person who comes in, meetings or workshops need to be held for staff in which these stories are revealed … who is this person? What is his or her special story?"

The size of a nursing home is a serious consideration when that selection must be made. Some people will do well in larger homes, while others will do best in smaller facilities. Staffing will likely be linked to what is called the 'census,' or having the appropriate ratio of staff to residents, as required by law. Some homes will have more, while others will skim to the bare minimum. While smaller homes can possibly provide more attentive care, this is not always the case, as Marti discovered. Larger homes can more easily afford a wide range of activities. A study published in the *Journal of Clinical Nursing* revealed that people with dementia coped better in smaller environments, where normal 'home' activities were encouraged, such as laundry and meal preparation, plus organized activities. Tensions, however, were more likely to occur between family members and staff over how much family were willing or able to be involved, since there was greater opportunity for this as well, including responsibility.[7]

Considering the very quiet nature of Marti's mother, she cannot imagine her mother that her mother would have done very well without her. "What do people do when they have no one? Who looks

---

[7]   Van Zadelhoff et al., "Good care in group home living for people with dementia: Experiences of residents, family and nursing staff," *Journal of Clinical Nursing*, September 2011, pp. 2490-2500.

after these people?" Marti also tells her children that that she hopes "they take as good care of me as I did my mother. Otherwise, I do not ever want to go through this."

Marti also criticizes nursing homes and facilities for focusing too much on the death aspects of the residents. It is obvious that, for many, these may be the last places they will live before dying. How old was Marti's mother -- who was facing 'imminent death,' according to the operator of the small nursing residence – when she finally died? She was 94, which means that she lived for five years after entering the nursing home.

"They had given up on her."

Dianne's mother was 85 years old and still mowed her own lawn. She was an active gardener and lived a full and healthy life. That changed radically when a dog bit her on the hand. Within two days, she was violently ill, curled up on her bed, and mobile only in a wheelchair. Her doctor started her on a series of antibiotics, but nothing seemed to work. Within two weeks, she was in the hospital. Dianne has several siblings, and they all had a lot of questions. Not all of them lived locally, and care for her mother was largely up to her and a nearby sister. She and her sister were very concerned that the antibiotics were not effective and were leading only to *clostridium difficile*. Generally, the treatment for c-diff is yet even more antibiotics. "We learned very quickly that the doctor did not like all our questions, and the more questions we asked, the ruder he got." It did not help that Dianne's siblings who did not live in the area were questioning Dianne and her sister as to whether they were really doing all they could and being pro-active with the doctor.

Dianne was alarmed at her mother's diet, which included copious amounts of dairy products – milk, yogurt, cheese, puddings, ice cream – and greasy-looking pork with gravy and mashed potatoes. Her mother enjoyed the diet, but it did little to abate her diarrhea, which was not subsiding. Dianne was not very successful with the hospital kitchen and decided to speak with the doctor, who appeared to assume that the new antibiotic had successfully treated the c-diff, which made Dianne wonder if he was reading her mother's medical chart. When she complained about the dairy products, he only said,

"Oh, is that what is going on?" Dianne decided she would bring nutritional food to her mother while she was in the hospital.

Meanwhile, Dianne's mother continued to be on antibiotics. Over time, antibiotics will destroy not only the bad bacteria in the body, but the good bacteria as well. Dianne wanted her mother also to take probiotics[8] and asked the nurse if this could start; the nurse replied that the doctor would have to order them, which he would not do. In his view, now was not the time for 'experimenting' with Dianne's mother. Dianne echoed what so many have said about the lack of nutritional training in medical schools, the overuse of conventional medicines that doctors prescribe, and their seeming unwillingness to consider alternative methods. The excuse may be that the prescription pad writes what has been approved by the Food and Drug Administration (FDA), but they have made well-documented mistakes.

Despite all the drugs, her mother's illness continued. Also, her joints began to swell and became red and hot. This was a brand-new symptom for her previously active mother. The doctors thought that perhaps the previous antibiotics were the culprit, so they were stopped for a new one, *Prednisone.* Yet Dianne's mother got worse: "The prescriptions were killing her." She was no longer in the hospital, but she was now in a wheelchair all the time, had lost considerable weight, and was disoriented. While she was home, she required care 24 hours a day. She could not be left alone. She could not care for herself. Four months had passed, and Dianne's siblings were madder than ever. What is going on? The doctors had a new answer: she needed to be in a nursing home. Dianne tried to point out that all of this only happened after the dog bite, only to be told: "Your mother

---

[8]   Probiotics are bacteria that help maintain the natural balance of organisms in the intestines. People who are taking excessive doses of antibiotics risk having the 'good' internal bacteria eroded, and probiotics help with this. For example, urinary tract infections are a frequent occurrence in long-term care facilities and usually require antibiotics. Probiotics can also help reduce the incidence of diarrhea.

is 85. What do you expect?" "They had given up on her," said Dianne as her mother asked, "Why doesn't someone help me?"

Dianne and her sister were desperate. They lived in a small town; while her mother had been seeing her family doctor for years, it was apparent he was now of very limited help. They had also seen a specialist in a much larger nearby metro hospital, but the treatment he had prescribed was not successful either. Dianne's husband had a classmate who served on the board of a major university that had a renowned teaching/research hospital. Surely someone there could help. Dianne and her sister traveled to Chicago with their mother, confident that help might finally be imminent.

What happened next left them in shock. While they had an appointment with this apparently excellent doctor, he was not prepared for their visit. He had not read any of the background material that had been sent to him and bluntly told Dianne and her sister: "I have no time for this. I only have about 4-5 minutes … and that's it. I have a room full of patients." Dianne learned that he was getting ready to go on vacation; he finally told them, "I cannot take care of her."

Dianne and her sister returned to their rural community to confront their siblings, who basically asked: "Why are you putting Mom through this?" Their rural physician was sympathetic, but admitted that they were probably better off returning to the specialist in the larger, metro hospital who now wanted to treat her mother with yet another drug, one used when other drugs fail: *Methotrexate*. Dianne did some research to find that the drug was used to treat certain types of cancer, which her mother did not have. The drug must be carefully monitored; it is potent enough to shut down an immune system and can be fatal if taken in wrong doses. That might be said about a lot of drugs, but Dianne had had enough: "You are not doing that," she told the doctor, and felt for the first time that she was out of alternatives.

Then a friend suggested Crossroads Healing Arts, which was connected to a conventional health system in a nearby community, but offered alternative medicine as well. Crossroads also worked with Born Preventive Health Care Clinic in Michigan. Dianne's mother began to work with an RN who was a lymphatic specialist, and the center asked for her medical records, the most recent of which were with the specialist at the previous metro hospital. His reply was blunt: "Come get your medical records. I cannot take care of [your mother]." Dianne was taken aback. Although she did not approve of the treatment he wanted to do, he had been very nice. All she was seeking at this point was a second opinion, and since all the traditional methods had not worked, she was seeking out alternative advice and possibilities. Her doctor in her rural hometown was more understanding: he would cooperate if he could, but he had limited knowledge or training in alternative methods of treatment. Furthermore, he had little time, given the demands of his practice, to learn much outside the circle of what was demanded of him to keep up with new treatment technologies, new drugs, and ever-pressing administrative demands from both insurance companies and the government. Alternative health treatment was not part of the new 'treatment technologies' he had time to learn; his patients expected to be 'fixed,' and drugs seemed to do that, for the most part. He did ask Dianne to send material to him about Crossroads and the Born Centers, so that he could "possibly refer." At least he was open to the possibility.

Dianne's mother was taken off all antibiotics and began a series of treatments that included nutritional IVs, a UVI machine, blood transfusions that involved her own blood, and peptide and prolotherapy injections. I asked Dianne if her mother's Medicare paid for any of this, and she said that only some of the office visits were covered under Medicare, but not the drugs. The FDA has not yet approved any of these methods. Just weeks before, Dianne's mother had become practically an invalid under drug treatments approved by the FDA and paid for by Medicare. Now she was recovering, but had to pay for this out of her own pocket. "I am convinced that if I had not found Crossroads and tried something other than traditional medicine, my mother would never have gotten well."

Dianne's mother returned home to again live an independent life. It had been two years since the dog bite. She did have issues with arthritis and her thyroid, but nothing serious. She also had problems with a heart valve, but that began 40 years ago. According to Dianne, her vigor and health returned, and she was an active 87-year-old woman. She continued to use preventive and alternative methods of treatment, with a nutritionally healthy diet that included "tons of Juice Plus," which is quite simply sixteen raw fruits and vegetables dehydrated and compressed into capsules and produced without sugar. She even continued to mow her own lawn. She died short of her 90th year.

"I put too much trust in the doctors and should have acted sooner," said Dianne. She has practiced preventive health for years, and felt all along that something was terribly wrong with how her mother was being treated, but few of us are prepared to act quickly when caught in an immediate health crisis. We tend to choose among the choices placed in front of us, because everything seems like an emergency. It is clear that conventional medicine has a pill for almost anything defined as an emergency.

Does residence in current long-term care facilities lead to premature death?

Holly's mother was a well-educated woman who loved classical music. Her home was full of books and the décor 'well appointed.' Holly knew that a regular nursing home environment of Bingo, linoleum floors, and institutional meals would not be well received. When the time came that her mother required support from a long-term care facility, Holly sought out one that was considered 'up-scale,' hoping at the very least for an environment that would be more soothing for her mother and the care more uplifting. However, soon after Holly's mother moved in, management changed hands and the difference in care and compassion became apparent. "They began to charge for things I found very odd," said Holly. "Everything was based on an economic scale and some services were considered 'extra.' Since she was in an assisted living facility, if she needed help walking down to the dining room, that was considered an extra service and became an extra charge on the bill." If arrangements were going to be that expensive, it made sense to Holly to move her mother to her own apartment in a retirement community. Unfortunately, while living on her own, Holly's mother fell and broke an ankle; after her hospitalization, she was sent to a rehabilitation facility. Within a short period of time, her mother began to contract urinary tract infections and developed hallucinations from the painkillers, which the doctor said was a 'normal reaction.' Holly's mother spent a long time in this facility, just learning how to use a walker; because it took such a long time, she lost her confidence in being able to walk more than a few steps. Meanwhile, she continued to hallucinate and hear sounds. In time, Holly's mother moved to yet another assisted living facility that Holly described as "just average," and the décor bothered her mother. Another place was tried because of her mother's growing dissatisfaction; living on her own was no longer an option.

Holly moved her mother closer to her own community, so she could be a more effective advocate. However, in this new facility, her once out-going and intelligent mother was not sociable. It was very likely that she felt she had little in common with other residents and did not find the activities stimulating, but shortly after moving in, her mother got a blood clot from a fall, which resulted in yet more fear of exercising and even less interest in socializing.

Because Holly was now able to see her mother more often, she began noticing other issues, such as that "the regimentation of the system takes priority over health and well-being." Holly observed that all the residents were 'wheeled' into the dining room an hour before dinner even began. Why? And why did everyone need to be in a wheelchair? Couldn't anyone use a walker, or a cane? Was everyone truly an invalid? And there they sat, staring blankly into space, "packed in," as Holly described it. "They can control the group in this way ... everyone is in one place rather than all over the floor, making the job easier for the staff."

Holly's mother continued to decline and become more 'confused,' which the doctors also continued to describe as "normal with elderly people." She also got pinkeye, which was not treated, since it was decided to "let nature take its' course," which infuriated Holly. Her mother's delusions were worse at night; new medications were tried to see if they could control her mother's growing mental deterioration. Meanwhile, the doctors were saying, "It's OK. We will take care of her," which Holly now recognizes as dangerous words. The nurses reported that her mother would not drink enough water or eat enough food, but "at 200 pounds, my mother loved to eat and always drank lots of water!" Holly was hesitant to criticize the nursing staff, mostly made up of aides or CNAs; after all, they were primarily taking orders and some of them she did like. To be too critical could have resulted in the nursing staff becoming hostile toward her mother, making matters worse. Holly came to feel that it was her own intervention that finally helped control her mother's urinary tract infections. Holly also had issues with the billing office, which each month "messed up the bills" to the point that Holly stopped paying until corrections were made.

As her mother's urinary tract infections lessened, she became "loving and happy again, and we had a great relationship ... for about six months." Her mother developed internal bleeding so severe that she was sent to the hospital. The bleeding would not stop. It was determined that an aneurysm had occurred in her intestine, causing the excessive bleeding; a colectomy was performed to remove all of her large intestine, following which she died without ever coming out of the anesthesia.

Throughout all this, Holly kept a medical journal. Her mother's 'long-term care' journey became part of Holly's own professional journey. She has been a life coach since 1990, and was a caregiver for her mother from 1996 to 2006. In that role, Holly integrated what she was learning about 'life among the elderly,' most especially when they lost their independence, into her professional work, which was also a personal commitment.

Over time, Holly became increasingly more involved with alternative approaches to long-term care. She was drawn into a movement started by Dr. Bill Thomas called the "greenhouse project," which radically changes the delivery of residential long-term care. Dr. Thomas argues that the current system is not 'people-centered'; the regimentation and lack of stimulation, combined with hearts that, in time, break, lead to what becomes labeled as 'confusion,' 'disorientation,' possibly even dementia, and in time, premature death. Dr. Thomas would 'tear down' current nursing homes and replace them with small, home-like environments where people live full and interactive lives. In 2005, the Robert Wood Johnson Foundation supported this vision, announcing a five-year $10-million grant to support the launch of Green House projects in all fifty states. Today, there are 100 Green Houses operating on 43 campuses in 27 states.[9]

For her part, Holly became an ombudsman, a caregiver coach, a speaker, and an author of several publications and book (see *The Caregiver's Reader: Thought Pieces on Family Caregiving* and *Exploring Hell and Other Warm Places: Redemption through Caregiving*) focused on alternative approaches to elder care. She also developed a survival toolkit for caregivers called *The Caregiver's Compass: How to Navigate with Balance & Effectiveness Using MindfulCaregiving*. As a change agent, she serves on the board of the New Hampshire Coalition for Culture Change and is currently developing the Eldercare Whole Health Alliance for The Lotus Healing Arts Foundation, bringing alternative healing to the residents of the elder communities in Newburyport, Massachusetts.

"I want to wake up this generation of caregivers," said Holy, "… so they can prepare themselves. They do not have to go through what I went through. I should have started reading more sooner, rather than wait until I was in over my head. I wish I had been more assertive earlier." Holly also feels she trusted the system too much. If she had asked more questions, she might have spared her mother unnecessary pain.

Overall, Holly tells everyone in this situation to "trust your instincts."

---

[9]   www.thegreenhouseproject.org

"Consensual Sex"

Caryl's mother was in a series of nursing homes as a private pay resident over twelve years before she died in 2003. As an RN with a Bachelor's in Science, Caryl advocated often on behalf of her mother, when she recognized inadequate care. The result of chronic understaffing most especially by large, corporate chains in order to boost profit margins was glaring. For example, despite being ambulatory, her mother was required to wear 'briefs,' or adult diapers. Although she recognized that incontinence develops with age and urinary tract infections are common in even the best facilities, these 'briefs' needed to be changed often. Despite Caryl's frequent requests to the nursing staff, her mother's briefs were not changed regularly and she developed sores. Helping her mother change her briefs became a part of Caryl's routine visits. While she assumed that this type of issue was likely common in many long-term care facilities, she was not prepared for what was to come.

Over time, her mother's advanced dementia required that she be moved to an Alzheimer's unit that was locked, a safety precaution to prevent those with dementia from 'wandering' and getting lost and possibly hurt in the process. What Caryl did not know was that in her unit was a repeated and known sex offender who proceeded to violate her mother at least 15 times. Finally, Caryl was called 28 hours after her mother's last assault and told to take her mother to the sexual assault center within the local hospital. The facility had already called the police, Adult Protective Services, and a local sexual assault center ... but not Caryl. Her mother had some awareness that she had been assaulted, but her dementia prevented full acknowledgment.

None of the assaults had previously been reported to Caryl; when she was finally informed, she discovered through the medical charts and conversation that the staff considered the violations "cute" and "consensual." The staff maintained that her mother could have retreated to her own room if she did not want to engage in this "consensual sex," although at this stage Caryl's mother was unable to identify her own clothes let alone find her own room when she felt 'lost' on the unit. The sex offender had the mental status of a twenty-year-old, and her mother that of a twelve-year-old. It was by accident that Caryl learned of the assaults, when a maintenance man was required to break down her mother's locked door to "get the assailant off my mother." When he was admitted to the Alzheimer's unit, Caryl also later learned that his chart reported that "he was asking for women" and he was "inappropriate with the staff." After the assaults on her mother were revealed, he was moved to the psychiatric unit of a local hospital, but there was no promise that he would not return. Caryl moved her mother out of the facility.

Adult Protective Services promised Caryl a grand jury investigation and criminal charges, but nothing came of this. Later, the prosecuting attorney claimed conflict of interest, because his wife saw her mother biannually as a part of a university research program. The Indiana State Department of Health found the incident "unverified and unsubstantiated," despite state law assurances that her mother had the right to be free of sexual abuse. Caryl consulted with an elder law attorney and filed a civil suit, which was eventually settled out of court, with $500,000 awarded to her mother. Shortly after this settlement, the facility declared bankruptcy and the owner died in "mysterious circumstances." Caryl had no confidentiality clause that bound her from talking about what had happened to her mother. After the case was settled, two articles appeared in the Indianapolis newspaper highlighting the case, and Caryl also appeared on CNN and ABC discussing her mother's assault: "It has become my mission that people know they cannot let their guard down while their loved one is in a facility," she said. "And I especially do not trust the large chains." In 2003, the year Caryl's mother died, Gannet News Service reported on their investigation on the status of nursing home violations that included dozens of interviews and an analysis of "four years worth of federal data on inspections and patient well-being at the nation's 1600 nursing homes."[10] Nearly three-fourths of the "most severe and repeated ... violations" were concentrated in a dozen states with residents in "for-profit companies [faring] worse in some ways than residents in government and non-profit nursing homes."[11] Indiana was among the worst states for violations. Findings included the following:

- For-profit nursing homes accounted for 83% of the more than 500 nursing homes with repeated, serious violations, yet were only 65% of all Medicare- and Medicaid-certified nursing homes; and
- Patients at for–profit nursing homes had, on average, higher rates of infections and pressure sores than those in government and non-profit facilities.

The study noted fewer incidents in homes that were monitored by councils of family members of residents and where advocates were more present.

Caryl discovered through her mother's chart that the staff knew of the repeated assaults and even reported hearing her mother's cries, but those who wanted to be more vigilant were warned to do nothing. The administrative staffs' credentials were dubious, according to Caryl: "An assistant social worker did not have a high school diploma; the Director of Nursing had an Associate's Degree; the head nurse was a Licensed Practical Nurse; and the social worker had a Bachelor's." Caryl even found the notes from the meeting where this group had

---

[10] Benincasa, Robert, and Wheeler, Larry, "Analysis finds clusters of nursing home violations by state ownership," *Gannet News Service*, 2003.

[11] Ibid.

decided that her mother could make a personal decision about the "consensual sex." Caryl told me that, "If my mom were in my home and I allowed her to be raped, I would be in jail."

Caryl moved her mother into a non-profit and faith-based nursing home that she liked until it was sold. The new owners insisted that her mother's medications be purchased through their facility, which Caryl discovered came at an exorbitant cost. When she confronted the administrator of the facility, he yelled at her. She also felt he was practicing medicine without a license, and reported all this to the office of the state Attorney General, to whom Caryl also reported Medicare fraud. Although her mother was still paying for herself and was also receiving services from hospice, Caryl discovered that the nursing home was charging Medicare $3000 a month for the following services:

- 30 minutes a month with a chaplain;
- A weekly evaluation with an RN;
- A weekly visit from a social worker; and
- An aide to assist with bathing.

These are services that should be routine in a nursing home. Meanwhile, the medical director was ordering bone density scans on all residents, whether they needed it or not. It turned out that he owned the scanning facility. Four months passed before Caryl could again move her mother, but not before she lost 20% of her body weight, with no alarm noted despite being "weighed monthly," according to the staff.

Her mother's next facility, another non-profit, was a "phenomenal nursing home." The residents were all women, and the staff "was wonderful." Her mother was there about fifteen months when the facility went bankrupt and had to close. Fortunately, her mother's final nursing home, again non-profit, provided excellent care. Caryl stressed that, although she would recommend non-profit facilities, her main objection was primarily to the large chains. A private for-profit facility, if small and not part of a corporate chain, could still be very manageable and caring.

Caryl started working with a small group of activists called United Senior Action, who are committed to advocating on behalf of "senior citizens and their issues and concerns." Founded in 1979 and still based in Indiana, these groups have grown all over the country. Caryl worked with the group to get a bill through the state legislature that made it a felony for failure to report or actually commit elder abuse.[12] According to Caryl, prior to this time, there was no such law, and its passage was a fluke: the legislature was concerned that, if such a bill passed, "it would be faced with an inundation of cases." The group was also up against a very strong state nursing lobby that fought against the bill. At this time, dementia training for staff was not required, and this was also changed.[13] In 2004, at the time of this ruling by the Indiana State Department of Health, 60% of all nursing home residents had dementia, with most of it caused by Alzheimer's disease or Alzheimer's combined with vascular disease. The Indiana State Department of Health sought the services of the Indiana chapter of the Alzheimer's Association to provide training via the state-funded *Alzheimer's and Dementia Care Training Program*, and the training is not restricted just to medical staff.[14] Many facilities involve all staff who work with patients in this training, including support staff; for example, the Indiana Veterans' Home includes its security guards and housekeeping personnel in the training because of their daily and close contact with residents.

---

[12] The Division of Long Term Care of the Indiana State Department of Health on reporting abuse, supported by Section 6703(b)(3) of the Patient Protection and Affordable Care Act, amending Title I of the Social Security Act, adding Section 1150B, impacting nursing facilities, skilled nursing facilities, hospices that provide services in long term care facilities and Intermediate Care Facilities.

[13] Comprehensive Care Facility (Nursing Homes) Licensing and Certification Program of the Indiana State Department of Health.

[14] "Directing an Alzheimer's Care Unit," Alzheimer's Association Greater Indiana Chapter, October 2004.

Caryl remains concerned, however, that the policy and laws are not being enforced: she would "fire everyone in the Department of Health [in the] long-term care division, replacing them with people who will enforce the regulations," charging that Medicare fraud continues to thrive, and abuse and neglect are still overlooked. Caryl claims this is often due to facilities being chronically understaffed for the benefit of profit margins in the large, corporate chains. This concern is substantiated by more recent research on nursing homes in the US. According to a study by the University of California at San Francisco and published in *Health Services Research*, the nation's largest for-profit nursing homes deliver significantly lower quality of care "because they typically have fewer staff than non-profit and government-owned homes ... [and] strive to keep their costs down by reducing staffing.[15] "Poor quality of care is endemic in many nursing homes, but we found that the most serious problems occur in the largest for-profit chains," said Charlene Harrington, RN, Ph.D., professor emerita of sociology and nursing at the UCSF School of Nursing. Harrington also is director of the UCSF National Center for Personal Assistance Services.[16] "The top ten chains have a strategy of keeping labor costs low to increase profits," Harrington said. "They are not making quality a priority." Low nurse staffing levels are considered the strongest predictor of poor nursing home quality.[17]

The ten largest for-profit chains in the US, which were selected for this study, represent about 2000 nursing homes, controlling 13% of the country's nursing home beds. In recent years, some of the largest publicly held chains have been purchased by private equity investment firms, investing funds from investors with whom they share profits and losses. These large chains were studied because they are the most influential in the nursing home industry and the most successful in terms of growth and market share, which has

[15] Fernandez, Elizabeth, *"Low* Staffing and Poor Quality of Care at Nation's For-Profit Nursing Homes," *UCSF News,* 29 November 2011.

[16] Ibid.

[17] Ibid.

boomed over the past few decades, most
has increased payments to these facilities.

Unlike in a small facility, the owner
largely invisible, hiding behind facility a
to ensure that profits are made. One c
satisfaction, but families and advocates
reasons for resistance or action are alm
of the 'protection of the resident and co
abuse, as in the case of Caryl's mother, might be glaring, but obviously
it is not always prevented. "You are fighting a disease process," said
Caryl. "You should not have to fight a system as well."

Beware nursing home diets.

Bonita's mother-in-law, Frances, was a diabetic for over 40 years. Frances had "learned' to 'manipulate' her blood sugar. If, for example, she was mad at her husband, which could be often, she knew how to elevate her blood sugar to create a crisis. When her husband died of cancer. Frances lived with her son and daughter-in-law. Frances did not like her doctor, so Bonita arranged for Frances to see her own primary care physician, who was proactive on preventive healthcare. Frances's diabetes was poorly controlled before she came to live with Bonita, with fluctuations in blood glucose levels from a low of 23 to a high of over 400 on a regular basis. With help from Bonita's doctor, who prescribed preventive medicine, major dietary changes, and exercise, Frances's blood sugar was controlled better than it had been in the previous ten years.

In addition to having become legally blind, Frances also had a stroke, and the demands of her care were more than Bonita could handle at home. She was moved to a nursing home that was supposedly one of the better ones in the area; it was also conveniently located across from the school where Bonita was working. Almost immediately, Frances began to complain that she felt her 'sugar' was either very high or very low and that the nursing home had to "take measures to correct it." Initially, Bonita was not concerned, as she was aware that a stroke can often create havoc with blood sugar levels, until she visited her mother-in-law during a lunch hour. Heaped on her plate were chicken and noodles, mashed potatoes, corn, and white bread and butter. Her dessert consisted of pears and a chocolate brownie. While Frances was thrilled with this hearty meal, Bonita was astounded at the vast proportions of sugar and starch: "This would be an overload for a normal healthy person who was getting plenty of exercise, but for a severely diabetic stroke victim confined to a wheelchair it was a diabetic coma just waiting to happen." She immediately contacted the kitchen staff and asked if Frances had the wrong tray; she was told 'no'; furthermore, Frances was not on a restricted diet for diabetics. Bonita was told by some that they did not know she required a special diet, or told "It was a special day," which was the reason for all the 'special food' like desserts. Bonita did some additional research and found that they had been feeding her this diet of 'regular' meals for some time; when her sugar spiked, the nurses would administer very high doses of insulin to counteract the sugar levels. Often in response to the insulin dose, Frances would bottom out and then be given a high sugar orange juice supplement. Her body was on a vicious cycle of high and low sugar on a regular basis. Bonita never received a clear answer to why the diet wasn't restricted. One of the aides had no idea her mother was a diabetic, which made Bonita wonder why this was not obvious just from the medical chart. One claim was that the doctor had not ordered a diabetic diet, which Bonita felt was not true. Another story Bonita thought more plausible came from a nurse's aide who told her it was "easier to just feed them and deal with a problem if it came up than to mess with a special diet," but this woman's credibility could be challenged because her job had recently been terminated.[18]

Frances's care was initially covered under Medicare; when the limits were reached, she had sufficient resources to become 'self-paying.' It was then that Bonita felt more troubling problems emerged. Bonita's doctor continued to remain involved in Ann's care to the extent possible, which was not a given, since many nursing homes do not extend privileges to doctors who are not contracted

---

[18] There are numerous websites devoted to this subject, including the regulations that residential facilities must follow regarding nutrition, and most especially facilities that offer services to people on Medicare and Medicaid.

by the facility. Bonita assumed that her doctor would also be in charge of her mother-in-law's prescriptions and medications, until she began receiving bills in excess of $700.00 per month, which "was amazing for a woman who took only one oral diabetes med and the occasional stool softener and Tylenol for headaches, along with her daily insulin." Bonita, along with a friend who was a pharmacist, both began to investigate what prescriptions were being ordered for Frances. They uncovered a list of nearly thirteen drugs, including "an $80 substitute for Tylenol." When Bonita asked about it, Frances said that she was not having headaches ... that the "stroke made my headaches go away." When Bonita pressed the nurses as to why she was being given a Tylenol substitute that cost $80, she was asked, "Oh, would you like [Tylenol] instead?"

Additional medications included three different oral drugs for diabetes, two of which required "at least partial pancreatic function or bodily manufacture of insulin – something Frances had not been able to do for years," said Bonita: "These medications are generally prescribed for younger, newly diagnosed diabetics and can be quite harmful for long- term diabetics, especially the elderly." Frances was also being given medication for high blood pressure, although there was "no indication it was needed, two different stool softening agents, a cholesterol medication – once again without any medical necessity – and the list went on." Bonita asked who had prescribed these medications and was told that the prescription order came from her family doctor. Highly suspicious, Bonita took the list directly to her doctor, who was appalled; she, too, asked who had been the prescribing physician, and when Bonita told her they were using her name, she was immediately on the phone with the director of the nursing home. The administrator told them that these meds were "typically" prescribed for stroke patients and that they didn't know what the "mix-up" was, but if Bonita's doctor – as primary care physician for Frances -- did not want her taking them, they would stop. There never was an adequate explanation of how or why they could legally use the doctor's name without her consent, but Bonita suspects that "this type of thing goes on a regular basis." Bonita believes that, since her doctor was not from the town in which the nursing home was located, it was easier for them to do this. She also believed there was money involved for them to administer the vast number of drugs they did. All incoming residents must post a financial statement that includes resources, and Bonita said they knew "Frances had money." Thus it was designed that she should "pay more" to offset those who did not have any resources other than Medicaid.

Bonita was surprised, because all this happened at "one of the larger more respected nursing home chains in the state of Indiana." Eventually, Bonita concluded that consumers needed to beware of nursing homes that were part of a "large corporate entity ... [whose] bottom line was the dollar." While Bonita was the advocate for Frances, her husband – Frances's son – had power of attorney; neither felt the nursing home listened to them. All communication had to be initiated by Bonita and her husband. When Bonita asked a lot of questions, she felt dismissed and told she was "too overly concerned." The administrator insisted that she "did not have the right to question." Reflecting on Frances's experience, Bonita says now she "assumed too much ... [and] assumed my doctor was more involved. I assumed they would offer a better diet." She realizes she should have been more pro-active and should have asked more questions.

Bonita and her husband once again brought Frances to their home. Within one week of a proper diet, her blood sugar level was back to 'normal'; although it was still high for a normal person, it was stabilized, without dramatic spikes, and reflected a profound improvement for Frances. She no longer took any medications for headaches and was only on a stool softener. Moreover, Frances did not take drugs for high blood pressure or cholesterol and showed no need for any other medication. The family doctor did try various oral diabetes medications over the next several years, but none of them seemed to be effective, and the risks outweighed the benefits.

Frances was in the nursing home only a few months. Bonita felt that they were "taking advantage" of her mother-in-law and were "writing Frances off." It is possible she might not have lasted very long given the dramatic spikes in her blood sugar while she was there, and the rush to use drugs unnecessarily. Once back with Bonita and her husband, Frances lived another four years. So much for being 'written off.'

"You're a bad boy!"

In 2001, Ruth's husband – John – had a heart attack and received five stents. On 2 September 2010, an aortic valve needed replacement, which required open-heart surgery. When he entered the hospital, at 6'2", John weighed 164 pounds, slightly under his usual 172. Ruth was aware that people who aspirate following upper body surgery have a high risk of dying; to aspirate means literally to 'suck in,' as when food or liquid enters an airway passage with the potential of chocking someone to death. John left Cardiac Critical Care and was transferred to a Telemetry Unit on 4 September. In these units, heart patients are connected to machines that measure heart rate, blood pressure, and breathing rate, as well as blood-oxygen levels and electrocardiogram data. The machines then send the data to computer screens monitored by doctors and nurses to better direct patient care.[19] Ruth was warned that her husband was allowed to eat only when he was able to feed himself; this would be the signal that he was alert enough to be ready to eat. Otherwise, he remained groggy and heavily sedated. As John was transferred to his new bed, although "half asleep," he answered correctly questions regarding where he was and the year; Ruth went home to rest. An older nurse was in charge, and Ruth felt confident in her care.

Ruth's son, Nick, visited his dad; while there, he observed that another nurse was attempting to feed John. Nick had not been present when Ruth was told that John could eat only when he was able

---

[19] "Telemetry Nursing," *DiscoverNursing.com*

to feed himself, and why. Ruth was already headed back to the hospital, when Nick called her to say that he did not like the sounds coming from his dad's throat. Ruth arrived in time to see John vomit, aspirate, and nearly die. Ruth told the nearest nurse that her husband had just thrown up, and the nurse said she would get a drug for nausea. Ruth quickly told her he had eaten and the aspiration had caused the vomiting. A second nurse had to literally "stomp" her foot at the attending nurse who had been feeding John to get her quickly to locate a suction kit. John was in "extreme distress," but Ruth was ushered out of the room. She later learned that the older nurse in whom she had confidence had ordered John to be fed … and this on a unit that should have known the procedures for heart patients.

While in the hallway, Ruth heard the Emergency Room doctor being paged; his notes later indicated a patient in a "nonverbal" status whose "heart sounds were present and little diminished" and required "emergent intubation." John was also returned to intensive care. "Just a few hours earlier, my husband had been lucid, relieved to be out of Critical Care, happy that his surgery was successful, and tired from the whole experience," Ruth observed. John remained in Critical Care from the 4th of September to the 17th for "aspiration pneumonia." Ruth ordered John's medical chart after his final discharge several weeks following this event; it read, "While on South Four, the patient appeared to be significantly sleepy and subsequently developed respiratory failure and required emergent re-intubation by the emergency room physician. He was transferred back to the critical care unit." Ruth was furious: "John didn't 'develop' respiratory failure. He choked [on food], vomited, couldn't breathe, and nearly died."

Because of being on the ventilator after returning to Critical Care, John experienced "significant deconditioning." Basically, he lost weight and became severely weak. Because of other complications and also fear of re-aspiration, John was being fed by IV for at least six days before receiving any other kind of nourishment, which Ruth read in the medical chart as a decision that "feeding was held off temporarily." Ruth's family "watched him melt during those days."

Ruth made it clear to everyone that she was her husband's advocate, which should have been obvious and respected; instead, she was ignored. When John was returned to Critical Care, the doctor talked "only to the nurse, using medical terms I didn't understand." Ruth asked to be informed of procedures and medications, which she was not. When Ruth later read John's medical file, she was shocked to read that he had been diagnosed with "acute systolic congestive heart failure." When, she asked, did this happen? He had a heart condition, but had never been diagnosed with congestive heart failure. Why had she not been informed of this, if that was in fact the case? She also learned that he had been prescribed a drug after surgery which caused delirium and agitation; his file revealed that he had "medication sensitivity to Beta Blockers causing profound hypotension and bradycardia." Ruth felt that, as her husband's advocate, she should have been informed: "If we hadn't ordered and paid for his hospital file, we still wouldn't know of ANY drug allergies."

On 17 September, John was returned to the Telemetry unit, and on 24 September, he was discharged from the hospital for a rehabilitation facility. Normally, a discharge would sound like good news, but Ruth was only informed two hours prior to discharge; she had no time to think about whether such a discharge was appropriate, and she clearly was not consulted. He was still on a feeding tube; Ruth would later read in the discharge summary that, "He has profound weakness that has been his biggest issue … and with the ability to feed through the feeding tube, he has greatly improved." John's skeletal frame and difficulty even holding up his head betrayed this medical note. He himself could not sit up alone, and had walked only a couple of times with a "cardiac walker in the hall with three people helping." Ruth inquired if the rehab facility would have such a cardiac walker, and the nurse dismissed the question as not being important, which baffled Ruth, since she read later in his charts that he was expected to "be out of bed as much as possible except for naps."

John's room at the rehab facility was "tiny," and the stand for the feeding tube was "wobbly." As John was trying to reach for the TV remote control, the feeding tube became detached, to which both the attending nurse and the doctor said: "You're a bad boy. You pulled out your feeding tube." This to a man with a Ph.D. who had spent much of his life as an educator and international development specialist in Africa and China! This incident created yet another medical emergency, which called for a return to the hospital Emergency Room, whereupon he was readmitted to the very bed he had left two days before and remained before being returned to the rehab facility on 29 September.

Ruth observed that John was spending too much time in his bed. Later Ruth wondered if this was a result of the medical chart they received from the hospital that stated erroneously that John had congestive heart failure; Ruth could only speculate that that was the reason he was not allowed to be ambulatory: "I had to repeatedly request that they help him get out of his bed and into a wheel chair and that they walk him. A meeting was finally called of all department heads and rehab personnel working with John where I pleaded for more effective PT and OT." He remained on the feeding tube, since the attending rehab doctor also determined that John had "left vocal cord paralysis" (which was not true) and thus could not swallow correctly. John remained weak. On 5 October, Ruth took John to his cardiologist, where he weighed in at 143 pounds, with his clothes on.

On 9 November, John was allowed to go home, capable of doing very little on his own and very depressed. They were able to find a Home Health Nurse who worked with John for four months Ruth credits this nurse and their internist with John's recovery. A Christmas card from Ruth, who is a family friend, read that John is "functioning again – reading books, helping around the house, exercising, wrapping Christmas presents – all those things he couldn't do even just six months ago."

Like so many other advocates, Ruth lost trust in the hospital, most especially after she felt they "stonewalled" following John's initial aspiration: "They were afraid they were going to be sued." Ruth also did not know that the hospital had an advocacy office until months after his discharge. The function of the office is not to serve as a patient advocate, but to offer support for families or friends who *are* the patient advocates; it would have been helpful had she known. She was also frustrated by the flippant nature of the hospital and healthcare professionals —most especially in rehab -- feeling that older or aging patients are treated with a dismissive disregard on the assumption that their age alone is a reason for many of their conditions. John was 83.

Ruth complained to the Medicare office for the state of Washington regarding John's initial treatment in Telemetry, which produced a positive outcome. A protocol has been established that no patient in Telemetry be fed when that patient is unresponsive – regardless of the reason. The hospital that treated her husband now has this protocol as part of its training for all medical personnel, including technicians, assistants, and head nurses who should know better. Most recently, Ruth received a letter from the hospital written by the CEO and Chief Nurse. It was a very patient-centered letter inviting families to be more active and visible: "You know your family member better than we do. Having you share with our team will make our care safer and better." Among the suggestions that would include family members was a listing of shift changes throughout the day, stressing the need for family members to be present for vital sharing of information. The letter said they needed to know about personal habits such as their family member's sleep and eating habits, and stated very clearly the desirability of "having someone stay with the patient as much as possible." The last line encouraged family members to "ask questions and share concerns." This was received a year after John's hospitalization: "It was not part of the picture in 2010 when John had his open-heart. At least the hospital is beginning to take notice of the need and function of advocates."

"Stop looking at the Internet!"

Nancy's daughter had a rare liver disease called *primary sclerosing cholangitis* (PSC) which affects six in one hundred thousand people. PSC is a chronic liver disease caused by progressive inflammation and scaring of the bile ducts of the liver; people with PSC will typically need a liver transplant at some point to keep on living. Her daughter's primary care physician since she was four did not detect this disease until Nancy's persistent prodding. Perhaps he did not consider the diagnosis of PSC because it is so rare, but Nancy continued to follow her instincts and the results of her research, which led her to view all her daughter's symptoms as PSC being "the only logical option." Once her doctor accepted this diagnosis, she was very comfortable with his care and treatment.

It is not uncommon for a rare disease like Nancy had been pleased with the care her daughter had received from this doctor of many years, so, rather than flee in search of other doctors, she wanted to help him with his future patients – that is, she wanted to "transform the doctor" rather than blame him for something so many others could have missed as well. Nancy has an interesting view on the training of doctors in this country. They receive their initial training in medical school, of course, but Nancy feels very strongly that "anyone can participate in the training of doctors." Nancy is referring to the life-long training that goes on after doctors leave medical school, which depends on an increasing population of well-informed patients and advocates who may challenge entrenched systems of beliefs and practices.

Nancy, whose daughter received treatment at a leading research/teaching hospital in the US, is an attorney with degrees (a BS and an MS) in mathematics and physics. As part of her legal profession, she is used to working "with rare diseases." While asking questions of one of the doctors she encountered at the research hospital, she was advised against "looking at the Internet." It is not uncommon for advocates who become intensely involved with care to search the Internet for answers and help, and doctors with their medical background do not like to be challenged by what they may view as an 'amateur prognosis.' Even university instructors advise their students to be very careful when conducting research on the Internet for serious papers; anything written by anybody is going to land in this huge depository of unedited information.

Nancy would agree with this: "A lot of information on the Internet has been cobbled together ... outdated, frightening and inaccurate." She advises anyone who wants to do their own Internet research to use Google as a "starting point," but not to take all that is available "as gospel"; rather, one should "follow the footnotes to the original article." Very often the original article is from a scholarly or professional journal. Nancy found relevant articles through *pubmed*, specifically through *pubmed.gov*, which she accessed looking for specific abstracts that she would then cut and paste to create a file of articles. Nancy's professional training enabled her to read scholarly medical journals; this may not be the case for many. Additional web sites that can be helpful include *webMD* and *medscope*, as well as sites that are associated with university teaching hospitals, which range across the country. One just has to be willing to move beyond the sensational articles with catchy headings to research with credible data; by doing this, one will get the respect and attention of the medical staff treating the person for whom one is advocating. It is critical that advocates know what is going on. Nancy urges people, if they are having difficulties understanding the medical research or are simply overwhelmed by the crisis of the medical condition, to seek – no, demand! – the services of the hospital ombudsman or social service office.

Nancy, who received tremendous support from a PSC support group, encourages everyone to seek out such a group. Her daughter's liver condition was so rare that there was not a local PSC support group, but she found one online and did not feel that was a detriment to receiving help. The PSC support group is a national organization that meets in person once a year, moving around the country to various locales in order to reach out to its geographically widespread members. Nancy said that it is common for 200 people to attend these annual meetings. The group is composed of patients, caregivers, and doctors, and also people who are very knowledgeable about the research and are able to interpret the scholarly material and make it understandable. Throughout the year, the group has a large list serve and stays in touch by email, online meetings, and discussion board postings, as well as by telephone conference calls. The PSC website also offers a great deal of help, connection, and information.

Doctors see many patients and associated illnesses; it is difficult for them to keep up with the latest studies on each and every disease, although we want this type of special treatment. Nancy feels that this may not be a realistic expectation, most especially in the case of a rare disease, which poses even further difficulty for the practitioner in keeping informed and up-to-date on the most recent medical research. Nancy feels that, given her own educational background and training and her profound interest in her daughter's medical condition, she can "keep up better than the doctors." And she is not afraid to assert herself. Her willingness to be assertive probably saved her daughter's life.

"Tell people what they did to me."

Jo's brother had a full life ahead of him. At 22, he was engaged, and, once through his rounds of chemotherapy, was scheduled to try out to be a pitcher for the Chicago White Sox minor league team – a lifelong dream. He did not like his treatments; he had already completed three rounds, and, because of his age, vigor, and health, all were confident that the outcome would be 'cancer free.' With any luck, this would be his last treatment.

The treatments were draining. Scott was to receive 55 milliliters of chemo liquid divided into three bags of 18.3 milliliters each, dripping continually for 24 hours, eight hours for each bag, for five days. No wonder Scott did not look forward to this, hopefully, final treatment.

Scott very quickly became symptomatic and nauseous. He complained how "bad he felt," that he was "on fire." He was also losing his hearing, while the blood coming from his urine was black and smelled like metal. This had not happened in previous treatments, yet they continued. He was given a medication to relieve the nausea, and Scott's family was told by the nurses that "he'll be OK" … they had sped up the IV drip so that he could get out earlier than anticipated, and that likely caused these reactions. The treatment "carried on."

Despite being "violently ill," Scott was discharged from the hospital, throwing up blood, unable to "feel his body." Staying at a local hotel, his parents were distraught and called the hospital. They were told they could bring him back, but the hospital could not provide transport. It was late, the middle of the night, during a frigid Minnesota winter, and Scott was in distress. He kept repeating, "There is something wrong with me … I think it is the chemo." Somehow they found transport to get him back to the hospital, only to be told, "Don't worry, Scott. You're not going to die. We're going to take care of you." He then began to hemorrhage from what seemed every part of his body.

Jo's parents were alone; she and her brother did not arrive for a couple of days, and by the time they did, they found Scott's room by his screams. He had lost his hair and 30 pounds; his skin was orange, and the staff was trying to keep his writhing body in bed. Over the next several days, Scott was attended by an endless array of nurses and doctors, but no one could stop Scott's pain and deterioration. He was initially placed on a ventilator to help him breathe, but later the family became aware that there was a hole in the ventilator tube inhibiting Scott's oxygen intake, even though at this urgent time he needed all he could get.

Scott was beginning to drift in and out, but he recognized his family. He also continued to argue that he felt the chemo had caused this eruption, yet the medical professionals were not ready to accept that. Finally, he was being weaned off the ventilator, replaced by a tracheostomy. Scott spoke to his sister one final time: "Jo, you have to tell people what they did to me." Despite his violent reaction to the last chemo treatment, he had been a virile, athletic young man. In the end, this blessing became a curse: it took almost thirty agonizing days for Scott to die.

And then it was discovered. The person who had mixed the chemo liquid had mistakenly put all 55 milliliters into a bag that was to have contained only 18.5 milliliters. Scott had been receiving three times the correct dose of an already potent chemical into his body throughout his entire treatment. The tragic irony is that the person who had incorrectly mixed the chemical *did* mark the bags correctly … each bag was labeled "55 milliliters" of chemo liquid. No one had noticed. The nurses just grabbed each bag without paying attention to the label. After all, Scott was in one of the finest research/ teaching hospitals in the United States … and when questioned later, none of the nurses believed it was possible that this kind of mistake could occur in such a prestigious place. It was "assumed" that someone along the way had checked the bags, so that the nurses could just administer the IV. "The nurses felt horrible. The nursing staff couldn't have been more accommodating and sorrowful. But not one doctor ever apologized."

Jo kept her promise to her brother and told his story, but it took 27 years. It never stopped being painful to write. Jo thought that the incidence of 'medical harm' would improve over time, but she felt it has not: it is a "$29 billion industry" as a result of errors with medication, infections, surgery, doctors, and other medical personnel and charts. In a study released by HealthGrades in August of 2004, an average of 195,000 people in the US died of potentially preventable in-hospital medical errors in each of the years 2000, 2001, and 2002, culled from a study of 37 million patient records.[20] Other studies reveal that, since 1999, 100,000 people die each year as a result of "medical harm" … the equivalent of about four jumbo jets crashing every week, doubled if hospital infections are included.[21] Approximately 1.7 million infections occur each year, resulting in 99,000 deaths.[22] Not all studies agree with these conclusions: the highly respected *Journal of the American Medical Association* reported on a study conducted in 1995-1996 by medical researchers to determine if these volatile numbers indicting healthcare as a public menace could be validated. Their conclusions suggest that many deaths occurred to people already not in optimal health, and that any errors that could have contributed to the death – while real – were low, the statistics revealing otherwise

---

[20]   "In Hospital Deaths from Medical Errors at 195,000 per Year USA," *Medical News Today*, 9 August 2004.

[21]   *dsc.discovery.com/videos/chasing-zero-part-1.*

[22]   "Deadly Infections: How good is your hospital at preventing them?," *ConsumersReport.org*, June 2011.

unreliable and skewed.[23] This study is outweighed, however, by others that continue to report an alarmingly high rate of 'medical harm,' albeit, of course, not intentional. More alarming, however, is the lack of transparency, especially regarding infections. As late as October 2011, only 27 states had laws requiring the public reporting of hospital infections; two others allow "confidential" reporting to state agencies; three have voluntary public reporting; five states have study laws on public reporting; and thirteen states plus D.C. have no laws on public reporting.[24]

Jo fulfilled her promise to her brother by completing his story – *For the Love of Scott*, published in 2011. She is also dedicating her life to fighting 'medical harm,' in memory of her beloved brother. She is very clear that that was what "killed" him and believes it can be eliminated. The Discovery Channel documentary she told me about ("Chasing Zero") is narrated by a host of people – including medical professionals – who believe that medical harm could be reduced to zero if certain precautions were taken. This sounds impossible, but it is also the goal of a large number of supporters of patient safety (see *Journal of Patient Safety*, edited by Dr. Charles Denham). A popular web site for more information is TMIT, which closely follows research and partnership programs to eliminate medical harm, led by prominent research/teaching hospitals such as the Mayo Clinic, the Cleveland Clinic, the Vanderbilt Medical Center, and Brigham and Women's Hospital; their plan is that each hospital will admit errors that have occurred within its own setting, and recommit to ending this tragic and unnecessary threat and fear.

---

[23] Hayward, Rodney, MD, and Hofer, Timothy, MD/MS, "Estimating Hospital Deaths Due to Medical Errors: Preventability is in the Eye of the Reviewer," *Journal of the American Medical Association*, 25 July 2001.

[24] Committee to Reduce Public Infections.

When neither the 'right' nor the 'left' hand talks to families

Lora's father had been hospitalized several times for various "heart issues," yet at age 88 he appeared to be thriving. Then he began to have reactions to some new drugs, including stomach problems and a vague sensation of feeling "crazy." Lora did some online research that revealed a "contraindication" among some of the drugs her father was taking. The prescriptions had been filled at a pharmacy which her father had used for many years, and Lora had been confident that, given the long-term relationship, the pharmacists would have been forthcoming about any issues related to the prescriptions.

Both the attending physician and the pharmacist turned out to be aware of the 'contraindication,' and the pharmacist stated later that the physician "waived" the concern, allowing the prescription to be filled and thus taken by the patient. Although Lora had done her own research, which alerted her to the contraindication, neither the pharmacist nor the physician had felt it necessary to mention this to her. She insisted, "*Both* should have told me."

It took Lora several days to sort this out between the doctor's office and the pharmacy. The doctor told Lora that he typically leaves drug contraindications "to the pharmacy to communicate with the patient" ... that the "pharmacy has the latest [list of patient] medications" to identify such dangers. This annoyed Lora, because the doctor's office had her father's list of current medications; she felt that this list should have been consulted prior to writing a prescription and any concerns then conveyed to her father. The pharmacist "assumed" that the doctor told the family about this contraindication, and Lora asked how the pharmacist could have 'assumed' this: "You would think [alerting the patient] would be a pharmacy protocol." The chief pharmacist also told Lora that "patients don't have access to the pharmacy file," which made little sense to Lora, since this seemed similar to having access to a patient file, which is allowed. Lora pushed the pharmacist even further, asking why, at the very least, a "warning label" had not been placed on the bottle; she was told they had no such labels, which struck Lora as odd, and to which she replied, "Do you have a pen?"

Fortunately, Lora's father did not have a serious reaction to this particular contraindication, but the incident did remind her of a potentially different outcome that happened to her sister over 25 years earlier, when she was hospitalized for a brain aneurysm. She was allergic to Demerol, and this allergy was clearly posted on a sign above her bed, in the front of her medical chart, and on a wristband. Lora was with her sister when a nurse came in the middle of the night with an injection of Demerol, for pain. Lora had the presence of mind to inquire what medication the nurse was about to give to her sister and was able to stop this potentially lethal step. Lora had always felt that, once in the hospital, families can be relieved that all would be well. That view radically changed with this one episode: "If anyone is in the hospital, unable to talk or care for themselves, someone must be there with them."

Approximately 1.3 million people are injured annually in the United States following "medication errors," defined by the National Coordinating Council for Medication Error Reporting and Prevention. In a study by the Food and Drug Administration that evaluated reports of fatal medication errors from 1993 to 1998, the most common error involving medications was related to administration of an improper dose of medicine, accounting for 41% of fatal medication errors. Almost half of these errors occurred in people over the age of 60, who may be at greatest risk for medication errors because they often take multiple prescription medications.[25] Patients should be fully informed of each and every medication prescribed, including dosage and directions, storage requirements, and any special instructions. When in the hospital, patients are encouraged to have a relative or friend keep track of the name and purpose of each drug administered, and to be certain that current medications are filed in the medical chart – although failure to read medical charts leads also to serious and sometimes fatal outcomes.[26] One must always ask questions, most especially if anything seems unusual or confusing … and must not be deterred by anyone who finds this annoying. A life may very well be saved: your loved one's life or your own.

---

[25] Medication error reports: U.S. Food and Drug Administration, "The Most Common Medication Errors," *MedicineNet.com*, Marks, Jay W., MD, Medical Editor, 28 September 2009.

[26] Strategies to reduce medication errors," ibid.

Sixth leading cause of death in the United States

Rob and Rosemary married when she was 18 and he was 20, straight out of their parents' homes. He has never lived alone and is now "very lonely." At age 48, Rosemary was diagnosed with early-onset dementia. She is well educated, with advanced degrees, and was very active and social. After initially ignoring the symptoms, she was clinically diagnosed in 2004 at age 52. Ron was able to take care of his wife in their home for many years, retiring as a successful salesman in 2008 to take care of her full-time. This worked successfully until 2010, when they both fell down the steps of their home while he was assisting her. Rosemary's mobility was becoming increasingly impaired, a symptom of the developing disease. Today, a lifelong vegetarian, she remains in superb physical condition but is unable to talk, read, or write … and does not recognize Ron.

Even though she is now in a facility, he is with her 40-50 hours a week. During the day he is doing laundry and housework and occasionally plays golf: he belongs to an Alzheimer's support group, which encouraged Ron also to take care of himself! He has arranged for a hospice service to help feed his wife breakfast and lunch during the day. Ron arrives at the facility by mid-afternoon to basically 'take over,' feeding her supper, reading her books and magazine articles, bathing her, and then preparing her for bed. He spends most of the weekend days with her. Their only daughter lives in the next state and visits when she is able.

Ron is aware that Rosemary is in the late stages of Alzheimer's and, although she remains in very good physical health, he does not anticipate that she can live very much longer with this advanced-stage disease. He is grateful to his Alzheimer's support group and the Alzheimer's Association for support and information that have helped him cope with his wife's disease. "People tend to generalize Alzheimer's," said Ron. "People think this occurs to older people, and it is true that early-onset dementia is rare in younger people." According to the Alzheimer's Association, 10% of people with early-onset dementia are under the age of 65, which is why early symptoms are ignored or missed ... people are not expecting to get dementia at a younger age. By the time the symptoms are properly diagnosed, they could be in a middle or advanced stage of Alzheimer's. The impact on one's life while still in what is considered 'productive work years' is dramatic: people afflicted with Alzheimer's may have to quit their profession or job; they may be denied medical benefits from traditional health insurance companies while they are too young for Medicare; they may quality for Social Security Disability Income (SSCI) but only after a waiting period that could take years; and, even with insurance, out-of-pocket expenses, co-pays, and deductibles may drain financial resources. Even after the waiting period, there is no guarantee of help, as the Social Security Administration may determine that the person with dementia can still work. Medicaid pays for long-term care services for people with dementia under age 65, but only if they first qualify for SSI and then meet any additional state eligibility criteria for specific services. The Administration on Aging pays for home- and community-based services, but only for people aged 60 and over. People who are under age 60 and their family caregivers are not eligible. Thus, people with early-onset dementia and their families must either incur very high out-of-pocket expenditures for long-term care or do without services that could help them.[27]

---

[27] "Early Onset Dementia: A National Challenge, a Future Crisis," Alzheimer's Association Special Report, June 2006.

In addition to the people *with* dementia, their partners or spouses are also affected, because they are with someone who will begin to need 24-hour around-the-clock attention and care, thus affecting the caregiver's job or profession. Ron, for example, retired before he was eligible for Medicare or Social Security benefits, so the drain on his life savings began at that time.

Rosemary eventually qualified for a Medicaid waiver, which would pay for her expenses in the long-term care facility. Ron sought the services of an 'elder law attorney' so that he could protect his remaining assets and not face his own senior years in poverty. He has adapted to many of the rules that apply to spouses of those who are on Medicaid and living in nursing homes. For instance, he has only one car; however, an elder attorney helped Ron with a 'quick claim deed' on their home, which basically transferred all ownership of the house to Ron, releasing Rosemary of this asset, on paper, which could have been a cause of denial of Medicaid. This is not illegal, and is a step that an elder law attorney can provide couples in Ron and Rosemary's situation to help prevent a spouse from spiraling into financial disaster.

Attorneys who work in the field of elder law bring more to their practice than an expertise in the law. They also have specific knowledge of the senior population and their unique needs as well as the myths and real barriers to receiving services and care. Competent elder law attorneys will consult with other attorneys if or when needs arise that are outside their area of expertise. Elder law covers all aspects of planning, counseling, education, and advocacy for clients and is a critical resource that will only increase in demand as the tsunami of baby boomers approaches the years of being 'senior citizens.'

Questions to ask an elder law attorney include:

- How long has the attorney been practicing law, and practicing as an elder law attorney?
- What percentage of the attorney's practice is devoted to elder law?

- Does the attorney's practice emphasize a particular area of elder law such as guardianship or assets?
- What is the attorney's experience regarding your specific need or case?
- How much elder law training has the attorney had and from what organizations?
- Is this particular attorney a member of the National Academy of Elder Law Attorneys?
- Will the attorney be able to work with any restrictions you may have? and
- What are the hourly fees![28]

Ask for references. If this offends or bothers the attorney ... walk away.

Elder Law is a growing industry. Choosing an elder law attorney must proceed with the same caution as choosing a primary care physician. Web sites that may help with this process include:

1. National Elder Law Foundation: www.nelf.org, and
2. National Academy of Elder Law Attorneys (NAELA): www.naela.org.

Local organizations can also help. Do consult with people within your support group, agencies dedicated to providing services to the elderly, even your church. Beware of referrals for the sake of a referral. People join 'networking groups' in order to build their businesses, which is fine ... but that does not automatically mean that they provide good service. We would probably not use a phonebook to find a babysitter for our children; the consideration is the same for our parents or spouse ... or our own needs, as we get older.

---

[28] Area Agency on the Aging.

"I am an advocate.
I put on armor and fight!"

Before Edith was a social worker, she was an advocate for Adult Protective Services, specifically in the medical and legal system. "Sometimes people feel that, if they just tell the right person what is wrong, then everything will be OK … the problem will be corrected," said Edith, as our interview began. "But each system has power differentials, and the real problem as an advocate is to find out who has the power." She began to realize that professional advocacy varied, depending on the person: "Is the client being served versus is the client being served well?" This insight, she feels, prepared her for her hardest advocacy, that for her own daughter.

Edith's daughter was an accomplished athlete and loved her job as a kindergarten teacher in 2002, when the pain began in her right ankle. She was 27 years old. The doctors thought she might have osteoarthritis, possibly exacerbated by her athletics, and she was prescribed *Celebrex*. This did not quell the pain. Edith's daughter was beginning to make frequent trips to the doctor with little relief. The horrendous pain she experienced over the weekend when her doctor's office was closed prompted visits to the Emergency Room. The doctors tried *Prednisone*, which brought little relief. Edith's daughter was then referred to orthopedic surgeons in a large and respected clinic, where she was told they wanted to test her for bone cancer. Feeling helpless, Edith drew on her role as an advocate for other people to become more intensely involved in her own daughter's condition. She began calling the clinics her daughter visited to follow up on the diagnoses and treatments, but this annoyed the physicians: they told her daughter, "Your mother needs to stop calling. Get your mother out of here." This only fueled Edith's anger, as she felt the doctors were not taking her daughter's pain and condition seriously ... perhaps believing she was just a hypochondriac. Her response was, "I am an advocate; I put on armor and fight!" At one point, Edith's daughter, who had not been able to put her foot on the ground with any pressure for six months, refused to see any more 'local' doctors; she was beginning to suspect they had been misdiagnosing her condition. She sought a consultation at the state's research/teaching hospital, where she met with a rheumatologist who prescribed a biologic infusion drug called *Remicade*, a drug for moderate to severe rheumatoid arthritis. Infusions last about two hours; after an initial 'three-starter dose,' relief can be documented with as few as six treatments a year, every eight weeks.[29] *Remicade* is prescribed when the daily pain and stiffness from rheumatoid arthritis are not responding to traditional treatments and the threat of permanent joint damage is possible. This is considered an aggressive treatment, and the IV infusions are expensive. Their generic name is '*infliximab*.'[30] At the time of her daughter's treatment, the infusions were $7000 each, and it took time for the insurance company to approve this expenditure; when they did, they only approved one treatment. By this time, Edith's daughter was no longer able to work. She opted for COBRA, so that she could continue the treatments. She also returned to the doctors whom she had been seeing in her hometown, to be told again that "nothing was wrong with her."

Meanwhile, Edith's daughter kept getting bronchitis and was referred again to the research/teaching hospital, where they suspected TB and put her in isolation. Her immune system was so depleted, she was vulnerable now to any infection, bacterial or viral. Tests revealed

---

[29]   Remicade Infliximad, Jansssen Biotech, 2012.

[30]   "Rheumatoid Arthritis: My doctor says I need Remicade," *EMedicineHealth: WebMD*, 2012.

that she had *histoplasmosis,* a fungal infection, not uncommon in the Midwest.

The rheumatoid arthritis or fungal infection never completely cleared up, and her daughter continued to take an anti-inflammatory that had been on the market for many years, as well as an anti-fungal drug. All her medications cost over $1000 a month. By 2010, Edith's daughter was on disability and eligible for Medicare, which that included a prescription drug plan to help with the growing financial burden of her illness. Throughout, according to Edith, her daughter remained "stoic": she refused to believe she was that sick … she did not want to be that sick. But now she fears she cannot have children, that she will never marry, since her poor health and the cost of her healthcare make her what she calls a "medical liability."[31] She has also gained weight, is often depressed, and sleeps much of the time. Gone are her athletic days and the joy she found in the classroom. For Edith, one of her biggest regrets is never having had enough money to make a difference in her daughter's life … to help meet her medical expenses and make things easier overall. "People do not know how hard it is for people who love people who are sick," she says. It is particularly painful when her daughter observes, "I don't think I am going to live a long time." We expect at some point to take care of our parents when they begin to age and become ill. This is not what we expect with our children.

---

31 In a phone conversation with Edith in September, 2013, her daughter is expecting a baby in November. Her health is still a major concern and everyone is cautious…….and joyful.

Beware of attractive
web sites.

Libby's husband, Greg, was airlifted to a major university research teaching hospital in Chicago following complications from open-heart surgery. While in recovery, he also experienced liver and kidney failure, and his condition was further exacerbated by multiple sclerosis. Greg spent several weeks in bed, leaving his muscles in a tight and cramped condition. He was still a fairly young man, and looked forward to aggressive physical therapy. He was hoping to get into one of the more highly rated physical therapy in-patient clinics in the hospital where his surgery was performed, but it was full. So Greg and Libby searched the Internet for an alternative, and found a rehab specialty hospital with an attractive and appealing web site. Although it was located several miles away in a small rural community, they were impressed by the commitment to a physical therapy regime: each patient received three hours of physical and occupation therapy a day, six days a week. The hours were divided between morning and afternoon, ensuring that the patients were not fatigued and their muscles and minds stimulated throughout the day. This sounded wonderful! It was advertised as a small facility, thus ensuring focused attention on individual patient care.

From Day One, however, Libby and Greg encountered problems. Greg arrived with severe restrictions that Libby felt were ignored by the medical and nursing staff. Greg was not to receive sleeping pills, yet her husband was administered a sleeping pill his first night as a 'matter of routine.' Libby is a teacher; it was July, and she would not begin teaching for weeks. So, after this initial medicine error, Libby decided to spend all her waking hours at this rehab hospital. She admits that the clipboard and file of her husband's medical records and charts that she carried with her probably unnerved the staff, but she was already suspicious. She also began to ask questions. For example, Greg was on diuretics and she was watching his lab work closely; why was he not on a potassium supplement? His lab work revealed a deficiency. The food appeared to be tasty enough, but he was not placed on a salt-free or cardiac diet: why not?

All this further annoyed the staff. Libby also attended all of Greg's physical and occupational therapy sessions; she was dismayed that these were frequently held all at once, sometimes very early in the morning, not scheduled throughout the day as advertised. On more than one occasion, the full three hours were not fulfilled. The excuse was often the same: special meetings intervened. She could not understand why a 'special meeting' would take such precedence over critical PT and OT – and so often. Greg also spent a considerable amount of therapy time in his wheelchair, again to her surprise. Greg was stiff from weeks in the hospital; he wanted to get up on the table and be allowed to stretch out his muscles. Why was this not being done? As her suspicions grew, she began to investigate the medical and therapy staff at this rehab facility. There appeared to be only one physical therapist with a full degree; most –including the occupational therapists – seemed just to have certificates. How could they have advertised themselves with such high levels of expertise, if their PT and OT staff had mostly minimum training? The consulting psychiatrist, who appeared on rare occasions, wanted to evaluate her husband: why? His MS was being treated by their primary care physician, and there was no indication her husband needed this type of evaluation. Meanwhile, Greg was evaluated by the consulting psychologist. Libby sought the help of the attending social worker, but felt ignored. Even calls to the CEO of this privately owned facility went unanswered. She did meet with a nurse practitioner, whom she liked and respected, but felt that her authority was restricted by the physicians who 'out-ranked' her.

After more than of week of growing concerns, space opened up at the original physical therapy facility they had wanted; the authorities there said they would hold the space for Greg. The insurance company would first have to release Greg from the specialty hospital in order for an acceptable transfer that would be covered by their insurance. This would take a couple of days. Libby was fed up with Greg's care, and was becoming both more assertive with the staff and protective of Greg. She did not want anything harmful to happen to him, which was her fear. The hospital resented her interventions and demanded that she abide by their rules. There was a stand-off, in which Libby locked the door to her husband's private room while she was attempting to reach their insurance company. The hospital had a response for Libby: they called the police to have her escorted off the premises, and she was not allowed to return to his floor. She could come to the receptionist area of the small hospital, but no further. The psychiatrist chose this time, in Libby's forced absence, to evaluate her husband, and the hospital tried to have Greg dismissed without awaiting final approval from the insurance company, a move which Libby was able to counteract.

Greg was finally transferred to the hospital in-patient rehab facility they originally wanted, and both felt there was a world of difference in care and professionalism. He was able to see his primary care physician, for instance, which was not allowed at the previous facility, where Greg was restricted to the network of doctors who appeared to be owners or contractors of the facility. Libby's investigation of some of their backgrounds was troubling. Since she concluded that their web site was misleading, she cautions people to probe deeply.

"No one helped me."

Bridget was a successful salesperson for a major telecommunications company, "awarded the designation of one of the best in the country." After several years with the company, given her success, she anticipated many more years there, when her dad died in 2006. Her mom and dad married when very young, and her mother had been completely dependent on her husband – she did not even know how to balance a checkbook. Now in her late 70s, Bridget's mother felt lost without her life partner. The youngest of six children and still single, Bridget had her mother move in with her so she could provide care and comfort. Within time, Bridget's mother started developing 'sundowner's syndrome,' the name given to an ailment that causes symptoms of confusion as the end of day approaches. These symptoms could appear in people who have Alzheimer's or other forms of dementia, although not all people with dementia have the syndrome. The symptoms vary; in addition to confusion, they can include agitation, fatigue, and even the inability to sleep due to stress. People may be up most of the night as a result of their confusion and fear, and then sleep much of the day; however, others may manifest symptoms throughout the day. Fear of the dark may provoke the symptoms, but sundowner's overall occurrence remains a mystery to medical science, although more studies are being conducted to determine the cause.[32]

---

[32] "Sundowner's Syndrome," *Everyday Health*, 2012.

Bridget left her job in 2008 to take care of her mother, which was now becoming a full-time commitment. Because of her mother's syndrome, Bridget herself was unable to sleep at night and was becoming exhausted. In order to take care of her mother, Bridget also needed to take care of herself. Therefore, she placed her mother in a local nursing home facility "just for respite," so that Bridget could catch up on her sleep. The plan was for her to stay only for a couple of weeks, and then return home. At 7:30 on the morning of 19 September 2008, she received a call from the facility that her "mother had passed." Her mother's health was declining and she still mourned the death of her husband. Although grief-stricken, Bridget assumed her mother just wanted to be with her dad. She was not prepared for a call from a coroner later that day, asking what she knew of her mother's death. He had received a call from the facility at 1:30 a.m. that her mother had died, and was shocked that they waited several hours before calling Bridget. When he arrived, she was lying in the middle of her bed, with a peaceful expression. An examination of her body, however, revealed bruise marks on her neck and hands, and he became suspicious. He advised Bridget to hire an attorney.

The official cause of death was listed as "positional asphyxiation." The coroner's report stated that Bridget's mother was laid on her side in a bed that had a six-inch gap between the mattress and the side bars. Her mother, who was of slight build, had slipped between the mattress and the railing and could not breathe. This, regrettably, is not an uncommon problem in nursing homes. While bed rails provide safety for some patients, they are potential death traps for others, most particularly if there is a large gap between the mattress and the rail. The Food and Drug Administration calls this "entrapment," and a special FDA division has been developed – the Hospital Bed Safety Workshop, or HBSW – to focus attention on entrapment and provide guidance and assistance to residential facilities such as hospitals and nursing homes. The HBSW has no legal enforcement authority.[33] One remedy would be to ensure that mattresses fit snugly within frames, but, if this involves purchasing new mattresses, it is easy to see why a facility would choose to save money and not do so, especially since this is not an issue most families and advocates are going to think of investigating when they are researching long-term care facilities. Some such facilities are exploring the possibility of adopting 'no rail' policies because of entrapment and other issues, such as when patients attempt to climb over rails to get out of a bed, possibly because of cognitive issues. Sufficient staffing really needs to be part of the solution.

At the time of her mother's death, there was no RN present in the facility. Nursing homes are notoriously understaffed, and non-profit or government facilities rank higher in this area than for profit facilities. Bridget's mother was in a for-profit nursing home. Federal law requires only that Medicare- and Medicaid-certified nursing homes have a registered nurse (RN) on duty at least eight hours a day, seven days a week. A facility can choose thereafter to have either an RN or an LPN (licensed practical nurse) on duty the rest of the time. There are no minimum staffing levels for nurses' aides, who provide most of the personal care.[34] Becoming a registered nurse can take three to four years; one can get a BS in Nursing, commanding the best salaries and jobs. LPNs may earn only a certificate or take more advanced training up to twelve months; they are paid significantly less than RNs and have limited duties based on their limited training. CNAs, or certified nursing assistants, have the least training and pay, yet in most facilities they provide the most direct hands-on patient care. There is a larger ratio of CNAs visible on shifts than either RNs or LPNs.

Although the facility did not call Bridget until hours after her mother died, someone besides the coroner called the police.

[33] "HBSW/FDA Frequently Asked Questions (FAQs) on Entrapment Issues," US Food and Drug Administration, US Department of Health and Human Services, 17 March 2010.

[34] "What nursing home staff levels are required?," ElderLawAnswers, *elderlawnet.com*, 2008.

Meanwhile, her mother's roommate remained in the room, in the next bed, while the room was being "taped off" as in a crime scene. She was in the facility for rehabilitation following a hip replacement. No one thought of removing the roommate, who became extremely distressed. She began to go about the facility immediately following the accident saying, "They killed Barbara! They killed Barbara!" The woman – age 65 – did not have a history of mental illness, but was nonetheless removed from her room and placed in a mental unit for several days because she was considered "uncontrollable."

Bridget followed the advice of the coroner to seek legal recourse. She charged the facility for "killing my mother," and the court agreed with the more legal terminology of 'wrongful death.' It was a victory for Bridget's advocacy, all the same.[35] Prior to this decision, the facility, which is part of a small for-profit chain in the Midwest, had filed for bankruptcy.

Bridget was not ready for her mother's death. When she quit her job to take care of her mother, this became her entire life. "I saw this as if we were a team, she and I," said Bridget. "I was going to take care of Mom." Bridget does not regret the decision to so this; she loved her mother, and felt this was a privilege. But she also feels that that people could have been more helpful and forthcoming with information: "My dad was a veteran, and I had no idea that Mom was entitled to VA Aid and Attendance, which would have made an incredible difference in taking care of her." Bridget would have gotten help with things she needed for her home, such as an appropriate bed or nursing assistance. "People need to speak up if their parent or late spouse is a vet, so that facilities know, in case they are eligible for things like VA Aid and Attendance." Bridget also lost her house and considerable savings, as much of this happened just as the economy was sinking into an historic depression; she moved in with her sister. But still, she has no regrets about taking care of her mother. She would do it again.

---

35   E-mail confirmation from Bridget on 2 July 2012 that she had won her suit "against the facility" by court action the previous week.

Bridget also did not reach out for support. Family and friends would have relieved Bridget for a few hours at a time, but she would return home thinking that only she could take care of her mother. She realizes now that she should have taken more breaks. Once her mother died, she was indeed alone and "fell apart." When she found her new career, she felt happy and fulfilled again.

One of the biggest changes that happened to Bridget as a result of taking care of her mother was a new career: "I was no longer interested in selling cell phones. That was no longer important." Bridget became a professional patient advocate, working as marketing director for a home health wellness group. She gained considerable knowledge while helping her mother and is compelled now to share that with others, so they do not make the same mistakes she did – and, especially, that they know there is help. "I felt no one was there to help me. I can now make a difference for other people … the people I work with do not have to feel they are alone." Bridget is also working with other advocates and legislators to lobby for better nursing home legislation; for example, she finds it appalling that an RN does not have to be on site more than eight hours a day and wants this changed. She also argues that staff ratios are too high, and that too many residents are assigned to each CNA per shift; this needs to be changed. While she has found support, she also feels she is up against the nursing home lobby, which she describes as a powerful force in her state, designed to protect the nursing homes and not the patients: given the growing number of for-profit facilities, investors' interests tend to win out over patient advocacy and care.

Making the Decision
for Home Care

Jonathan cited the 1974 doctors' strike in Los Angeles as the reason he decided he would never put anyone he loved in a long-term care facility, and only for the briefest possible stay in a hospital. The story became legendary that, during the month-long strike, the mortality rate for patients dropped by 18%. A 1979 study in the *American Journal of Public Health* showed that the *overall* death rate remained unchanged. During this time, there were 11,000 fewer operations performed in which there would have been a statistical number of deaths; additionally, the Emergency Room continued to function. Other studies reveal conflicting opinions on whether a doctors' strike results in reduced patient mortalities.[36] Still others conclude that the risk of infections and errors with medical charts, medical staff, and medicines is sufficient for people to fear being confined in hospitals and long-term care facilities.

Jonathan's wife was in a wheelchair when they married in 1995. As he took care of her during their courtship, he became prepared to continue this care once married. Indeed, he found that personal caregiving was "a calling." For several years he worked as a caregiver in an adult foster care home run by a local Indian tribe, which further deepened his commitment to providing his wife care at home throughout their entire marriage. Eventually, his personal caregiving

---

[36] "When doctors go on strike, does the death rate go down?," *thestraightdope. com*, 4 January 2008.

included his own mother and his mother-in law, who also lived in his home to enable him to provide direct care. This meant that Jonathan was no longer able to work outside the home, but he was willing to make this sacrifice. "Caregivers have tremendous power in doing the right thing for the right reason," he said, which essentially meant to him keeping people you love out of residential facilities. Jonathan stated that people have to "do this from the higher side of who you are to make a difference," forsaking their own needs to provide this care. The case for taking care of parents is easy: they took care of you while you were young and helpless, and when they get older and sick, then it is your time to take care of them the same way … in the home. "If you do this with love, then it is rewarding and fulfilling."

Jonathan admits that there is a cost: he suffers from sleep deprivation, he has had cancer surgery and a double hernia while caring for his wife and relatives, and he is constantly struggling to make financial ends meet. But he finds a way, and he thinks others should as well. When someone in the family becomes dependent as a result of mental or physical disease or illness, a family council must convene, first, to make the joint decision to keep this family member in the home (in whose home must also be decided), and, second, how the necessary care will become everyone's commitment. He mentioned that perhaps someone in the family making a substantial income might be willing to trade their career to take on home care, but that income might also be critical to meeting bills, and that really is a personal decision. No can pass judgment. Jonathan's concern remained that if you want the best care to be given to a loved family member, it has to come from the family and in the family home. He feels that hospitals are so rampant with infections and medical errors that one cannot choose otherwise, and statistics do support Jonathan's argument that long- term care facilities are understaffed and increasingly dollar-driven.

Jonathan feels that family care giving is "my expertise"; he has written a series of e-books on in-home personal caregiving: *Commitment to Compassion; Doing Good Words; God Knows Why;* and *Turning Toward the Light.*

This is a personal choice. Jonathan is fully committed to his belief that we must take care of those we love in our homes and avoid nursing homes or other similar facilities. I agree that the news regarding mishaps, infections, abuse and just general decline of residents is not encouraging. I still cringe when I hear others say they fulfilled a promise to their spouse or someone they loved that they would never put them in a nursing home. I often felt I broke a promise to George who I knew hated this possibility, and still carry that guilt. But guilt is not healthy. Not one person I interviewed complained for the sake of complaining. Resentment and frustration are real and a part of the grieving process that happens when you watch someone you love 'slip away,' if you make the choice that Jonathan did, and it is possible, that is wonderful. One way that would make this kind of decision more feasible is a long term care insurance policy. A good policy is designed to help keep you out of nursing homes and in your own home for as long as possible, as well as financial support once a decision has to be made about nursing home facilities. A good policy can provide the equipment and nursing assistance required to allow someone to stay in their own home, or that of a relative. When I purchased my long term care insurance policy several years ago – and assuming I would outlive George – I told my children that I had purchased a gift for them as well as a policy for me. It just helps during a very difficult time. I wish George had such a policy when he became so ill.

I have listed Jonathan's books which you may find helpful and supportive. He is dedicated to his work. If you decide that you cannot provide 24/7 care and the person you are caring for must have nursing home care, please avoid feeling guilty. I know that will be hard! But guilt can lead to misery and shame, and those are not useful emotions.

Is it Possible to be a Self-Advocate?

Being a self-advocate is not necessarily an intentional choice; very often we assume that going to the hospital is OK and we are going to be taken care of. For the most part, we are. Hospitals save more lives than not, and that is what we count on. We will have our procedures or tests, and leave. It is likely we may need someone to drive us home from the hospital, but many of us may not consider that we need an advocate or that we may not be of sound enough mind to be our *own* advocate.

Kip was his own advocate. Recently divorced, he was close to his brother, who was willing to help and did … even though he lived in another state. Kip also had a bevy of friends, and they helped as well, but Kip realized only after his hospitalization how much he could have benefitted from an advocate and why.

Kip had a vicious cancer of the tonsils that was treated at the renowned M. D. Anderson facility in Houston, Texas, where between September and December he received 47 doses of radiology and three treatments of chemotherapy. An avid sports athlete, his photos on Facebook frame Kip against his bicycle. He looks robust, and, like many who also feel this way, did not think he was going to be vulnerable enough to need that much help through his cancer treatments.

'It is more than just someone driving you home," said Kip. "That is easy to figure out. But you are literally addled after some of these procedures!" Kip remembers being in a recovery room when someone began to give him instructions on how and when to clean his feeding tube. Later he could not remember what to do and had to return for further instructions. He had the feeling this was a bother, as he was in so many words literally asked, "Weren't you paying attention?" He also recalls another time lying on a stiff recovery room gurney, wearing only a hospital gown. He was given the business card of a doctor he was expected to call later. Into what pocket or wallet was he to put this card? And what were the chances that he would leave it in the recovery room … because he was, after all, in Kip's own words, "addled"? After undergoing many of these procedures, Kip strongly feels that people should not be allowed to make any kind of major life decision when there are drugs in their system and they are having a host of reactions – a further reason to have an advocate with you for support. Typically, medical personnel are 'firing away' with a host of instructions; an advocate can be taking notes on all this because, again you as the patient are in a hospital gown and just waking up from a procedure.

Kip also feels that someone's higher socio-economic status provides an advantage that is not fair. "I had a bunch of friends who were medical professionals or Ph.D.'s who were able to give me invaluable information that I know helped improve my recovery. If I were homeless, what are my chances of having that kind of support?" How can a more equitable healthcare system address that gap?

Sometimes an advocate is important just for being there. Kip recalls being in an Emergency Room late at night. He was seriously dehydrated from his treatments and required immediate attention. It was late, and the treatment was making him sleepy … .but he was afraid to go asleep. He might not wake up. He was alone, it was too late to call a friend, and he had not thought of calling someone before he went to the hospital. No one knew he was there. One of the attending nurses picked up on this fear. Staying with him, she rubbed his arms until he fell asleep. She is just one of the 'medical angels' we have all met who try to make a difference.

The Final Story

A poignant reason to have a patient advocate, and reason to be alert. Also the reason for the title of this book.........

Stand in the Way!!!

Carla is an experienced RN and health care administrator. She has managed wards and divisions in large medical settings and is also a health trainer and educator. And she was her son's advocate following a serious accident: "I was the advocate for my son and the medical staff knew it. I questioned each and everything they did for my son. There was a family member 24/7 from the first day of the accident." The severity of her son's injuries necessitated a four month hospitalization; it was not practical that Carla give up her job and become his full time advocate. Other members of the family and friends filled in, but Carla was always the authority in charge, and she made sure the hospital knew this. She called the hospital every day to see what was being changed and why. And she did not worry if this was bothering anyone. As far as Carla was concerned, her son was her number one concern......not whether she was a nuisance to the hospital. She knew when to get 'out of the way' and when to 'get in the way'.

Early on in her son's hospitalization, she had one serious issue with a doctor. While still in ICU (intensive care), her son was "extubated"....that is, a tube had been removed from an airway, a passageway. His vitals were responding better since admission and while his oxygen levels were still slightly low, he was as Carla put it, "livable." His lungs were clear and he was on low levels of oxygen, which helped reinforced his breathing. Carla did not observe that he was in critical danger. Then an intern entered the room, listened to her son's lungs, turned to Carla and said: "I will have the surgery consent form ready for you to sign in a few minutes." Carla was shocked. and asked "What for?!" The intern replied that her son needed a tracheostomy[37] to which Carla firmly said "No!!" She explained to the doctor that her son was NOT in respiratory distress; his lungs were clear, he only needed low levels of oxygen. She was observing her son constantly and this would continue and if his condition called for a tracheostomy, then it would be addressed at that immediate moment of time. Not now. This upset the intern, not expecting to be addressed this way. His only reply was "I guess you no longer need my services "to which Carla replied – "I guess not." She never saw the intern again. Nor any other doctor who felt the need to support this intern's recommendation. Which left Carla feeling that given the age of the intern, perhaps he was looking for an opportunity to practice inserting a trach tube? This seems horrifying to suggest, but this fear is substantiated by yet another health professional who took the survey who spoke of a real fear of teaching hospitals with too many new young doctors in need of training. Was her son about to be someone's teaching moment?

Those who are not health professionals like Carla may feel they do not have this authority; however, we are likely to be a patient advocate for someone who is either a family member or someone we know and care for a great deal. It is a good thing that hospitals have ombudsmen and professional patient advocates......but that does not replace having your own personal patient advocate who knows

---

[37] A tracheostomy is a surgical procedure to create an opening through the neck into the trachea (windpipe). A tube is usually placed through this opening to provide an airway and to remove secretions from the lungs. This tube is called a tracheostomy tube or trach tube.

you very well. AND also has medical power of attorney which will enable your patient advocate to see your medical chart and make medical decisions when you are unable to do so. An ordinary 'power of attorney' will not allow this.

We all have 'radar' for sensing trouble. We all have instincts that tell us when something is either right, or wrong. As a patient advocate, we must learn that when we sense something is not right, to seek - perhaps even demand – a second opinion. Carla did not need to insist on this. She could trust her own judgment and training. We may need to trust our instincts. The most important 'take away' that I can leave you after reading this book is to know when to get out of the way when you trust your instincts that the quality of care the person for whom you are advocating is OK and appropriate, and when to get in the way. ....to literally 'stand in the way' when you sense something is wrong. This important step could mean the difference between recovery and serious impairment. Between life and death. You can do it!

About the Author

Dr. Betty Tonsing has an extensive background as an academic and researcher, international development specialist, and senior executive manager in the public sector with specific experience in the marketing and fund raising arena. Serving as a Fulbright Scholar in Lebanon and Senior Fulbright Specialist in Kyrgyzstan and South Africa, Dr. Tonsing has also worked with the United Nations, USAID, Catholic Relief Services and the National Democratic Institute for International Affairs. Widely published in both national and international publications, previous books also include *The Quakers in South Africa: a Social Witness Against Apartheid* by Mellen Press and *Let's Visit Lesotho* for young readers, published by Macmillan of London. Dr. Tonsing's pioneering initiatives with interactive high-technology linking hundreds of university students and faculty in the US together with students and faculty in Afghanistan, the Middle East and Africa (*How to Internationalize the Classroom Without Leaving the Room*) led to recognition as a best practice teaching tool by the International Institute of Education. Currently Dr. Tonsing directs a non-profit, international Quaker initiative that provides micro finance to women's self-help groups in Africa and India. She lives in metro Indianapolis, Indiana. Her daughter, Eva, is completing a Ph.D. in pharmacology at the Indiana University School of Medicine and her son, Joe, is an assessment worker with the Indiana Department of Child Services and serves as a First Lieutenant for the Indiana National Guard.